D1212447

THE KING OF THE WORLD
IN THE LAND OF THE PYGMIES

The King of the World
in the Land of the Pygmies

Joan Mark

University of Nebraska

Lincoln and London

B -Put

∞The paper in this book meets the minimum requirements of American National
Standard for Information Sciences—Permanence of Paper for Printed Library Materials,
ANSI Z39.48-1984.

Library of Congress Cataloging-in-Publication Data
Mark, Joan T., 1937–
The king of the world in the land of the Pygmies / Joan Mark.
p.   cm.
Includes bibliographical references and index.
ISBN 0-8032-3182-2 (alk. paper)
1. Putnam, Patrick Tracy Lowell, 1903 or 4-1953.
2. Anthropologists—Zaire—Biography.   3. Anthropologists—Massachusetts—Biography.
4. Mbuti (African people)   5. Ituri Forest (Zaire)   I. Title.
GN21.P88M37   1995   306'.092—dc20
[B]   94-16285   CIP

Book design by Wesley B. Tanner, Ann Arbor

1. [Frontispiece] Patrick Tracy Lowell Putnam. Formal portrait, c.1945. Photographer not known.
By permission of the Houghton Library, Harvard University.

Contents

Illustrations

Acknowledgments

My first debt is to Rodney G. Dennis, Curator Emeritus of Manuscripts at the Houghton Library, Harvard University, who recognized the interest and potential significance of Patrick Putnam's papers, set in motion the process of acquiring them for the Houghton Library, and urged me to have a look at them. Several members of the Putnam family talked with me about Patrick Putnam and the family or offered help in other ways. I am particularly indebted to Marley Putnam de Castro (since deceased) and her husband Ramon de Castro, Anna Lowell Tomlinson, Harriet Bundy Belin, Augustus Lowell Putnam, Jr., George Sturgis, Anna Lockwood Putnam Seamans, and Charles R. L. P. Finnerty. John McDonald, Patrick Putnam's brother-in-law, holds the literary rights to the Putnam Papers and gave me permission to publish excerpts from them. He also shared reminiscences of Patrick and Anne Eisner Putnam. Christie McDonald allowed me to read and to quote from the papers of her aunt, Anne Eisner Putnam, talked with me about the Eisner family, and kindly put me up for the night in her Vermont home. Colin Turnbull, who died on July 28, 1994, talked with me at length about Patrick Putnam. I am grateful for his enthusiastic support of this book and regret that he did not live to see it in print. Other friends of Putnam's with whom I have talked most profitably include Emily Hahn, Milton and Vivian Katz, Gordon and Elinor Browne, and Julian Apley.

Josephine Baca, a sister of Emilie Baca Putnam, offered me warm hospitality in Santa Fe as well as reminiscences, photographs, and family papers. John and Terese Butler Hart talked with me about Epulu today, shared their research, and allowed me to intervene in a Butler family reunion. I am also grateful to Terese's parents, Arthur and Kathleen Butler, for their kindness and hospitality. Among those who have corresponded with me or offered information in other ways are Janet E. Baldwin (librarian at the Explorers Club), Curtis Benjamin, Jean R. Boise (librarian at the Farlow Herbarium), Ruth Chapin, Christopher Gray, Roy Richard Grinker, Schuyler Jones, Pen La Farge, Frank L. Lambrecht, Ruth Rees, Eulalie Regan (librarian at the Vineyard Gazette), Harry L. Shapiro and Enid Schildkrout (at the American Museum of Natural History in New York), and Louis G. Wells. Robert Cogan and Pozzi Escot helped me to begin to understand the music of the pygmies.

The manuscript was read by Edward Mark, Jessica Mark, and Anne Bernays, three expert and caring critics whose advice I treasure.

The project was supported by two Scholar's Grants from the National Science Foundation, which I gratefully acknowledge.

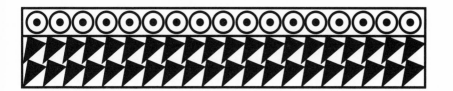

Introduction

In 1927 an American woman journalist set out on a six-month journey across equatorial Africa. "At Buta," Grace Flandrau wrote, "we met Americans—rarest of all encounters in this part of the Congo. Three of them were members of a scientific mission sent out by an American university to measure Bantu skulls and test the blood of Pygmies." One of these was

> a young man who had grown an immense, curly beard and was a most charming and cultivated person. I particularly remember him because he had the curious habit of eating ants—ate them, in fact, before coming to Africa, where, of course, grilled ants are a favorite native dish. American ants, he assured us, were much the better, and he said that he ate the African varieties only in order to test their relative merits. Also, this young man was very scornful of the so-called dangers of the tropics—scoffed at sun-helmuts, quinine, boiled water, and even at elephants, which, although armed with a very light gun, he was planning to shoot. We wondered how long he would beat a game that has never been beaten, and many months later we learned. He had had malaria, had been wounded by an elephant, his wounds had become infested, he had contracted a parasitical disease

of the intestines. Then all news of him had failed, and his father had sailed to Africa to look for him.[1]

Flandrau's unnamed bush-bearded ant-eater can only have been Patrick Tracy Lowell Putnam, a member of the three-person anthropological expedition sent by Harvard University to central Africa in 1927. Putnam had a bushy brown beard. He liked to eat ants, although in Africa they were likely termites. And other parts of Flandrau's description point to Putnam, including the fact that she wrote nothing whatever about the other Americans who were on the expedition. Wherever he was, Patrick Putnam was always the center of attention.

In 1928 Dr. Charles Russell Lowell Putnam of Boston and New York sailed for Africa to hunt for his son. He found him in a native village in the Ituri Forest, living with a native woman. Dr. Putnam managed to bring Patrick home, but his victory was only temporary. Within a year his son had returned to Africa. Patrick Putnam would spend most of his life there. He would become the world's leading expert on the pygmies and on the equatorial rain forest they inhabit in the northern part of the Belgian Congo, which today is Zaire.

Patrick Putnam moved through life with the casual bravado that Grace Flandrau noted, but people were immediately won over by his intelligence, his warmth, and his intense interest in everyone and everything going on around him. A very slight stutter made him appealingly vulnerable. Longtime friends and new acquaintances alike were captivated by him, and again and again they wrote about him. Emily Hahn visited him for eight months in the early 1930s and wrote about him in her book, *Congo Solo*. Martin Birnbaum, an American traveler, described Putnam's camp on the Epulu River in the Ituri Forest in the late 1930s. DeWitt Wallace, editor of the *Reader's Digest*, sent a reporter out to find him and others like him for a series on interesting Americans in far-flung places. A Danish journalist, Olle Strandberg, and a young American traveler, Schuyler Jones, described Camp Putnam in the early 1950s. The columnist Max Lerner wrote about him. A German big-game hunter, a South African Boer farmer and novelist, and an American documentary filmmaker (Bill Longenecker) wrote scandalmongering accounts. Colin Turnbull, a young Scottish student of Indian philosophy and ethnomusicology, stopped in at Camp Putnam for a night, stayed for several months, and returned to write a best-selling study about the pygmies, *The Forest People*. Putnam's third American wife wrote a book, *Madami*, about her experiences.

Of all the stories that circulated about Patrick Putnam, the most intriguing originated after his death. In 1960, when Patrice Lumumba's picture was on the front page of American newspapers (as leader of the fight for independence and the Congo's first prime minister), several of Patrick Putnam's friends were struck by his resemblance to Putnam and wondered if Lumumba might be his son. The evidence was circumstantial but cumulative. In photographs Patrice Lumumba and Patrick Putnam looked alike, apart from skin color: both tall and thin with long arms and legs, their delicate facial features strikingly similar particularly in profile. Their names appeared similar as well. Was "Patrice Lumumba" an African variant on "Patrick Lowell"? To Putnam's friends, it seemed even that their personalities were alike. Lumumba had extraordinary abilities as a speaker and organizer but also a tendency (at least as portrayed in the Western press during the Congo crisis of 1960) toward irregular, unpredictable actions. He seemed to be Patrick Putnam all over again, his charm alternating with moodiness, touched with genius and at the same time slightly mad, brilliant but on an erratic course.

Was Patrick Putnam the father of Patrice Lumumba? The answer is no. Lumumba was born on July 2, 1925, in the village of Onalua in the Sankuru district of Kasai Province. This is south central Zaire, several hundred miles from the Ituri Forest, where Patrick Putnam lived. Most telling is the date: July 2, 1925. Patrick Putnam first arrived in Africa in November 1927. He could not have been Patrice Lumumba's biological father.[2] What the rumor does confirm is the hold that Patrick Putnam had on the imagination of his friends, as well as their fanciful wish that the influence of the old shipping and mercantile families of New England might be as potent as ever in world affairs. "There is always something new out of Africa," was Pliny the Elder's famous phrase. What better "something new" might there be than that one of the first and most powerful leaders of the Pan-African independence movement would turn out to be a Lowell from Massachusetts?

While others were writing about him, Patrick Putnam himself wrote almost nothing. He died in the Belgian Congo in 1953 at the age of forty-nine in despair and madness. He died of a disease that he had had for ten years, a disease with a vague name, emphysema, and in his case no known cause. As his lungs lost their elasticity and his body became starved for oxygen, he could not walk across a room without gasping for breath. As his body became frailer, his prodigious energy expressed itself in an increasingly tyrannical will. He spent the last years of his life reigning over his small kingdom in the forest from his chair.

Patrick Tracy Lowell Putnam bore some of the proudest names in New England. His father, his mother, and his dowager aunt plied him with attention, approval, and implicit expectations. He basked in their attention, fled from it, and sought it out once again. He went as far away from his family as he could get, to an isolated riverbank in a tropical rain forest in the center of Africa. Once there he recreated his family's way of life, practicing medicine as his father had and managing a household-become-village in the manner of his mother. He could not escape his family, nor ultimately did he want to. In the last year of his life he waited helplessly in a hospital room in a little African town, thinking that his eighty-four-year-old father might once again be able to rescue him from this last, worst scrape he had gotten himself into.

As Putnam struggled with his family and his disease, he struggled with the complexities of his chosen profession. Anthropology was a child of the colonial empires of the nineteenth century and of western expansion in the United States. At Harvard in the 1920s when Putnam was a student there, it still had the aura of a profession for gentlemen, a way to have foreign adventures—rather like exploring or big game hunting but in the guise of a scholarly pursuit. But anthropology was changing. The traditional division of labor between field researchers and armchair theorists was giving way to the performance of both tasks by professionally trained anthropologists. The new model was Margaret Mead, not Sir James Frazer. Anthropologists were expected both to gather the data and to theorize about it, and to do this they had to move back and forth between the "field" and the academic community at home. Anthropology was no longer an accumulating body of data but an ever shifting playing field of theoretical interpretations. It was a change Putnam was never able to accommodate himself to or even really to understand.

When Patrick Putnam died in 1953, he had long been written off as a failure by most of his anthropological colleagues, for he had published virtually nothing of what he knew. But looked at in other terms, his life was not a failure. In his last years he willingly became a middle-man in the production and distribution of anthropological knowledge, a businesslike activity that his Boston Brahmin ancestors would have respected. If he could not write about the pygmies and the Ituri Forest, he could help others do so. At Camp Putnam he established a tradition of research in an atmosphere of mutual trust and respect, a tradition that has been revived there several times since his death. Patrick Putnam was one of a little-heralded corps of idiosyncratic and far-flung people: missionaries, traders, government agents, and other expatriates-by-choice who are the bridges between cultural worlds. Anthropology is and always has been far more dependent on them— on their knowledge, their ideas, their good will, and the good will they elicit toward foreigners among the people with whom they live—than most official accounts acknowledge.

But Putnam's life transcends his contribution to anthropology. For a brief shining time he created at Camp Putnam on the Epulu River in the Belgian Congo a world that seemed a virtual paradise in the colonial Africa of the 1930s. Patrick Tracy Lowell Putnam was a stylist of his own person, creating his legend as he created his life. He liked dramatic entrances and dramatic exits. He liked to startle. He loved to shock. But his favorite role, the one he played longest, was that of the New England gentleman in the heart of Africa. There on a public stage he created a world to his own measure, a world in which he was both master and public servant, judge and defender, creator and, ultimately, destroyer.

Journey into Africa

The Harvard Expedition for Africa set out in the fall of 1927. At its head was Frederick R. Wulsin, a genial and independently wealthy Harvard graduate in engineering, former big game hunter in Africa, and veteran explorer of China's inner Asian frontier, who had decided at the age of thirty-six to become a graduate student in anthropology. To go with him Wulsin chose Patrick T. L. Putnam, a twenty-three-year-old Harvard graduate who had just returned from a family- and self-financed anthropological expedition to Java and New Guinea.

Behind the expedition to Africa was Earnest A. Hooton, controversial and beloved professor of physical anthropology at Harvard. Hooton's interest in human evolution, in the differentiation of existing races, and in subsequent "race mixtures" in the United States and elsewhere naturally led him to an interest in Africa.[1] In 1924, when Patrick Putnam was a junior at Harvard, Hooton gave for the first time his course "Races and Cultures of Africa." Two years later he had the idea of sending an expedition to the bend of the Niger River in French West Africa, where from medieval times onward a sequence of cultures had flourished, including the legendary Timbuktu. Hooton wanted one man to take physical measurements of individuals in different tribes to try to determine their racial affinities, and another to excavate archaeological sites. For the necessary funds he applied to the Rockefeller Foundation, calling field research "the vital essence of anthropology."[2] He confessed himself, however, to be "one of that drab female type of anthropologist who remains at home and reproduces the species while the more brilliant male roves abroad both in quest of adventure and of food to be brought back for home consumption."[3] In the *Harvard Alumni Bulletin* around the same time, Hooton added: "I have plenty of vicarious, second-hand adventures through the talented young trouble-seekers whom I send on anthropological expeditions. They are welcome to the adventures provided they bring home the data."[4] The Rockefeller Foundation granted him $7,000 for his roving male trouble-seekers, and Hooton passed the money on to Wulsin.

The original plan was that Wulsin and Putnam would enter Africa from Dakar in Senegal and take a train 700 miles inland to Bamako at the bend of the Niger. But two days before sailing from New York, Wulsin learned that the port of Dakar was closed because of yellow fever. Since Putnam was already in Europe waiting for him, rather than delay their journey Wulsin decided to change the route. Instead of entering Africa from the west they would go in from the north. They could go up the Nile, cross the northern part of the Belgian Congo to French Equatorial Africa, and return home from Lagos in Nigeria. This meant that their area of study would be not the Niger River basin but an area to the east where they could study the intermixing of pygmies, Sudanic peoples, and Bantus in the transition zone between the grassy savanna and the equatorial forest.

In October 1927 Wulsin spent three days in Brussels inquiring about conditions in the Congo, three days in London buying hunting guns, and several days in Paris making diplomatic contacts. The guns were his personal contribution to the expedition—a contribution he later regretted, for they created red tape everywhere and were a temptation that Patrick Putnam could not resist. In Paris, Wulsin met Putnam, whose parents, a sister, and a pet monkey had all come to see him off. On November 12, Wulsin and Putnam sailed from Marseille.

The two-person party soon became a threesome. As they were crossing the Mediterranean a cable arrived from twenty-year-old Harvard summa graduate in anthropology Milton Katz, who had spent the summer at the Peabody Museum doing readings on Africa in several languages for Wulsin. That fall he had gone to Europe on a fellowship, but he was restless and more intrigued by what Wulsin and Putnam were planning to do in Africa than by what he was doing in Europe. He offered the rest of his fellowship money if they would let him join them. Wulsin and Putnam agreed and cabled Katz to meet them at Luxor.

Wulsin had decided from what he had learned in Europe that they should measure pygmies near Avabi in the Belgian Congo and do their archaeological work farther north near Lake Chad. On their way through Egypt they toured recent excavations near the pyramids with George Reisner, world-famous archaeologist, who gave them tips on archaeological methods. At Luxor, near the Valley of the Kings, where Milton Katz joined them, they stopped to visit one of Putnam's Harvard classmates who was working as an assistant to the director of an expedition sponsored by the Metropolitan Museum in New York. The Metropolitan expedition was spending $80,000 per year and hiring 150 to 500 people at a time. Its members "live in a delightful house, built for the job, as does Reisner, and they come back year after year," Wulsin noted in his journal.[5] It seemed a good life.

At Khartoum at the southern edge of the desert the three men took a Sudanese government steamer up the White Nile through grasslands and equatorial swamps to Rejaf, almost on the Uganda border. At stops along the river they made observations on the Shilluk and the Dinka, whom they later compared with the forest peoples. Their presuppositions about African body types were soon proved wrong. They had expected these Nilotic tribes to be tall and thin, with sooty black skins and fine features, but instead of this distinct type they found mostly intermediate physical characteristics, blending gradually from one physical type to another. What they were seeing, they realized, was physical evidence of migrations, intermixtures, amalgamations, and redivisions across a vast portion of the African continent. "A tribe, as we find it today, is primarily a political and social unit held together by common customs and common interests," Wulsin wrote. "Common descent is of course present in most cases, but one cannot be certain how far back it goes, or how pure the blood has remained." He urged the tracing of the history of each tribe as far as possible "to study the forces which have actually been effective in bringing about changes, before resorting to linguistic, ethnological or somatological inference."[6] An awareness of the vast and complicated history of Africa stayed with Putnam all his life. He never forgot that he was witness to one particular moment only, not an observer of a timeless primitive ethnographic present.

At Rejaf they traveled west for two days, to arrive at Faradje, which was to be their headquarters for several weeks. In crossing from Rejaf to Faradje they moved from the basin of the Nile River to that of the Congo. Faradje was in the extreme northeast corner of the Belgian Congo, in the Haut-Uele district. The southern part of the district was equatorial forest, a damp, dimly lit world beneath a canopy of treetops 120 feet overhead. The forest abruptly gave way in the north to "bush," a horizontal terrain of tall grasses and small and medium-sized trees. The whole province had been the scene of an extraordinary transformation in the preceding few years, owing to the building of some 5,000 kilometers of improved roads. Porterage, the carrying of goods by native bearers, had been forbidden, but they found it difficult to get an automobile. Eventually they were able to buy a Ford touring car from a chief who had paid several hundred pounds of ivory for it. They were told that when the motor did not run, the chief's solution was to have the chauffeur flogged. Once the car was theirs, Putnam

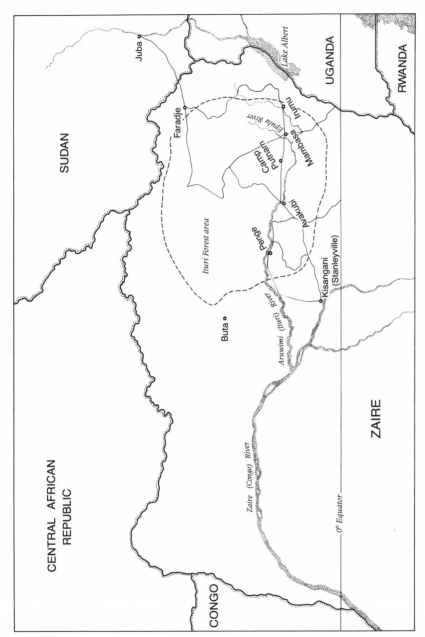

Map of northeastern Zaire

disappeared under the hood and emerged several days later, smiling triumphantly. The motor was running. Repairing automobiles was a skill he prided himself on.

"We are in a most interesting region with pigmies, Azande, Mangbetu, and all sorts of other people to study," Wulsin wrote in his journal.[7] For two weeks he drove the touring car around Faradje and made an ethnological collection among the Mangbetu, while Putnam and Katz measured eleven adult male pygmies and visited a pygmy village several hours away in the forest. They had intended to collect blood samples; a Dr. Miner at the Harvard Medical School thought it might be possible to distinguish races by the prevalence of certain blood types, and he was particularly eager to get samples of pygmy blood. Putnam and Katz practiced on one another—unfortunately choosing the earlobe as a likely spot for taking a sample—and had so little success that they abandoned the attempt to get blood from the pygmies and reverted to the traditional techniques of photographs and body measurements. Here too they were soon disillusioned. In a group of twenty pygmy men they could technically define three nose types but could see that, in fact, no two noses were alike, and they were really learning nothing.[8]

At Christmas the three explorer-anthropologists gathered at the home of District Administrator Albert William van Zuylen van Nyevelt, a Belgian baron, to consider their future plans. They took stock of their work to date: 450 photographs, 100 ethnological specimens (tools, weapons, cloth, and the like), 11 measurements of pygmies, a short pygmy vocabulary, and miscellaneous ethnological information. Putnam argued strongly that they had only scratched the surface of pygmy studies. Since they were in an area where pygmies were numerous and friendly, he thought they should stay and continue research in physical anthropology and particularly in pygmy culture; the influx of European civilization was changing the area so rapidly that pygmy culture, "slight and rudimentary" as it was, was in danger of vanishing altogether.[9]

But Wulsin was eager to move on to the western Sudan and Lake Chad, the real goal of their journey. Finally, reluctantly, they decided they would split up. They divided their equipment, their guns, ammunition, cameras, photographic supplies, medicines. Putnam was given two guns (a 35 Winchester and a 22 Winchester), two cameras, all the reserve medicine he would take, one full set of anthropometric instruments, 500 blood tubes, two servants, some 30,000 francs (about $900), and the Ford touring car. Wulsin and Katz bought a Ford truck in which they and the cook and his assistant and their guides could continue the journey. To simplify accounts and because the expedition was running out of money, Wulsin undertook to finance Putnam's work out of his own funds.

The three men made one last brief trip together to Stanleyville and to Buta (where they met Grace Flandrau, the American reporter who was charmed by Putnam but wondered about his foolhardiness). At Buta it was so hot that the three anthropologists took a brief trip up a tributary of the Uele River in a hired dugout canoe. The native paddlers said the river was full of crocodiles, but Putnam slipped swiftly over the side of the canoe for a swim, then just as swiftly bounced back up into it. From this and many other incidents Wulsin had come to understand thoroughly both the strengths and the peccadilloes of his young associate. Putnam refused to observe even the most elementary rules of hygiene, and he was immediately and often ill. On the steamer going up the Nile he had come down with the grippe and a fever. When they got to the Belgian Congo, Putnam was ill enough to be admitted to the local hospital, where his complaint was diagnosed first as malaria and then as amoebic dysentery. Putnam jeopardized freely not only his own health and safety but the future of the expedition. Milton Katz was alarmed when a native said there were some buffalo nearby and Putnam handed the man a rifle and told him to bring in some proof, for the Belgians were intent on keeping guns out of the hands of natives. Though Wulsin knew Patrick Putnam's faults, he admired the young man's obvious talents, including his exceptional mechanical ability and his flair for languages. Of Putnam's first attempts to learn and speak KiNgala, one of the Bantu languages, Wulsin wrote, "I have never seen a man who learned a native language so rapidly."[10] Above all, Wulsin understood that Putnam would do what he would do. There was no point in trying to talk him out of anything.

When the party split up at Monga in the Bas-Uele on January 27, 1928, and Wulsin and Katz headed north for the French border and French Equatorial Africa, Wulsin wrote in his journal: "Pat saw us a couple of miles on our way, and then turned back. I felt quite a wrench at parting from him. He is a lovable sort, and has gifts which should make him a most remarkable ethnologist."[11]

Wulsin and Katz spent two months, as they had planned, doing archaeological work around Fort Lamy in French Equatorial Africa. When Putnam did not appear at their appointed place of rendezvous, they waited around for a couple of days and then headed home. Putnam's mother, when she heard about it, was greatly incensed that her son's traveling companions had left Africa without bothering to find out what happened to him, but they had assumed, in accord with what they knew of his character, that he had simply found something better to do. Wulsin and Katz had a safe trip, apart from the malaria Katz contracted, and a relatively successful one. Wulsin wrote his doctoral dissertation on the archaeological work he had done in the Shari basin in French Equatorial Africa, then settled into an academic career first at the Peabody Museum, later at Boston University, and finally as a professor of anthropology at Tufts. Milton Katz, the youngest member of the party, decided to abandon both anthropology and his first love, creative writing, and to set out on what would be an illustrious career in government, law, and international relations. He became a professor at the Harvard Law School, and after World War II he succeeded W. Averell Harriman as head of the European operations of the Marshall Plan.

In 1928, meanwhile, four months went by with no word from Patrick Putnam. His combination of inexperience and overconfidence was nearly fatal. He had previously done little reading about the Congo, so he spent his first couple of "solo" weeks in libraries in Buta (at the district headquarters and at the Premontrean Mission) and in Stanleyville, the provincial capital. He also bought a permit to kill two elephants. After many local inquiries, he learned that there were pygmies near Kole, on the road between Buta and Stanleyville, and in late February 1928 he set out in search of them.[12]

Putnam went into the equatorial forest on foot, accompanied by porters (porterage was legal where there was no road). On the first day out he sprained his ankle so badly that he was forced to rest for several days in the village of a local Bobua chief named Dunggu. He rested again at Kanwa, an isolated gold-mining post. Almost immediately he found himself short of provisions. He had expected to live off the land, but it was March, and in that region and season the Africans did not have enough for themselves; it took him time and diplomacy to get even a starvation diet. The sneakers he was wearing fell apart, and he had to go barefoot. Then he was plagued by recurrent fevers and general mental lassitude, which weeks later he learned were symptoms of hookworm disease.

On March 29 Putnam crossed the Longgele River and for several hours continued along a path through tall trees that shaded tangled underbrush and an occasional small stream. Suddenly the path swelled out into a broad clearing, "white and hot under the sun suspended overhead."[13] Along each side of the clearing in the forest was a long row of low, leaf-thatched huts. A few goats and chickens ran about, and an old man lolled under a hangar, an open-sided shelter near the center of the clearing. Behind the huts, paths led out to plantations on the edge of the forest. He had reached the village of Buondo, named for its chief, the head of the Mboli clan of the Makere. The Makere were non-Bantu, non-Sudanic people who had been in the area before the Bantus had moved up from the south and the Sudanic peoples down from the north. The Mboli (or BaMboli) were farmers, growing primarily plantains but also maize, manioc, and sweet potatoes. They shared many cultural characteristics—including house decorating styles and artificially elongated heads for women—with a better-known branch of the family, the Mangbetu, who lived to the north.

Buondo's village was the first Putnam had found that had pygmies associated with it. Within a half hour of his arrival the pygmy chief, Nóolo, came in with one of his men. Nóolo saluted Putnam smartly and shook hands, and they tried to carry on a conversation, but the pygmy chief apparently spoke only Makere. Through a Mboli villager who knew some KiNgala, Putnam asked Nóolo a few questions and presented him with a gift of salt. Putnam later wrote "Nóolo accepted it and asked why I did not give more, as he had many people. Then they went home."[14]

The next day Putnam walked through the forest to the pygmy camp, ten or fifteen minutes away, and tried to make a census of the pygmies who were there. He invited them to Buondo's village to dance, and about twenty of them came, men, women, and children, wearing plumes of green leaves. They borrowed Buondo's drums and did a single-file dance round and round in circles and figure eights, and then Buondo paid them with a bowl full of palm oil. Later Putnam passed through their camp several times, and he saw them one or two more times when they came into Buondo's village, but he felt he had made no significant contact with them. He was frustrated by his inability to speak their language, which was Makere, the language of the Mboli. In the Mboli village itself, he could talk to a few people in KiNgala, but he found that KiNgwana, the Congo variant of Swahili, was the more common trade language, so he began to learn it.

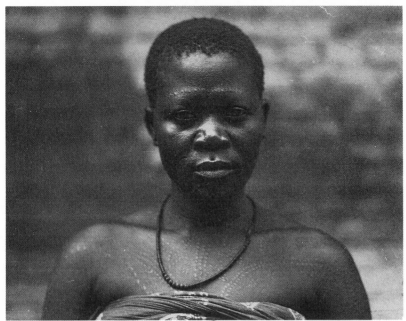

2. *"Abanzima, a Mboli of Buondo's village near Panga, Stanleyville District."* —*P.T.L.P.*

3. *"BaMboli of Buondo's village."*—*P.T.L.P.*

4. *"BaMboli of Buondo's village in the chief's parlor."—P.T.L.P.*

5. *"Houses, people, goats, hanger of chief," Buondo's village.—P.T.L.P.*

6. *"Houses, decorations, people sitting by door, fibre cloth trees," Buondo's village.—P.T.L.P.*

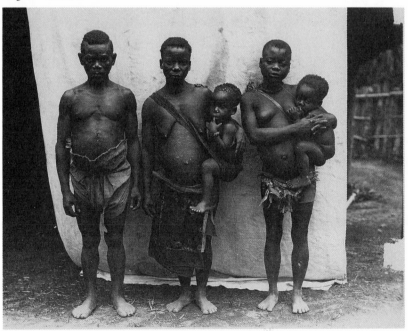

7. *"Three Gombari pygmies and two children. The adults are Magoratora (male) and Kundaluse and Kambaruse (females)."—P.T.L.P.*

At about that time, however, Putnam's fevers and mental lassitude began in earnest. Not knowing what was wrong with him, he decided that the excitement of hunting elephants might cure him. It was
his worst mistake. He went out with a native gun bearer and two
pygmy guides. On his third day out he very nearly got a large elephant.
The next day he and his guides were following an elephant track when
suddenly they came upon the elephant they had pursued the day before, feeding in a banana grove. It turned on them, and as they fled,
Putnam tripped on a root and fell. The elephant gored him, a giant
tusk ripping across the flesh of his back, buttocks, and thigh. Only a
guide's frantic noise finally distracted the elephant and kept it from
trampling him.[15]

Putnam fainted, and his pygmy guides thought he was dead. They
carried him back to Buondo's village, where Buondo's daughter, Sofia
Abanzima, packed his wounds with herbs and native medicines. Several days later, when Putnam was able to persuade Buondo to call for
porters, he had himself carried down to the Aruwimi River, a few
hours' walk through the forest. There, he waited two days with Abanzima for the canoes to the nearby Belgian post of Panga. They arrived
at Panga in early May, about a week after the goring. The Belgian administrator at Panga, E.M.F. Bock, and his wife were remarkably kind
to him, Putnam wrote later, for he "came like an apparition and looking like a tramp out of the forest."[16] He could walk a few steps when he
arrived, but almost immediately he came down with a high fever and
spent the next two weeks in bed. Then by tepoy (a portable chair) and
porters, he was carried to the government post at Poko, still accompanied by Abanzima. At Poko his fever became even worse. After two
more weeks in bed he hired a Greek trader to drive him to Dili on the
road to Buta, where there was a competent physician. He was treated
for hookworm and allowed to go on to Buta, where he learned that official inquiries had been made as to his whereabouts. He immediately
sent telegrams to Wulsin and to his parents. It was late June 1928, two

months after he had been wounded by the elephant and four months since he had set off into the bush. Wulsin's answering telegram gave him permission to stay for two more months in the Congo. His father wired that he and Patrick's younger brother Sebastian were on their way to Africa to meet him.

Putnam spent the three and a half months before his father's arrival in October alternately waiting around for automobile parts and nursing fevers. At Gombari he tried again to measure and photograph pygmies, but he found they would not stay around the post long enough unless he fed them, and there was no food to be had. Gombari was in the middle of great fields of rice, but the growers were obliged to sell all they had to the colonial government, which in turn sold it— at below market prices—to the gold-mining companies.

In mid-October Putnam's father and brother arrived at Aba, near the border between the northeastern Congo and the Sudan. The afternoon they arrived Patrick casually mentioned to them that the vision in his left eye was blurred. His father rushed him to the nearby mining town of Watsa, where the mine physician had ophthalmological instruments and diagnosed what his father suspected: tubercular retinitis, a disease that can cause blindness and death. At this Patrick capitulated to his father's care. Dr. Putnam prescribed rest and good food. "I had countless eggnogs thrust at me," Putnam reported to Wulsin. "The diet, moderate daily quinine, and the fear which the perpetual presence of a doctor seemed to inspire among the spirits of sickness, must have had an almost magical effect, for from then on, during the months that my father stayed with me in the Congo, I had nothing more serious than a cold."[17]

While they were waiting for his health to improve, Dr. Putnam and Sebastian got Patrick's life in order in other ways. They settled in around Arebi, making camp in a Mangbele village in the northeast corner of the Ituri Forest. Sebastian took charge of the camp, while Pat and his father went off on a two-week trip to find a dentist for Pat's teeth. They returned to find Sebastian running a well-ordered ménage with newly built furniture, ample supplies of rice, and great quantities of plantains ripening to make wine. Sebastian was deaf—"stone deaf" in his mother's words[18]—but what was a handicap in the United States was an advantage in the Congo. For him there was no language barrier, because he was accustomed to communicating with signs and gestures. Sebastian was easygoing, likable, and as popular with the porters and servants in the Congo as he was among family and friends in America. The African men who took orders from him all day taught him their gambling games at night, and he in turn taught them to his brother. Patrick Putnam's only formal publication in anthropology is a brief letter to *Man*, the British anthropology journal, describing "A Mangbetu Game," which he learned in 1928 from Sebastian.

Since Patrick was supposed to rest his eyes, Dr. Putnam did his reading and writing for him and tried to help him get his ethnographical notes together. Among the books Dr. Putnam read was Henry Morton Stanley's two-volume *In Darkest Africa*, and he made notes for Patrick on the pages that mentioned pygmies.[19] Meanwhile, Patrick spent most of his time hunting elephant and buffalo. His excuse was that the porters needed meat, but later, trying to justify himself to Wulsin, he would write: "Those who know Africa know that to hunt with a native is one of the best ways to acquire his friendship and confidence."[20] They stayed around Arebi until December 17, 1928, when a telegram arrived from Wulsin, ordering him to return home as soon as he was well enough to travel, and it had the desired effect. "Regretfully following orders," Putnam cabled back.[21]

Although Patrick did not know it, the telegram had been instigated by Dr. Putnam, and it broke the stalemate. Patrick wanted to stay in Africa. His father wanted him to return home. The telegram from Wulsin gave Pat an excuse to do what his father wanted him to do, while seeming not to be capitulating to him. But it worked only temporarily. He would soon be back.

Of the four tasks Wulsin had assigned to Putnam when they parted
—to measure pygmies, study archaeological sites, ship his specimen
collections back to America, and make such ethnographical observations as he thought fit—Putnam could claim to have done only the latter two. One of them was specific and managerial, the other pleasingly
vague. What Putnam could not do was follow orders, particularly if
the order involved a goal set by someone else. This refusal to take orders was characteristic of Patrick Putnam all his life. Its roots lie in his
childhood, in his relation to his father and mother.

As the only natural child in the family, Patrick was the one who
counted and the center of virtually suffocating attention. To cope with
this surfeit he developed a pattern of rebellion followed by a need that
would bring his parents running, so that he was not left out on a limb
of his own making. Charles Putnam, like his wife Angelica, was willing to do virtually anything for Patrick, including leaving his family
and his New York City medical practice for six months in order to find
and take care of his son in Africa. Frederick Wulsin thought that Pat
Putnam's disdain for personal safety, his neglect of personal hygiene,
and his often unkempt appearance were his way of rebelling against
an overprotective mother and the covey of nurses and governesses
who had surrounded him as a child. The accidents and sicknesses that
resulted would then bring his father to his side. Patrick seemed almost
deliberately to expose himself to dangers, confident that whatever
scrape he got himself into, his father would rescue him. Although he
was being playful when he wrote Wulsin that his father's very presence seemed to frighten away the spirits of sickness, he did have an almost childlike faith in Dr. Putnam's ability and willingness to provide
for him, care for him, and get him out of trouble and to do so again and
again without complaint. More generally, his feeling of invulnerability, of being able to do anything he wanted to without serious cost
to himself, was a not untypical legacy of a pampered childhood in a
wealthy family.[22]

The one thing his father would not allow him was an African wife. In the Makere village after he was wounded by the elephant, Putnam had fallen in love with Abanzima, the village chief's daughter who took care of him. He was twenty-three, and she was about twenty-five, although she looked older, as African village women do. Pampering care through extended periods of illness was familiar in Putnam's life, for he had been a sickly child. For six months, until his father arrived and probably afterward, Abanzima was nurse and lover. She treated his wounds with native herbs. He later felt that he owed his life, or at least his health, to her skill and knowledge. As he grew better, he queried her about native customs, and she became his teacher as well.

Meanwhile, though he did not let his parents know where he was, he began to think of marrying Abanzima and taking her home with him as his wife. In the native village in the heart of the Ituri Forest in the Belgian Congo, Patrick Putnam imagined that his parents could be brought around to his point of view: they would see that Abanzima had saved his life; that skin color, family, and culture were irrelevant; and that he should have, as he had always had, whatever he wanted. But he had not reckoned with the racial climate in New York and Boston.

Patrick, his father, and his brother spent Christmas with the van Zuylens at Faradje—as Wulsin, Putnam, and Katz had done the year before—and then packed up camp. With them they took "Chimpy," a young chimpanzee. They decided to go home via the Congo River rather than down the Nile, and on January 11 they took the steamer from Stanleyville to the coast. Along the way they stopped at Boma, then the capital of the Belgian Congo, and Patrick made official calls, not so subtly signaling to his father his intention to return to Africa. He had lunch with the director of agriculture and called on the district commissioner and on the governor general. District Commissioner Charles Delhaise turned over to Putnam a sheaf of manuscript including notes and measurements of pygmies and villagers in the Stan-leyville District which he had taken twenty years before, and Governor A. Tilkens told Patrick Putnam what he wanted to hear, that he "should return to the Congo."[23]

In Belgium, as they prepared to cross the Atlantic, Putnam made another round of official visits. The American Embassy gave him a letter of introduction to the secretary general of the Ministry of Colonies, who in turn arranged for him to meet two influential men: Josef Maes, the ethnographical director of the Museum of the Congo at Tervueren; and Edouard De Jonghe, an official in the Ministry of Colonies, editor of the review *Congo*, and Belgium's leading Congo ethnologist. "I was able to correct certain details in an ethnological map of the Congo, which the Ministry is preparing," Putnam reported to Wulsin.[24]

On March 12, 1929, they arrived in New York, and Patrick Putnam's struggle with his parents began in earnest. He told them he wanted to marry Abanzima.

The Family

And this is good old Boston,
The home of the bean and the cod,
Where the Lowells talk to the Cabots,
And the Cabots talk only to God.
                    —John Collins Bossidy

Patrick Putnam's sense of self rested secure in the knowledge that he was a Lowell from Massachusetts. The public prestige of the Lowells was at its height during Patrick's childhood. The family included James Russell Lowell, recently deceased diplomat and revered New England poet; A. Lawrence Lowell, the president of Harvard College; and Amy Lowell, the Imagist poet. The very name conjured up visions of wealth flowing from the manufacturing town of Lowell, Massachusetts. The doggerel about the Cabots and the Lowells (in the epigraph above) was first given as a toast by John Collins Bossidy at a Holy Cross Alumni Dinner in Boston in 1910, when Patrick was six years old.[1] It shows the combination of awe and irreverent mockery with which more recent immigrants into Massachusetts regarded the Lowells. The family's own sense of the importance of being a Lowell can be seen in Patrick's name: all three of Patrick Tracy Lowell Putnam's given names came from the Lowell side of the family, represented by his paternal grandmother, Harriet Lowell, although that was only one-quarter of his heritage.

The Lowell family of New England stems from Percival Lowle, a merchant who moved from Bristol, England, to Newbury, Massachusetts, in 1639 at the age of sixty-eight, bringing with him two sons, one daughter, and their families. Although the Lowles were well-enough off when they arrived in America, like other old New England families they stagnated in the New World for more than a century, for commercial opportunities were few. Not until after the American Revolution, when the old families merged with the newly rich families of shipbuilding and seagoing merchants, were the wealthy patricians of New England born. In the Lowell case, the founding event occurred when one branch of the family, that founded by John Lowell ("the Old Judge"), began to intermarry with the descendants of an Irish immigrant named Patrick Tracy, who had transformed himself into the wealthiest man in Newburyport.

Although Patrick Tracy arrived in Newburyport a common sailor, he soon became the commander of his ship and then the owner of many sailing vessels. During the American Revolution he raided British ships, selling the goods afterward at enormous profits. He never forgot his humble origins. He was said to be a man of fighting spirit and also generous and liberal. In his will he left an annuity to the black man, Apropos, who had been his slave, an abolitionist act that was much commented on at the time.

John Lowell's son, Francis Cabot Lowell, married Patrick Tracy's granddaughter and went into business with her brother, Patrick Tracy Jackson. The company they founded revolutionized American manufacturing. On a visit to England undertaken for his health, Francis Cabot Lowell secretly memorized the design of power looms used in manufacturing cotton cloth and recreated the looms when he got home. Lowell, Jackson, and some Boston friends who were persuaded to invest in their venture transformed the farming village of East Chelmsford into America's first factory town, and in 1816 Lowell went to Washington and persuaded John C. Calhoun and others in Congress to add a duty on cotton cloth to the Tariff Act of that year. This hit directly at the prosperity of the New England shippers who imported large amounts of cheap Indian cloth, and the irate shippers began to regard Lowell and his associates as "industrial radicals." But the enterprise at East Chelmsford prospered. After Francis Cabot Lowell's death in 1817 the town was renamed Lowell in his honor, and by 1845 it was the world's leading textile center. From textile mills the Lowells, the Jacksons, and the Boston families with whom they intermarried branched out into shipping, railroads, banking, and mutual funds.[2]

Harriet Lowell Putnam, Patrick Putnam's grandmother, was a direct descendant of Patrick Tracy (her mother, Anna Cabot Jackson, was Patrick Tracy Jackson's daughter) and of Francis Cabot Lowell's younger brother, Charles. The poet James Russell Lowell was her uncle. Amy Lowell, A. Lawrence Lowell, and the well-known astronomer Percival Lowell were her cousins on the slightly more distant family branch stemming from Francis Cabot Lowell's older brother, John. Her brother Charles Russell Lowell, Jr., was a Civil War hero (although mortally wounded he led a cavalry charge at Cedar Creek, Virginia, in 1864), and she named her second son, born in 1869, Charles Russell Lowell Putnam in his honor. This was Patrick Putnam's father.

The eminence of the Lowells came not just from inherited wealth, which many other New England families had, but from a tradition of leadership in war and in peace, in business and the arts, in education, benevolence, and public welfare. To be a Lowell was to be the New England equivalent of a European gentleman. This ideal of the gentleman, a direct legacy from the Renaissance, developed in the Italian courts of Mantua and Ferrara in the fifteenth century. It was carried to England by Roger Ascham, tutor to Queen Elizabeth I, and from there it passed to the thirteen colonies, where it produced the liberal arts curriculum and the emphasis on sports and games so characteristic of elite colleges and prep schools in this country. A gentleman was expected to be a learned humanist and at the same time an active man of affairs; a man courteous to women, faithful to his friends, and respectful of all persons; a man able to control his passions, remain cheerful under adversity, and be sportsmanlike and manly under all circumstances.[3]

In 1948 Patrick Putnam told Anne Eisner, a New Yorker whom he was courting and eventually married, that if she wanted to understand him she might read Cleveland Amory's *Proper Bostonians,* which had just appeared.[4] Anne did so and was baffled. She could not see what the anecdotes about tightfisted millionaires, formidable women, and favorite charities had to do with Patrick Putnam, whom she thought the most original man she had ever met. Certain traits such as family pride and loyalty to Harvard were evident, however, and some of his habits were amusing. Whenever Patrick sat down to play chess with Anne's cousin, he would raise his glass and make a toast, "To your defeat, Sir," which the cousin thought was very "proper Bostonian."[5]

Earlier, and with a different wife, Patrick Putnam used a different book to explain himself. En route home from Africa he and Emilie Baca Putnam read *The Late George Apley,* by John P. Marquand, an ironic fictional memoir of a Boston man of good family who lets the social dictates set out for him—first by his parents and then by his wife—guide virtually everything he does. Emilie wrote her mother, "I really believe it gives me a better understanding of Pat and his Boston background," and added perceptively, "Because his whole background is not Bostonian he clings all the more tenaciously to that which is for he feels great pride in it."[6]

Although the Lowell side of Patrick Putnam's heritage was the more illustrious, the Putnams too were an old New England family. Divisions over inheritance within the Putnam family of Salem Village (later Danvers) in the seventeenth century have been called one of the prime causes of the Salem witchcraft trials.[7] The family also included Isaiah Putnam, a famous Revolutionary War general who founded Putnam, Connecticut. Isaiah was considered slightly mad, and it was family tradition, which Patrick Putnam delighted to repeat, that all Putnams were either touched with genius or a little mad.[8]

George Putnam, Patrick's paternal grandfather, was the son of a Unitarian clergyman in Roxbury. He attended Harvard College, studied law, and married the sister of his classmate Charles Russell Lowell, Jr. George Putnam and Harriet Lowell had five children. Their eldest son, William Lowell Putnam, also married a Lowell—Elizabeth, the sister of Percival, Abbott Lawrence, and Amy Lowell. Patrick Putnam could therefore claim while he was at Harvard that he was a nephew of the husband of the sister of the president of the college—or, as he preferred to put it, "a nephew of sorts"—as well as a distant cousin of Harvard president Abbott Lawrence Lowell.[9]

Charles Russell Lowell Putnam, George and Harriet Putnam's second son, chose his own course. He did not study law or go into the family financial business. Instead, after Harvard College he attended the Harvard Medical School and then did post-graduate work in surgery in London and Vienna. He shocked his family by traveling through Europe with a woman to whom he was not married, and when he returned home he shocked them again by marrying not a proper Bostonian but a divorée from Albany, New York, whom the family regarded as disturbingly unconventional, perhaps even a little bohemian.

Angelica Talcott Rathbone Putnam, Patrick's mother, was a tall, slender woman with reddish hair and blue eyes. Family tradition credits her with being a model for Augustus Saint-Gaudens's statue of the Winged Victory leading General Sherman, which stands in front of the Plaza Hotel at the foot of Central Park in New York City. Patrick Putnam, with his blue eyes, long limbs, and long tapering hands, resembled her more than he did his short, rotund, genial father.

Angelica was born outside Albany at Kenwood, the family estate built by her grandfather, Joel Rathbone, who made a fortune in the wholesale stove business and retired at the age of thirty-five. He and his wife, Emeline Weld Munn, had five children. Their eldest son, Clarence, was wounded slightly in the Civil War. He returned to head the family stove business, but in the prime of life he too retired to Kenwood. His wife, Angelica Bogart Talcott, was the daughter of a civil engineer in Albany. Their third child and first daughter, named Angelica after her mother, was born in 1871. The family religious tradition was Presbyterian (through Emeline Rathbone inclined to the Baptists), but young Angelica was sent to a convent school, perhaps because of her rebellious nature. In 1893, when she was twenty-two, she ran off and married fellow art student Charles Sydney Hopkinson, and they went to Paris.[10] According to a family tradition, Angelica wanted to go to Paris to study art but could not do so as a single woman, so she accepted Hopkinson's proposal with the condition that the marriage not be consummated. In Paris, Hopkinson asked his best friend, Charles R. L. Putnam, who was studying medicine in Berlin and Munich, to come and talk some sense into his wife. Charles came but fell in love with Angelica himself.

Charles Putnam and Angelica Talcott Rathbone Hopkinson were married on December 25, 1899. They were well matched. Charles was congenial and energetic and not at all stuffy, cold, or rude as Angelica thought most New Englanders were—including his family. Charles delighted in having his domestic affairs managed by a strong-minded woman, and when he wanted to, he held his own simply by ignoring her. Charles interned at Massachusetts General Hospital in Boston, but on looking around, as he later told his nephew, he could see so many men who had to die or move on before he could be promoted there that he decided to relocate to New York City.[11] In New York the young Putnams turned their backs on society, preferring to seek out interesting people among artists, composers, singers, and even boxers whom Dr. Putnam met in the course of his work as an ear, nose, and throat surgeon.

The Putnams' first child, a girl, died during delivery. Stung by this experience, Angelica Putnam refused to go to a hospital for the birth of her second child. She locked herself in the bathroom and, alone, delivered Patrick Tracy Lowell Putnam on September 4, 1904. Thereafter she regarded Thursdays, the day of his birth, as very special days.[12]

When Patrick was four, the Putnams adopted Sebastian, the two-year-old son of friends who had been killed in an accident. Patrick was so pleased to have a sibling that they decided to add more children to the family. Instead of seeking healthy infants, they looked for children who needed them. Dr. Putnam was assistant surgeon in the children's ward of Postgraduate (now University) Hospital in New York, and Angelica Putnam often did volunteer work in various baby hospitals in the city. They began to bring home abandoned and sickly children. The first to arrive, in February 1911, was Christine, aged four, abandoned in a boardinghouse by her Italian mother when she was a month old. In November, Angelica brought home Marley, an abused toddler who had been picked up on a New York City street by a policeman. She was not expected to live, but Angelica insisted that her husband could treat her, and he did. Soon afterward a boy, Russell, and then twin baby girls, Arabella and Julia—who had been taken to a hospital nearly dead from malnutrition—were added to the family. When the required waiting period of one year was over, the Putnams legally adopted each of the children, giving them all the rights that their own child Patrick had. The Putnams did this quietly and managed to avoid publicity until 1913, when the legal proceedings were picked up by the *New York Times*. In 1915 the children ranged chronologically from Patrick, aged eleven, Russell, nine, Sebastian, eight, Christine, seven, and Marley, five, to the twins, two.[13]

The Putnams always liked to say that Patrick was the impetus for the adoptions, but they were doing what fit their own personalities. Dr. Putnam was eager to help some of the children he came across in his practice. He was also a convinced environmentalist in the heyday of the heredity-versus-environment debate, and he believed that he and his wife could compensate for whatever hereditary weakness or early damage the children had suffered. Angelica Putnam was not interested in social life or cultural pursuits. She liked children, animals, landscape gardening, home renovations, and an active life. She liked to buy a house in an unpopular area, fix it up, sell it when the area improved and prices rose, and then move on.[14] She had enough money to employ an array of servants, nurses, governesses, carpenters, and yard men, and she managed this small domestic army, along with her husband and seven children, with zest and skill.

When Angelica decided that it would be better for Patrick and the other children to live in the country, the Putnams bought a farm on Martha's Vineyard—Valleydale Farm at Chilmark—which had previously been in the Hammett family for at least four generations. The farm had an old rambling house, more than 200 acres of land, 5,000 feet of shoreline, a hill that looked out over Vineyard Sound, and two ponds.[15] Angelica renovated the house, and the family lived there year round for several years. They raised Shetland ponies, and on Sundays people came out from Vineyard Haven and paid a small fee to ride them around an exercise ring. Angelica Putnam also kept several monkeys and chimpanzees. She liked to say she could never resist a monkey in a pet store window.[16]

At Valleydale Farm there was an old Indian graveyard, where Dr. Putnam, ever the curious scientist, dug up a complete skeleton. He strung it together with wire and hung it in his New York office as a demonstration aid, but then, equally characteristically, he began to feel that he might have been guilty of vandalism and desecration. He finally took the skeleton back to Martha's Vineyard and returned it, still wired, to the grave from which he had taken it.[17]

Patrick and his siblings who were old enough attended the North Road and West Tisbury Schools on the Vineyard. Angelica Putnam also hired a German governess for the boys and a French-speaking governess for the girls. Every year Charles and Angelica brought all the children into New York City to their home at 121 East 38th Street for the Christmas holidays.

In self-reflective moments in later years Patrick Putnam recalled two incidents in particular from his childhood. He remembered that he had written "Patrick Putnam, the King of the World" inside his geography book at the Tisbury School.[18] It was either an early indication of his adventurous explorer spirit or, more likely, an expression of his perceived place in his own small world, the world of his family, where he indeed was king.

The second incident also took place on the Vineyard, and Patrick recounted it when he was accused by a friend, Emily Hahn, of being so intent on his own concerns that he ignored the legitimate rights of others. One day when he was twelve, Mademoiselle Blanche Coulon, the stocky, blonde, French governess from the country near Belfort, called him to lunch, but he refused to move from under a bush in the yard until he had finished turning over, one by one, each page in the rather large book he was reading. The governess complained to his mother about how naughty and unreasonable he had been. "Mother, though, beside being authoritative and, to some people, rather formidable, also had some ideas as peculiar as my own even if not always the same," Putnam wrote Hahn. "So I told her why I had looked at each page,—that it was because I thought that a gnat had alighted on a page and had perhaps been caught and that I wanted to save him from death at my hands."[19] His mother accepted the explanation as perfectly reasonable. Putnam conceded that he had trouble drawing lines between what was reasonable behavior and what was not, and he hinted that it came from having a mother who preferred interesting ideas and a concern for animals to good behavior.

Thinking back on this incident, Putnam insisted that it was not pity for the gnat that had motivated him but a twelve-year-old boy's fear of the fires of hell. He added this comment on the religious environment of his childhood: "I had been born and brought up in a household of which the father believed in atheism; and the mother, with venomous hatred of God-palaver, preached it bitterly even if she did not believe in it. But at twelve for a time I wondered if perhaps there was not truth in what so many people said they believed in—in a hell into which were thrust when they died, by a Creator of Hell, Men and Gnats, and the whole Univ[erse]."[20]

Patrick had succeeded in surrounding himself with siblings, but he continued to be the one who really counted in the family. He gloried in this. He liked being "Patrick Putnam, the King of the World." At the same time he knew that this was not a feeling he was supposed to have; he was not supposed to dominate his brothers and sisters. In theory, at least, they were all equal. This double message could leave him feeling torn with conflict and guilt. In the summer of 1922, several weeks before his eighteenth birthday, his father chided him for not being very nice to his brothers and sisters. Patrick's response was to run away from home. He simply vanished.[21] Charles and Angelica Putnam went up and down the East River in New York trying to find a ship he might have sailed on. They asked the police to trace him, describing him as a tall, thin boy who "sometimes stammers when excited."[22] They received one report that he had been killed in an automobile accident.

Months later Patrick returned, and his father found him calmly sitting on the sofa in the family living room. He had been working in a factory in the Middle West. His parents could say little, for flight was a family tradition. Both of them had at one time or another run away from home. Charles had run away when he was ten but was found and returned by authorities in Nova Scotia.[23] Angelica had eloped when she was twenty-two. Patrick Tracy Lowell Putnam was to make flight from the world into which he had been born and from its demands on him a way of life. But he never left without keeping open the option of coming back.

"Desiderata in the Choice
of a Vocation"

After four years in Vineyard schools Patrick Putnam was sent to a preparatory school, the Gunnery, in Washington, Connecticut. From there he went to Harvard College, entering in 1921 during the tenure of A. Lawrence Lowell, his "uncle of sorts."[1]

Abbott Lawrence Lowell was an imperious figure who presided over Harvard University for almost twenty-five years, from 1909 until 1933. In accord with his belief that the goal of a liberal education should be to know a little of everything and one thing very well, Lowell replaced Charles Eliot's elective system with a program of major and minor fields of concentration and a general examination to be given to all graduating seniors. He raised the money to replace the snobbish eating clubs at Harvard with a more democratic "house system" in which students and tutors would live together in an intellectually richer and socially less discriminating atmosphere. He believed in First Amendment freedoms, strongly supporting the rights of socialist and pro-German faculty members during World War I, and he gave vigorous public support to Woodrow Wilson's proposal for a League of Nations.

Other aspects of A. Lawrence Lowell's tenure were less happy. He supported the right of black students to attend Harvard but would not allow them to live in the dormitories. In 1924, during Patrick's senior year, Lowell tried to establish a quota system for Jewish students at Harvard, a proposal that was rejected by the Board of Overseers, the governing body of the university. Lowell was a longtime member of the national committee of the Immigration Restriction League, and in 1927 he was the dominant member of the three-man investigatory committee that upheld the conduct of the Massachusetts judiciary during the trials of Nicola Sacco and Bartolomeo Vanzetti and allowed these two Italian-born anarchists to be executed.[2] A Brahmin distaste for outsiders disturbing the waters in which he swam so contentedly at the top marred an otherwise impressive career. It was a distaste that Patrick Putnam as an undergraduate saw no reason to challenge.

At Harvard, Patrick majored in chemistry in his freshman year and then switched to anthropology. The department was small, with perhaps twenty undergraduate concentrators in any given year, but it had three distinguished professors: Roland B. Dixon, Alfred Tozzer, and Earnest A. Hooton. Dixon had been there the longest, ever since his days as an undergraduate and graduate student. A small, reserved man, he was professor of ethnology and "a passionate bibliographer" with an unsurpassed knowledge of anthropological literature from around the world. He lived with his sister in what a colleague described as "a beautiful country home, intentionally selected for its remoteness from Cambridge."[3] Three times a week he ventured in to give courses in the races and cultures of North America, or South America, or Oceania, or Asia, but he tended to be overshadowed by his two more flamboyant colleagues.

Alfred Tozzer was the archaeologist, a specialist in the ancient Maya, and one of a handful of eminent people on the Harvard faculty who were always addressed as "Mister" rather than "Professor"—the implication being that the designation of a gentleman ("Mister" or "Master") was preferable to that of a mere professor. Tozzer's reputation rather outran his actual qualifications. The son of a pharmacist and drugstore owner in Lynn, Massachusetts, he was not wealthy himself, but not long after getting established at Harvard he married a wealthy woman, Margaret Castle of Honolulu, and gave up active research in favor of a leisurely academic life. One student from the 1920s remembers being invited to Tozzer's large home a few blocks from the Peabody Museum to discuss whether he should become an anthropologist. A uniformed maid ushered him into the library, where after a couple of routine questions Tozzer asked him abruptly, "How much money has your father got?" Other students later explained to the still indignant student that Tozzer thought anyone coming into the Department of Anthropology ought to be a gentleman with sufficient money to support himself as a scholar.[4]

The third and best-known member of the department was Earnest A. Hooton, who taught physical anthropology. Hooton was a Methodist minister's son from Wisconsin and had joined the Harvard faculty after studying at Oxford on a Rhodes Fellowship. Like Franz Boas at Columbia, Hooton was a pioneer in the use of statistics in the study of human beings, but whereas Boas used statistics to emphasize the effects of the environment, Hooton used then to stress the importance of heredity. He was an outspoken advocate of eugenics and a popular and controversial writer and speaker.

Hooton's classroom lectures, delivered before all male undergraduates, deliberately bordered on the vulgar. Hooton would imitate a gorilla, recite his own doggerel, and read from exotic and sometimes sexually explicit travel accounts, all in an effort to get undergraduates curious enough to want to go and see for themselves. He peppered his lectures with suggestions of peoples who should be studied, of distant places where it would be interesting to go. Outside the classroom Hooton was "an extraordinarily loving and concerned professor."[5] He and his wife served tea to students every weekday afternoon. Once a week either Hooton or Tozzer hosted a seminar where the guest of honor was likely to be one of the great names in anthropology: Marcel Mauss or Bronislaw Malinowski or Franz Boas.

Between classes anthropology students gathered on the steps of the Peabody Museum to smoke and talk. Patrick Putnam is remembered (not altogether kindly) as an exhibitionist intent on being different. He liked to pick up ants crawling along the steps of the museum and eat them. He often had a pet monkey or chimpanzee with him. Once he and Tom Scudder, another undergraduate and perhaps his best friend, popped out of a sixty-floor attic window of the Peabody Museum and chased each other around the two-foot-wide, downward sloping zinc ledge that circles both the Peabody and the Museum of Comparative Zoology some sixty feet above the ground. Scudder chased Putnam around the entire complex before he caught him, and then the two wrestled on the ledge high above a lip-biting audience.[6]

In the summer of 1924 Patrick Putnam and Tom Scudder traveled together to England, France, and Germany. On board ship Putnam started a journal but kept it up only until they reached land. Their shipmates included two girls who paid no attention to them, several "freshwater college boys [who] have improved on acquaintance," and some "Tech men," whom he thought "very nice chaps." But Putnam was most impressed by a young Mexican businessman, "a near approach to a cosmopolite," who gave them advice on where to find cheap hotels, good beds, and "erotica, as he calls them in Berlin and Paris." Putnam continued, "He is, to me, a great relief in his freedom from American 'mores.' He is frankly and joyfully unmoral, yet fair."[7] It was a persona he wanted to emulate.

In the tradition of the gentleman scholar, Putnam did not work very hard at Harvard. In the late fall of his junior year he reported to his father that he was expecting a C in English, an E in history, a B in Anthropology 1, and D, C, and C respectively in his other two anthropology courses and his statistics course. His debts, he admitted, were "enormous," including a $50 garage bill for repairs on his automobile.[8] Putnam managed to graduate with honors (*cum laude*) in anthropology but not with the *magna cum laude* that his friend and classmate Carleton Coon took at midyear before going on rapidly to earn an M.A. and a Ph.D. In the end it was only through administrative courtesy that Putnam was allowed to graduate at all, for he had steadfastly refused to sign up for the required freshman writing course, saying it did not interest him at all and he saw no reason why he should take it. Finally, a special course was created for him, and he was allowed to receive a degree. He broke other rules as it suited him. He joined, for no reason that any of his friends could figure out, the Reserve Officers Training Corps (ROTC), but soon tired of it and stopped going. When the officers came to look for him, he was having tea with President Lowell, who allowed him to slip out the back door while the officers waited at the front.[9]

In a letter to his father near the end of his life Patrick Putnam mentioned his "Dutch courage" in college, which he called the result of excess drinking.[10] Two other clues to his college life survive in his personal papers, termite-eaten and covered with mildew from years in Africa. One is a packet of several dozen printed invitations to debutante balls, teas, and dinners in Cambridge, Boston, and New York, nearly all dated 1925, Putnam's senior year; on each card he noted whether the invitation was "accepted" or, in a very few cases, "declined." The other is a written wager, signed by two students and formally witnessed by two others at 11:38 P.M. on January 26, 1925. In it, two friends promised that they would pay Putnam $25 each if within a year from that date he had visited New Guinea. A Harvard professor (surely Hooton) had said in an offhand way that New Guinea was the wildest bit of land on the surface of the globe.[11] That was all Patrick needed to choose it as his next destination.

Patrick Putnam did spend nearly a year in Dutch New Guinea and Java. He went alone, taking with him such official credentials as he could get. His uncle, James Putnam, gave him a letter of introduction to Gen. Charles L. McCawley "in the hope that you can direct him to the proper people in Washington for his purposes. I am a little vague about his purposes but understand that he wants to meet some of the Smithsonian people among others."[12] Eventually, the American Geological Society made Patrick Putnam a Fellow and gave him a letter to take with him to the East Indies. He sailed to Singapore, where he hired a Javanese guide, a sailor who knew some of the languages of southern New Guinea, and they took a steamer to Merauke on the southern coast of New Guinea.

Patrick Putnam spent two or three months among the Papuans of New Guinea, but he thought them, according to the *Boston Post*, "the dumbest and laziest people on earth."[13] He made his base on the southern coast of the island, and from there he and his guide traveled inland, up rivers, in dugout canoes. He spent a week at one village about seventy miles from the coast, sleeping in a tent and bartering copper wire, mirrors, knives, and cotton cloth for string and fiber skirts, necklaces, amulets, drums, mats, and other items to take back to the Peabody Museum. The *Boston Post* reporter made much of his spartan diet—dried fish, lemons, and rice—and of a rumored attack in one village which he deflected by making a great show of loading the clip of his automatic. Little else is known about this period in his life other than that he frequently visited prostitutes and that in Jakarta he picked up the gonorrhea to which he later attributed his apparent sterility.[14]

Putnam became very ill in New Guinea and was cared for by his servant and guide, Mohamed bin Tjatoer, who brought him back to Singapore and then returned with him to the United States for a long visit.[15] This rather endearing pattern of becoming ill in an inaccessible place, being nursed back to health by someone on the scene, and then wanting in his gratitude and affection to continue to keep that person as part of his life would be repeated two years later with Abanzima. In a larger sense it was an aspect of his capacity for friendship. Putnam's friendships with all kinds of people were beyond counting, and they were for life. He was always interested in news of his friends, and he would turn up abruptly at various times in their lives.

Patrick Putnam was back in New York early in 1927. It was the Jazz Age, and with college friends and younger brothers Sebastian and Russell, he drank Prohibition whiskey and pursued women until one morning, he later told a reporter, he woke up sober and decided to go back to anthropology.[16] The actual decision, although it may have been made that suddenly, was the result of considerable thought. In the Hotel Vereeniging in Indonesia, Patrick Putnam had sat down to assess his future. On a sheet of hotel stationery he made a career chart, a remarkable document headed "Desiderata in the choice of a vocation for myself." It reads:

1. The possibility of being self supporting as soon as possible
2. The pleasing of my father
3. The pleasing of my relatives
4. The pleasing of myself, in that it shall be:
   1. lucrative
   2. interesting
   3. not able to be called or considered as humanitarian
   4. conducive to, or at least not prohibitive of travel
   5. not tending to separate me from friends

Next Putnam listed the career possibilities he was considering: anthropologist, practicing physician, research physician, lawyer, curiosity dealer, planter, contracté (abroad), consular service. In columns he noted whether each possibility "Does not fulfill," "Completely fulfills," or merely "Satisfies" his desiderata.

None of the possible professions proved to be completely satisfactory. Being an anthropologist would be interesting and conducive to travel, and it would not separate him from his friends, Putnam noted. But it would not be lucrative, might be considered humanitarian, and would definitely not please his father. The profession that would most please his father was medicine, and Patrick Putnam rated both research and practicing physician as "interesting." But they would be considered humanitarian, and neither would allow him to be immediately self-supporting, which was his number one criterion. Law would satisfy all his own desires as expressed in desideratum 4 and would please his relatives (his uncle, Albert Rathbone, was a lawyer). But again, it would not soon make him self-supporting, nor was he convinced that law would please his father. And so it went through the list. The professions of curiosity dealer, planter, and contracté abroad would please neither his father nor his relatives, nor were they likely to be lucrative. The consular service would please his relatives but would not be lucrative and would separate him from his friends.

At the end of the chart he added some epigrams, expressions of his personal philosophy:

> Everybody in the world except a tiller of the soil is a parasite whose host is man. And everyone without exception is a parasite on earth.
>
> Enthusiasm cannot exist without faith, and faith I have not.
>
> I have neither love nor hate for my fellow man; my tolerance is too all inclusive: by it I condone my own and the sins of all the world.
>
> There are many who believe, and glory in their beliefs. I believe, also: I believe that nothing matters, and despair in my belief.
>
> Ambition is a faith in one's destiny.
>
> Curiosity invites me to examine, but nothing makes me build. An empty belly calls to me to fill it, and I hear the call and obey. The voice of achieving, which is heard by the fortunate, never calls to me. Or if it does it is faint and soon forgotten. I do not like to follow it because I do not know from whom or where it comes.[17]

The chart and the accompanying philosophical statements are those of a rebellious but still family-bound young man, whose first concern was to become free of his father by becoming self-supporting, but whose second and third concerns were to please that same father and other "parental" figures such as his mother, her brother Albert, and his father's sister Elizabeth. Only after all these authoritarian figures were accounted for could Putnam get around to pleasing himself. And pleasing himself he set forth in a casually cynical fashion: he wanted to do something that was interesting and lucrative, that would allow him to travel and be with his friends, and that could not remotely be considered noble.

Patrick Putnam's relation to his father is easy to find in this document. But there are echoes of a second voice as well, a voice that disdained flowery talk of ambition, achievement, faith, and serving humanity, the voice of someone who had idealistic, moral, even religious concerns but would not admit it, for she hated pious cant and would attribute to herself only the most self-serving of motives. It was the voice of his mother.

Angelica Talcott Rathbone Putnam was regarded by people outside the family as a formidable and determined woman whose willful actions sometimes appeared to "stop just this side of insanity," as one friend put it.[18] Her letters to her son show her endearing side: her forthrightness, her indifference to what others thought, her lack of pretension, her single-minded and clear-eyed pursuit of what she wanted and considered important. She who had adopted six destitute children would tolerate no talk of benevolence; such talk she considered pious nonsense. Their coming was for Patrick's pleasure and her own. She gave the children everything that money could buy, and she gave them of herself in full measure. She supervised their school work, planned outings and family festivities, and kept them all occupied in a constant round of activities. Angelica Putnam had neither moral nor intellectual pretensions. The intellectual in the family was Aunt Elsie—Charles's unmarried younger sister, Elizabeth—of Commonwealth Avenue in Boston, who liked to discuss books and current events with her nieces and nephews and take them to plays and museums. Angelica Putnam preferred outdoor activities. "I should have known your mother. Wasn't it she who said that many books were a burden to the mind," one of Patrick's friends wrote him.[19]

However much Patrick Putnam may have been like his mother and eager to please his father, what he wanted to do when he was twenty-two years old was get out on his own as soon as possible. Accordingly, on his return from Indonesia in January 1927, and after an interlude of social life in New York, he took an apartment in Cambridge and started work at Harvard toward a master's degree in anthropology. That summer he and several other graduate students made 35-mm black and white movies for anthropology classes, using footage acquired from the Pathé Film Exchange. It was a Hooton project, a farseeing one (although it foundered with the coming of sound and the Depression). Putnam looked at card catalogues and films in the Pathé offices in New York. When he found promising footage shot in Africa, Melanesia, Polynesia, or elsewhere, he sent it on to Hooton, Carleton Coon, and Douglas Byers in Cambridge, and they turned out seven or eight films, including their own version of Robert Flaherty's *Nanook of the North.*[20]

Then came the expedition with Wulsin and Katz, followed by Putnam's ten months on his own in the Belgian Congo. In 1929 he returned to Cambridge for a few months. He brought with him the young female chimpanzee Chimpo, whom he had toilet trailed and taught to eat at a table with a knife and fork. Chimpo went everywhere Patrick Putnam did, and stories are still told about her activities, from correcting the table manners of Pat's friends to throwing rocks at black maids on their way home from work in college dormitories—for in Africa the villagers tormented chimpanzees, and Chimpo had learned to respond in kind. The stories emphasize both Chimpo's uncanny cleverness and her unruliness, which could be destructive. If pets are chosen, albeit unconsciously, as an extension of their owner's personality, Chimpo was an apt choice for Patrick Putnam.

Meanwhile, Putnam was making plans to return to Africa and to the village woman he loved. He had decided to live permanently in Africa; there seemed to be no other way to keep Abanzima in his life. "I'm not saying I'm beaten," Putnam told Emily Hahn in New York in the fall of 1929. "I may marry her yet, but even so I certainly won't be able to bring her home. I realize that now. . . . I used to think that if I gave my father and mother enough time to get used to the idea—But it wouldn't have worked. I've found that out by trying to talk it over sensibly with them."[21] Putnam told Hahn that when his mother heard about Abanzima, she fired the family's black maid and vowed never to have another black servant in the house. After that she simply would not discuss it.

Putnam was trying to work out a way to live permanently in the Belgian Congo. If he had any illusions about going back to the Congo as a Harvard-sponsored anthropologist, these were dispelled in a conference with Hooton. Putnam had returned to Harvard with two kinds of material. He had scattered notes on pygmies, and he had notes and an outline for a book on the Mboli, Abanzima's people, based on his two months' stay in Buondo's village. When he showed the outline to Hooton, the professor told him coolly that everything he had could be found in a book written four years earlier by a Frenchman.[22] Hooton suggested he write up what he had anyway, for possible publication in the Harvard African series, but Putnam soon realized that he did not have nearly enough material for a serious study. He finally wrote a seven-page essay, "Mboli Science," mainly a collection of what he had learned from Abanzima about food taboos and prohibitions against sexual intercourse before going on a hunt or before planting. Apologetically, Putnam sent this modest effort to Diedrich Westermann, professor at the University of Berlin and codirector of the London-based International Institute of African Languages and Cultures, asking him to look it over.[23] The essay was never published.

Putnam's other topic was the pygmies, a people whose real or imagined presence in Africa had been part of the lure and romance of that continent since the beginnings of recorded human history. The Egyptians knew as early as the Sixth Dynasty (c. 2300 B.C.) that a small people who liked to sing and dance lived in a great forest in central Africa to the west of the Mountains of the Moon. This was reported to Pharoah Pepi II by an Egyptian noble and caravan leader, Harkhuf, during his fourth trading expedition to Nubia. Pepi II ordered Harkhuf to bring one of those dancers back with him, to treat the dancer well and to guard him day and night so that he would arrive in good health. Whether or not he was able to comply, Harkhuf was so pleased by this correspondence that he had both sides of it added to the inscriptions on his tomb, where, squeezed in around the other inscriptions, it was first noticed and published by the Italian archaeologist Ernesto Schiaparelli in 1892.[24]

For several millennia after Harkhuf's correspondence, North Africans continued to have some knowledge of a small people who lived south of the desert. Herodotus reported that he had heard of five Nasamonians traveling south of the Libyan desert who were seized and carried away by a band of diminutive men.[25] A mosaic from the dining room of a Roman house in Tunisia dating from around 250 A.D. shows a hunting scene on the Nile in which little men with large heads, long trunks, and short legs are attacking a hippopotamus.[26] A wall painting from Pompeii, now in the National Museum at Naples, shows a river landscape in which short men are fighting crocodiles and a hippopotamus.[27] But neither the Egyptians nor Herodotus called these small people "pygmies."

The name "pygmy" comes from the Greek word *pygmē*, which means "fist" and also a short unit of length, the distance between the elbow and the knuckles. In the *Iliad* Homer described men of Troy coming out to battle like cranes flying "over the streams of Ocean, hoarsely calling, to bring a slaughter on the Pygmy warriors."[28] It has been suggested that Homer's offhand mention of Pygmy warriors may have alluded a story widespread in northern Europe in ancient times that at the edges of the world where the great dome of the sky approaches the flat earth, the sky is so low that only dwarf-sized human beings can live there. Between the earth and the sky great winds and migrating birds (Homer's cranes) rush in and out, and tiny men do battle with them. Homer's Pygmy warriors, then, having no geographical location other than the periphery of Earth around which "the streams of Ocean" flow, belong to the world of myth, not that of ethnographic reality.[29]

It was Aristotle, writing around 340 B.C.—some five centuries after Homer—who connected both the cranes and the Pygmies of myth with empirical reports of short people in central Africa, thus placing them geographically. In his *Historia animalium* Aristotle wrote, "The cranes fly to the lakes above Egypt, from which flows the Nile; there dwell the Pygmies, and this is no fable but the pure truth."[30]

As the Roman Empire collapsed and the Muslim world expanded around the Mediterranean, Europe was increasingly cut off from Africa. The voyages of exploration in the fifteenth and sixteenth centuries brought Europeans into contact with the coasts of Africa, but the interior remained unknown to them. By the eighteenth century, European scholars were convinced that pygmies were mythical creatures like elves and one-eyed men, despite an occasional unsubstantiated traveler's description of them. Not until the German explorer and botanist Georg Schweinfurth published his two-volume work, *In the Heart of Africa,* in 1874 was it definitely established that there were small peoples in central Africa. Schweinfurth could simply have described a people four- to four-and-a-half-feet tall who were called "Akkas" by their Mangbetu neighbors, but he had had a classical education and knew what would draw the attention of his readers. He called them "pygmies" and wrote that he had found "living evidence of a truth that lay under the myth of some thousand years."[31] His book became a best seller, and the people he described have been popularly known as pygmies ever since, although anthropologists prefer the KiNgwana name Mbuti or BaMbuti (Ba is the plural prefix).

Immediately after Schweinfurth several other explorers traveled through central Africa, including reporter Henry Morton Stanley (sent out by the *New York Herald* to search for the supposedly lost missionary David Livingstone) and Venetian geographer Giovanni Miani. Miani died en route, but when his collections arrived in Khartoum they were accompanied by two young pygmy boys whom Miani had purchased from a Mangbetu king, intending to turn them over to the Italian Royal Geographical Society. The boys were examined and measured and quizzed at length in 1873 by scientific societies in Khartoum and Cairo, where one doctor was particularly concerned to learn if they had anything resembling the beginning of a tail.[32] They were then sent on to Italy for more of the same by scientists in Naples and Florence.

The two boys, named Thiebau and Keralla (from Cher-Alla, "favored by God"), were discussed by scientific societies in Paris, Madrid, Berlin, and London, for they were the first pygmies to reach Europe. At issue were several momentous questions. Were they true representatives of a pygmy race, or sports of nature? If they were true pygmies, did they belong to a separate branch of the human family, perhaps the last remnant of an ancient but now nearly defunct Ethiopian race? Or were they a degenerate form of some other race? Or were they a form intermediate between humans and monkeys—the missing link? This last Darwinian speculation was tempting to many, but it had frighteningly large ramifications, from the philosophical to the mundane. One immediate practical question was what should be done with the two pygmy boys. If they were considered less than human, would they end up in a zoo? The president of the Italian Royal Geographical Society, Cesare Correnti, settled that concern by insisting that from their eyes, their smiles, the grace of their movements, and the splendor of their intelligence, it was obvious that the pygmies were human.

The two boys were given over to the care of the vice-president of the Italian Royal Geographical Society, Count Miniscalchi Erizzo, who took them to live at his villa in the Veneto. Thiebau died in Italy of tuberculosis in 1893.[33] In the 1950s Colin Turnbull, inquiring of the Miniscalchi family as to what had become of the boys, learned that Keralla had returned to Africa, where he became a saddler in the Ethiopian army. He was last heard of shortly before World War II.[34]

Other pygmies were brought to Europe for study in the following decades. In 1893 Franz Stuhlmann, who had been with Emin Pasha in Africa, brought two pygmy women to Europe. In 1906 an English big game hunter, Colonel James J. Harrison, got permission from the Belgian authorities to bring six pygmy volunteers to England. They stayed for eighteen months and then went apparently happily back to the Ituri Forest. During their stay in England their health was said to improve, and they gained an average of nine and a half pounds each.[35]

Through these decades the main interest of anthropologists was in the physical characteristics of the pygmies, their origin, and their possible genetic relationship to other peoples, including the Bushmen of the Kalahari desert and hunting peoples of small stature in the Philippines, Celebes, and New Guinea. It was Patrick Putnam who first insisted that pygmy "culture," the way pygmies lived, was worthy of study on its own account. In the essay he wrote for Hooton, "Pigmies of the Ituri and Neighboring Forests," he duly noted their small size and distinct physical characteristics, but only in the most general of terms, and without the physical measurements and blood types he had been sent to get. The pygmies were the smallest people in Africa, about four-and-a-half-feet tall; they were lighter in skin color than most black Africans; and they had lips that revealed the red membrane inside the mouth, a bulging forehead, wide eyebrows, very large bright eyes, and a hoarse constrained voice as if their speech were repressed. But to Putnam, what truly set them apart from other groups living in the Ituri Forest was not their short stature or how they looked but how they lived. The pygmies did not plant gardens or work iron or make pottery. They lived by hunting and gathering in the forest and on such vegetable foods as they could beg, barter, or steal from the villagers. They hung around the villages, and a group of them would have long-established ties to a certain village but, if offended, would vanish into the forest. The villagers tolerated them but considered them pesky raiders who were more animal than human, rather like crocodiles, gorillas, chimpanzees, and leopards.[36]

Putnam had tried to study their customs and traditions, but he had learned very little, for he was not yet able to talk to them except through a village interpreter. He did have one interesting hypothesis. During his weeks in Buondo's village in 1928 he had tried to puzzle out the exact relation between the Mboli villagers and their pygmies. In the Congo he had read some notes on pygmies by a Belgian civil servant who called that relationship "symbiosis": the pygmies brought meat from the forest and received in return plantains, salt, and old pots and tools from the villagers; the relation was one of mutual benefit, in which each participant needed the other in order to survive.[37] Putnam disagreed with that analysis. "In the first place," he wrote, "the pygmies bring small and occasional gifts of game, but receive from the negroes a regular and substantial ration. . . . In the second place, the negroes are pretty good hunters and get for themselves far more game than they receive from their pigmies." He thought the pygmies were parasites on the villagers, who could easily get along without them.[38]

The question, then, was why the villagers tolerated and even wooed them. The relationship was not symbiosis; it was not charity; nor was it that of master and slave, for the pygmies could leave at any time. What did the pygmies give the villagers that was of value? In Buondo's village Putnam answered his own question. He listened to the men of the village talking about the old days, about almost constant warfare between tribes and neighboring villages and against the

Arab slave traders, the BaNguana, who came in from the East coast of Africa to get ivory. The Mboli had fought the BaNguana bitterly, and in their struggles the pygmies were valuable allies. They moved silently through the forest, alert to any changes and quick to warn the villagers of enemy approach. They would return to the forest, hide in the thick undergrowth, and ambush the attackers with their arrows, which were deadly at close range. But "nowadays," Putnam wrote,

> since the white man has come and put a stop to all this fighting (and well does the negro, in the midst of his discontent admit this benefit of the white man), the value of the pigmy has declined to almost nothing. But this was only a short time ago, and the habit of feeding the pigmies is so ingrained in negro life, that they still go on doing it. However, it is bound to come in time, that the negro will see his economic error, and stop supporting the now worthless pigmies. In that case, the pigmy will have to go to work for the white man, which he has been averse to doing heretofore, or to learn agriculture, which certain groups have already attempted with some success, or to live entirely on the forest, and whether to live or die we do not know.[39]

Patrick Putnam reported to Hooton his intriguing hypothesis on a question that would be much discussed in pygmy studies over the next decades, but he had only the scrappiest of data. Instead of narrowing his topic to something that was manageable, as Wulsin had done in limiting himself to the archaeology of the Shari River valley, Putnam had broadened his to include not only the pygmies but the villagers with whom they lived. He insisted that one could not be understood without the other, and he was right, but he had also set for himself—particularly as a beginning anthropologist—an impossible task. Hooton was vaguely encouraging, but Putnam knew that measured by what the Peabody Museum expected to get for the research money it expended, he had been a failure. Both Frederick Wulsin and Carleton Coon, whom Hooton had sent to Morocco, were soon to publish the results of their work in the Harvard African Studies. Putnam had

nothing to publish. His career as an anthropologist was at an end unless he managed somehow to redeem himself.

He could not go back to Africa immediately as an anthropologist,
so he looked for other possibilities. Putnam thought again about international diplomacy, especially after reading a book about Thomas
Raffles of Singapore, which he borrowed from the Harvard College Library. Sir Thomas Stamford Raffles (1781–1826) was a British empire-
builder in the area where Patrick Putnam had done his first exploring,
the East Indies. Raffles was governor in Sumatra and the founder of
Singapore, a neglected island that he had turned into the key British
foothold in the Far East. He was known for his friendliness to the native Malays and for his interest in natural history. He kept four men on
the colonial payroll whose only job was to go into the forest to collect
natural history specimens: plants, insects, fishes, mollusks, birds, and
mammals. The larger specimens were sent back to London to become
the nucleus of the Zoological Gardens in Regent's Park, London's first
zoo, which Raffles established in 1826. Raffles built a model plantation in Java on land that had been leased to him, more eager to show
what could be done than to derive profit from it. A local admirer reported that Raffles "hated the habit of the Dutch who lived in Molocca
of running down the Malays, and the Dutch detested him in return: so
much so that they would not sit down beside him. But Mr. Raffles
loved always to be on good terms with the Malays, the poorest could
speak to him." It was said that "he governed to promote the good of
the people."[40] Patrick Putnam made these notes and others on the
manner of ruling of Sir Thomas Stamford Raffles and kept them in his
papers. If there was one single model for the way he would attempt to
live in the Belgian Congo, it was Raffles, the British son of a merchant
seaman who one hundred years earlier had shipped out to the Malay
archipelago as a clerk with the East India Company and had risen to
become England's foremost statesman in the Far East.

But first Putnam had to find a way to get back to the Belgian

Congo. He could not go as a clerk and move up in the consular or diplomatic service, for he was not a Belgian. Nor could he go simply on
his own, as a would-be settler; the Belgian government did not like
people hanging around in their colony who had no official reason for
being there. But they did need medical personnel so badly that they
were willing to take people who were neither Belgians nor medical
doctors. Putnam decided that the quickest way to return to Africa and
to be paid for being there would be to enroll in a three-month course
given by the Belgian Red Cross in Brussels, after which he would be
qualified to work in the Belgian Congo as an *agent sanitaire*.

Repeatedly, Putnam sought to convey to his family and friends his
sense of how safe, how easy, and how civilized life in Africa was. "An
excellent gravel highway connects the Nile with the River Congo," he
told the Harvard Travelers Club before he left. "Hostile natives are a
thing of the past. The last rebellion in this part of the Congo was that of
the Bobua in 1915, and the last in the whole country was one down
here [pointing to a map] in the Kasai in about 1921."[41] Putnam
showed the Travelers Club photographic slides of life in a Mboli village, Abanzima's village, pointing out their houses, plantations, the
hangar where the men gathered, and a dance in the center of the village. This "simple brutal people," as he called them, had lived in "a
happy state of intertribal war" in the Ituri Forest along the equator in
Africa, a tropical rain forest so impenetrable that it was one of the last
regions to be encroached upon by conquerors. Invaders eventually
came: first the hosts of Bantus from the South and Sudanese from the
north, followed in the nineteenth century by Arab slave catchers and
raiders and ivory traders, both BaNguana Zanzibars from the southeast, and Egyptian Arabs from the north. Then came European explorers, missionaries, soldiers, and, in turn, Belgian rubber gatherers
and tax collectors.

By the 1920s in the Ituri Forest, Putnam continued, there were
Greek traders, mining companies, agricultural companies that export

cotton and coffee, and an enlightened Belgian administration more put upon than exploitive. The Belgians were trying to stamp out such native customs as intertribal warfare, cannibalism, trial by poison, slavery, and polygamy. They had been successful, except for polygamy, which Putnam called the most deeply rooted and the least harmful. It was, he thought, a natural consequence of the unequal sex ratio resulting from constant warfare; as warfare ceased, he told the Harvard Travelers Club, it too would fade away.

In New York, Putnam called on African experts, including James Chapin, ornithologist at the American Museum of Natural History, who with his colleague Herbert Lang had been in the Congo from 1909 to 1915 on a scientific expedition sponsored by the museum. Chapin immediately proposed Putnam for membership in the Explorers Club in New York, and the two became lifelong friends. In Washington, D.C., Putnam spent an hour and a half in conference with the Belgian ambassador to the United States.[42] Then he "said goodbye to the friends of his Falstaffian life"[43] and headed off—by way of Belgium—to the Congo and the woman he loved.

The course at the School of Tropical Medicine in Brussels ran from October 1929 to February 1930. The lectures and readings were in French, which Putnam had learned from the family's French governess. He rented a spacious apartment in a large suburban house in Uccle, and he and Chimpo moved in. Bored and restless, Chimpo escaped whenever possible and harassed the neighbors, who in turn called the gendarmes. Angelica Putnam came for Christmas in a last desperate attempt to get Patrick to change his mind. She found him in a nearly empty apartment, for Chimpo had done so much damage to the furniture that most of it had been removed. One morning when Angelica was alone in the apartment, the chimpanzee grabbed her and hung on with arms, legs, and teeth for five hours, until Pat's voice on the phone ordered Chimpo to let go.[44]

For six weeks Angelica Putnam tried without success to get Patrick to forget about Africa and return home with her. She went back to America alone and threw herself into renovations on the house and garden at the new family place in Bedford, New York—including a 12-by-12-foot addition to Patrick's bedroom, "the grandest in the house," she wrote him, "where you and Seb will be happy together but room for Chimp too. It is to have doors opening out where Chimp can walk in and out without going through the rest of the house."[45] (Chimpo's destructiveness had caused considerable tension on Patrick's most recent visit to Bedford.) Other letters continued the theme. A luxurious room and anything else he might want were waiting for him at home. "I do hope you are happy and that you are glad that you went for I am not.—everytime we are having a good time I am wishing you were here to enjoy it. Strawberry mousse for dessert for tonight—doesn't that sound good."[46] She reported that Patrick's friend Mary Linder and her roommate had been there, and the roommate was trying to psychoanalyze Angelica: she "asks leading questions but doesn't seem to make much headway."

Later that summer Angelica Putnam decided suddenly to build herself a shack on the beach at Martha's Vineyard as a place of refuge from the demands of her family. She and a workman went down one night and hid some furniture in the bushes. At eight o'clock the next morning she had four carpenters on the scene; the plumber drove a well at 2:20 P.M. and put in a pump and sink; by the end of the day the shack was finished, decorated with flotsam from the beach, and she had moved in. It was an example of her impulsiveness, the resources that money put at her command, and her managerial skill.

In mid-August 1930, preparing for a party, Angelica Putnam wrote Pat, in doggerel, as she often did:

> I've laid the glasses and silver
> but what I want is you!
> Many guests are coming from places near and far
> but what I want at my table is just YOU and me and PA.

Won't you ever come home again?
and can't you stay when you come?
With our love and our food and our beds and our board,
are you really quite so dumb
as to think that Nigs and bugs and the Pigs
are *quite as nice as home.*

Now you see I've burst into poetry again," she added, and went on with details about family matters. Then a serious note again: "It is so long now since we have had a cable from you and all our cables are returned. Pa and I are pretty worried and discouraged. Pa insists you have not arrived yet at the Red Cross. As you were due there June 1st and as it is now almost September I can't see what is wrong."[47] Finally, after more than two months of silence, "longer even than the Hookworm and elephant time," his father complained, Patrick Putnam cabled his parents.[48] He was at Wamba awaiting assignment.

From Wamba in the Belgian Congo that fall Patrick Putnam sent a report on some of his activities to the *New Yorker.* He and Abanzima spent Christmas in Faradje as guests of the local Belgian administrator, Baron van Zuylen and his family. "Billy" van Zuylen was fond of Pat Putnam and intrigued at Putnam's insisting on living openly with a native woman. And Christmas with him had become a tradition: in 1927 Wulsin, Putnam, and Katz had been van Zuylen's guests; in 1928 it had been Putnam, his father, and his brother; in 1929, when both had been in Belgium, van Zuylen invited Putnam to his ancestral home at Breda for the holidays. Now in 1930, back at his station in Africa, he invited Putnam and Abanzima for Christmas. Patrick Putnam rewarded his host by writing him afterward that Abanzima liked Mrs. van Zuylen "more than the other white ladies."[49]

Agent Sanitaire

Around the end of January 1931 Patrick Putnam moved from Wamba to Penge to take up his first official assignment as *agent sanitaire* for the Belgian Red Cross.[1] It was the only regular job he ever held in his life; his other periods of employment, most of them brief, were temporary, and he was paid by the day or the task. As *agent sanitaire* his job was to keep census and health records, to treat leprosy and wounds, and to give injections twice a week for syphilis and yaws, an infectious tropical disease that causes severe skin and bone lesions.

Penge, on the Aruwini River, had once been but was no longer an important trading center. Putnam lived in a brick house, surrounded by a veranda, which had once belonged to the local Belgian administrator. He set up his hospital in an old two-room schoolhouse. He had Abanzima with him and also several "boys" (employees) whom he had brought from Wamba. They included Helafu, Sabani, and Abanzinga, who was in charge of his menagerie of animals: the chimp, a monkey, a baboon, a slothlike creature called a parasseux, a donkey, and a guinea pig. Putnam was the only European in the area.[2]

Putnam's "Report from the Field," written while he was still at Wamba, was published in the *New Yorker* in February 1931. It was a breezy piece but carefully crafted. Putnam described a *New Yorker* cartoon recently sent to him showing two cameramen trying to get a group of pygmies to pose for them, while the pygmies are saying, "Nothing doing! We can do better with the Paramount-Mayer-Goldwyn people."[3] He hinted that this cynical view was closer to the truth than the frequent Sunday supplement reports of intrepid explorers encountering fearful dwarfs in the depths of unknown forests. He ended by making fun of a French film company that trained the pygmies to act like primitive arboreal men and then filmed them doing so. Ironically, within a few years he would be providing similar, although slightly more restrained, opportunities for film companies.

Putnam wrote his "report from the field" for two reasons. He wanted to establish himself as an expert on the pygmies. "I've had a good deal to do with pygmies, plentiful enough around here," he wrote. He also wanted not to be forgotten by the world he cared about at home, including the readers of the *New Yorker*. His plan succeeded. The world he yearned for did not forget him. Within a month of his arrival at Penge a young reporter for the *New Yorker*, Emily Hahn, came to visit, and soon the popular press began to call him the world's greatest expert on the pygmies, a title that he would carry to the end of his life.[4]

Emily Hahn had met Patrick Putnam in New York City in the fall of 1929 through Tom Scudder, his college classmate. She was interested in Africa; Putnam described himself as living there. They met several times, to look at the African animals in the Bronx Zoo and to visit the Africa exhibits in the American Museum of Natural History. He took her to the apartment he was sharing with several friends to introduce her to Chimpo. One night in 1929, shortly before he left for Belgium, Putnam told Hahn about Abanzima and about his family's intense opposition to his proposed marriage to her. To Hahn it seemed a wildly romantic and intriguing story.

Emily Hahn arrived in the Belgian Congo a little over a year later, in January 1931. Wandering alone and lost up the hilly streets of Matadi, the port city at the base of the rapids on the Congo River, she ran into the trading company official who had been sent by Patrick Putnam to look for her. It was her first experience of the way news traveled among Europeans in Africa and of the unspoken convention that they looked out for one another. With the young official's help she slid through customs, which otherwise would have kept her out, for the Belgian bureaucracy regarded any young, casually dressed woman traveling alone as a threat to public order.[5] From Matadi it turned out to be a six-week journey to Patrick Putnam's station in the bush. The trip began with fourteen hours on a train around the rapids on the Congo River to Kinshasa, the trek that had taken Joseph Conrad six weeks on foot forty years earlier. At Kinshasa she waited a week for the boat up the Congo River. After ten days on the river steamer, she arrived in Stanleyville, where eventually another emissary from Pat Putnam met her—a member of the Belgian consulate, who drove her as far as his home at the small settlement of Avakubi. There, finally, she was met by an elephant hunter who accompanied her on a three-day journey by motor-driver pirogue (canoe) and portage on foot through the forest to Penge.

As her pirogue neared Penge, several smaller pirogues shot out from the bank toward them, a grinning Patrick Putnam paddling one of them furiously. "Dr. Putnam, I presume?" she yelled back, "You've no business being here until six o'clock tonight."

"I never thought you'd get here," Patrick Putnam told her, "but now that you're here I'm going to chain you down. Lots of people *said* they'd come, but you're the only one who did."[6]

Putnam called Abanzima over and introduced her to their American visitor. Abanzima was older than Hahn expected, with shriveled breasts. She had decorative scars on her face and chest, and her teeth had been filed to points. Her head was temporarily shaved smooth, for she was in mourning for a relative.[7] Two other women were around the household and helped with the cooking: Nambedru, a cousin of

Abanzima's, and Ceci, a young girl whose father was a member of the local tribe and whose mother was a pygmy. Nambedru had an elongated, melon-shaped head and long eyes from the custom of infant head-binding practiced by her people, the Mboli. Putnam told Emily Hahn that Abanzima's head had not been bound only because her mother died in childbirth and no one else had bothered to do it.

Emily Hahn settled in at Penge for an indeterminate time. She was a journalist looking for a subject for her first book and in no hurry to get back to Depression America, where there were few jobs. Putnam took her on his census expeditions. He taught her how to give injections and keep records in the clinic. If a medical emergency arose in the middle of the night, he would wake her and ask her to hold the lamp while he treated the injury. Or he would want simply her company while he kept vigil at the bedside of a very ill patient. Often they talked about his work and medical ethics. He would ask whether it was foolish for him to wear himself out treating an old woman who was likely to die within a day or two when so many other people needed his attention. He wondered if it was malpractice when he made a mistake, as when he inadvertently gave an overdose of medicine to a woman who died as a result.[8] Emily Hahn read the books in Putnam's library—an unbalanced library all about Africa until he sent for the *Encyclopaedia Britannica.* When it arrived, she read through more than half of it, getting as far as "Pottery." She made a pet of a baby baboon whom she named Angelique, at Putnam's suggestion, after his mother, who loved apes.[9] Hahn worried about Putnam's repeated illnesses, dysentery and a suspicious lung ailment that he tried to hid from his superiors. She admired his single-minded interest in Africa, and in general she liked his attitude toward Africans, which contrasted markedly with that of most of the Europeans she met.

Putnam treated Africans fairly and with respect. He insisted on paying good prices for chickens, eggs, bananas, and other food supplies, instead of simply taking what he wanted and paying little or nothing as most whites did. On one census trip, they met some pyg-mies. One pygmy woman was very shy, but she liked the generous present of salt that Putnam gave her. Then, as Emily Hahn described the scene, Pat "made a little speech to her and said that I had never seen pigmies so that he wanted her to stand close to me; he pointed out that she had never seen a Madame either, so it was a good chance for both of us. For the space of a few minutes we inspected each other solemnly."[10]

Putnam behaved like an anthropologist, Emily Hahn thought, asking many questions and having long conversations with local people. But she noticed that his work was "scrappy": he gathered in-formation but did not write it up in any coherent fashion.[11] He had vo-luminous notes, particularly on linguistics, but he lost them in a ca-noeing accident on the Ituri River. He had been transporting native women and their babies from one village to another near Penge when the pirogue tipped over. Putnam managed to save the women and children, but his notes were swept down the turbulent river. Ever af-terward, when he tried to account for his publishing so little, he would say that he had lost much of his early work in this accident.[12]

Sometimes Emily Hahn was angered by Patrick Putnam's need to dominate other people and his occasional cruelty in doing so. When an awkward boatman pulled the pirogue the wrong way as they were going through rapids, Putnam lost his temper and threw a paddle at the man. When he thought discipline among his workers at the infir-mary was sloppy, he drilled them and made them stand at attention for ten minutes. Putnam had tough and, Hahn thought, "very inflex-ible theories" about colonialism. He claimed that he did not object to the pitiless exploitation of natives, for it was a law of nature that the strong should prey on the weak; what he objected to was the hypoc-risy that sometimes accompanied it, as when missionaries claimed purer motives.[13] The country needed roads and sewers and trains. The natives had to be forced to provide the labor for these. Putnam approved in general of the colonial policy of the Belgian government but was critical of the private companies; he believed they merely wanted to get all they could as fast as possible, with no thought for the devastation they left in their wake.

With a Belgian miner and his mulatto traveling companion, Putnam and Hahn discussed "the eternal subject of the ménagère [native woman who was mistress and housekeeper]."[14] The Belgian miner said that during his first sixteen months in Africa he had not touched a woman. The idea of a black woman had filled him with disgust. Putnam said that most white men seemed to feel that way. But gradually, the Belgian said, he had become accustomed to it, and now he had no desire to return to Europe. The workers he supervised were terrified of him. He no longer believed in beating them, but "Ah, before I took the woman, you may be sure I was terrible to the blacks."[15] Afterward, Putnam admitted to Emily Hahn that he was attracted to black women, and the uglier the better.

Buying a length of printed cloth one day in the market, Putnam remarked casually, "It's a funny thing how much three wives can cost a man, even in the Congo."[16] Hahn was surprised, even slightly shocked, for she had not realized that the other two women in the household were also his wives. Putnam assured her that none of them objected. It was an African custom to have several wives. Putnam thought Europeans were hypocritical about black women. They kept them in semi-secret as mistresses. He preferred to live openly with them as wives in the African manner. Abanzima had brought a cousin to be her co-wife, as was customary among the Mboli. As for Ceci, the young girl who was part pygmy, Putnam said, "I only got her last week," apparently meaning that he had just made an appropriate marriage payment to her family and perhaps also to her village master.[17]

Emily Hahn had left a fiancé of her own back in America. Her role at Penge became that of confidant to Putnam about his wives and increasingly that of intermediary between him and them. Putnam and Hahn nicknamed the two wives who spoke Makere and KiNgwana, calling them Prudence and Ophelia, so that they could discuss them in English without letting the women know they were being talked about. Hahn was indignant when Putnam, to punish Nambedru for falsely claiming to be in mourning in order to receive a new length of cloth, cut off her hair. Abanzima sided with the younger wife. "There's one good thing about it," Putnam told Hahn, "they're not quarreling any more: they're too mad at me. . . . I am a hen-pecked man."[18]

One day Emily Hahn returned home to find Abanzima chained to a tree trunk in a clearing near the house with a collar like Chimpo's padlocked around her neck. Putnam had found her with one of the local men. He did not want to send her away; instead, after beating and near-strangling her in his rage, he tied her bed to her back and made her walk through the village. Then he decreed that she must spend every day for a week tied to a tree from sunrise to sunset. And since Nambedru had been in on the affair, he had sent her back to her native village and was trying to get her parents to return the bride price.[19]

What particularly upset Putnam was the realization of how little he understood his African wives. He told Hahn, "What drives me so crazy is the way she lied."[20] He had thought they were all honest with one another. He knew Abanzima had been with other men when he was away for a year, and he had often told her that he would understand and make it possible if she wanted a temporary "vacation." But "she says everything in that honest way that I used to love so much," and now he no longer knew what he could believe. "Tell me what you really think," Putnam begged Hahn. "Should I give up my whole plan of life and go back home? Or should I stay here?"[21] Hahn told him that she thought he should go home, but she doubted that he would do it. The household gradually called down, and daily life went on as pleasantly as before—until one day on a whim Putnam announced that he was going to cut off her hair as he had cut off Nambedru's. Emily Hahn thought he was joking and then realized he was not. It was time for her to leave, and she did, rather abruptly, after having been at Penge for eight months.[22]

Meanwhile, Putnam had increasingly gotten himself in trouble with his superiors in the Congo Red Cross. In part it was because he had so openly taken African wives, in part because of a misunderstanding about the work he was to do. The Belgian authorities wanted him to be a census taker and move from one area to another. Putnam thought of his work as primarily medical and wanted to homestead in one place. He concentrated his efforts on his hospital-dispensary, but the Congo Red Cross officials chided him for spending so much time and money there. When Putnam did do the census, he included long reports on the ethnography and history of the area, which the officials considered unnecessary. Putnam tried at first to bend to their wishes, but his distaste for authority, his reluctance to take orders, and a tendency to "meddle with politics" when he saw an injustice done all continued to get him into trouble.[23]

After Emily Hahn left Penge in late November, Putnam became increasingly reckless. In January he took off on a three-week expedition to visit some nearby caves. His traveling caravan included three wives —Abanzima, Asumini, and Mada (the latter two having replaced Nambedru and Ceci). Along the way he bought and tried *bangi* (marijuana), which was very popular among the Africans but illegal under Belgian law.[24] The outcome was predictable. En route and almost exactly one year after his arrival at Penge, Patrick Putnam was fired by his regional superiors in the Congo Red Cross. "This day I found the letter announcing my discharge from the C.R.C. An unpleasant shock, but I feel as if heavy chains had been thrown off," Putnam recorded in his notes.[25] He wrote his father immediately to tell him the news.

It did not take him long to make other plans. Severe toothaches and a swollen face from seven bad teeth led him to walk an old Arab trail to the eastern side of the Ituri Forest, where the missionary dentist named Woodhams, who had treated him before, was stationed. Along the way Putnam came to a beautiful spot where the trail forded the Epulu River. The site was deserted, for some years earlier the inhabitants had all been killed, he was told, and the area was considered cursed. He noticed that the elevation was higher there than at Penge and the climate better. It was still damp, in the middle of the dense rain forest, but the nights were cooler. The Belgians were building a road through the Ituri Forest, and Putnam learned that the road was to pass near the site he had found. At Penge all supplies came by river, and the water was low, they were held up for months and sometimes spoiled before they reached him. If he could station himself along the new road, getting supplies would be easy. On February 15, 1932, he telegraphed Baron van Zuylen, "Am applying for *concession agricole vivrière* [permission to farm and reside] this side Epulu."[26]

What he wanted to do was to establish a small tourist hotel in the Ituri Forest, at the point where the main road from Stanleyville to Irumu crossed the Epulu River. He got the idea from the dude ranches of the American West, where cattle ranchers, after one particularly sharp drop in profits, had the idea of inviting urban dwellers as paying guests in order to bring in some much-needed extra income. Putnam proposed a similar sort of "dude-plantation" in the African tropical forest. His would be a modest establishment but with "all sorts of little pleasures and luxuries, such as running water, electricity, tennis, horse riding, motorboating, swimming, tropical fruits of all kinds." He wrote the Belgian colonial authorities, "My studies having pertained to natural history, I will continue to occupy my leisure time in making botanical and entomological collections, as well as linguistic and demographic studies." He intended to acquire scientific apparatus (a microscope) and resources for photography—including a dark room and African clerks trained in developing photographs—and to build a reference library. "With these tastes, the visits of scientists of all kinds will give me particular pleasure," Putnam wrote, but he also promised to try to attract to his hotel in the Congo the big-game hunters who "spend several millions in East Africa each year."[27] He hoped that wandering tourists, mail carriers, truck drivers, and colonial officials would also find Epulu a convenient wayside stop.

Putnam spent most of 1932 trying to secure the concession— thirty-six hectares (eighty-nine acres) of agricultural land and two hectares (five acres) for a hotel—which he wanted at Epulu. His father came eagerly back to Africa to help him when he heard the news. Dr. Putnam came alone, for Sebastian, the brother Patrick was closest to, had died the previous October. Sebastian Putnam had had a heart condition since childhood, and in Africa he had contracted a fever from which he never really recovered. He died of bacterial endocarditis in October 1931 and was buried in the Indian graveyard at Valleydale Farm on Martha's Vineyard, overlooking the sound. His was the first of the Putnam graves that would be dug there.[28]

Dr. Putnam and Patrick together packed up the contents of the two medical wards Patrick had built at Penge, and with an entourage of a dozen loyal employees and one pygmy family who had attached themselves to Patrick after he gave them medical care, they walked the Arab trail again through the forest to the chosen site at Epulu. Dr. Putnam was his usual curious, interested, and kindly self. He helped Patrick plan the layout for the new compound, with a lawn sloping down to the river and the rocky brook nearby. He learned some KiNgwana and made friends with the workmen, employees, and neighbors. Hubert Smet, a white elephant hunter and merchant at nearby Mambasa, wrote Patrick in late August, "I hear that your Father is about to depart," and added, "I am very curious to see your installation at Epulu." Smet sent greetings "to all the family and to Abanzima."[29]

After three months in the Congo, Dr. Putnam headed home. On his way back to the United States, he called on officials in the Congo and in Belgium, hoping to gain support for his son's petition. At home he had his nephew-in-law, Harvey H. Bundy, assistant secretary of state, secure a letter from Henry L. Stimson addressed to American diplomatic and consular officers, asking them to extend such courtesies and assistance as they were able to Dr. C. R. L. Putnam of New York.[30] Armed with this letter, Charles and Angelica Putnam packed up their remaining responsibilities at home—two children, Christine and Marley, and Mrs. Putnam's mother and her nurse—and headed for Europe, hoping to influence the Belgian government to grant Patrick the concession he wanted.

At first the concession was refused.[31] At Epulu, meanwhile, Patrick Putnam succumbed to a new illness that resulted in a stiff leg. Feeling very sick and not knowing what was wrong, he discharged all but thirteen of his workmen and medical personnel. He sent 5,000 francs to Hubert Smet, asking him to make periodic visits to Epulu to give out monthly wages, forward the mail, and look in on Abanzima and the other wives.[32] Then he flew to Europe to join his parents.

In Toulon, France, the puzzle of Patrick's illness was solved. He wrote Hubert Smet, "My leg has been diagnosed as poliomyelitis, what is called in English infantile paralysis. It usually gets children, but is known to occur fairly often up to about 30 years of age. The new president of the United States, for example, Mr. Franklin Roosevelt, acquired it when he was about my age. I am afraid that there is nothing to be done for it, so I shall soon return to the Epulu, crippled but healthy. I think that a good deal of what the natives call 'esumba' is the same thing." Dr. Putnam again took his son under his care, prescribing hot baths and muscle treatments for his leg. When Patrick was better, they went to Belgium, where he had interviews with the minister of colonies and with the head of the Belgian Red Cross, the latter in an attempt to explain what had gone wrong at Penge.[33]

While they were waiting for a final decision on the concession, a new crisis arose in the form of an urgent letter and then cables from Emily Hahn. Her publishers wanted Patrick's permission before they would publish her book. It was a matter-of-fact account, based on her journal, of her trip across Africa, of Pat Putnam's work at Penge, and of daily life there with Pat's three wives. Putnam had told her that she could write anything she wanted to, for he was not ashamed of anything he did, and she had taken him at his word. But Dr. and Mrs. Putnam were appalled. Dr. Putnam implied that life would not be worth living if such a book about Pat were published. Under this heavy pressure from the family, Emily Hahn made the extensive changes in the page proofs that they wanted.[34] She changed Pat Putnam's name to Den Murray, changed the name of the place from Penge to Sanga, attributed some of the story to "an Englishman from South Africa" who was passing through Wamba, and removed any hint that the three native women in the household at Penge were wives. The result was a published book, *Congo Solo: Misadventures Two Degrees North,* that was in places nearly incomprehensible. Thirty-three years later, after Dr. and Mrs. Putnam and Patrick were dead, Emily Hahn again wrote about Patrick Putnam at Penge, this time calling him "Stewart." Her second account was published under that title in the *New Yorker* in 1966.[35]

Hahn had told Putnam that she thought he should go home but that she doubted he would. As it turned out she was both right and wrong. Patrick Putnam did go home, but only to find an American wife to bring back to the Belgian Congo with him. He was enamored of life in the Congo and wanted to stay on, but he was no longer spellbound by one particular African woman. He needed a companion such as Emily Hahn had been for eight months, someone who spoke English, someone he understood and who understood him. In short, he wanted a woman he could talk to.

And he had a certain woman in mind. One of the friends Patrick Putnam had said goodbye to when he left for Africa was Mary Linder, a landscape architect from Canton, Massachusetts. While Dr. Putnam was at home after helping to get Patrick established at Epulu (and before returning to Europe), he wrote back to Pat, "I have written to

Mary Linder to try to arrange to let me see her."[36] Not long afterward Dr. Putnam went to Boston. He had tea at Hooton's, where he enjoyed being introduced all around as "Pat Putnam's father." He also had dinner, along with Mary Linder and other friends, with his sister Elsie. Then, Dr. Putnam reported to Patrick, he rode the train halfway out to Canton with Mary, and they both got off and talked for a while on the platform.[37] Dr. Putnam was courting her on behalf of his son.

Paradise on the Epulu

While Patrick Putnam was in Belgium awaiting a final decision on the concession he wanted on the Epulu River in the Belgian Congo, Crown Prince Leopold and Princess Astrid of Belgium were visitors at what was already being called "Camp Putnam." The royal pair were on an official tour through the Belgian Congo, and the prince decided that while inspecting the road being built through the Ituri Forest he wanted to spend a day in the dark forest with pygmies. District Commissioner Colonel Henri-Martin Hackers found a site he liked and sent workmen to prepare it for the visitors. They widened the little road leading out to the main road, built a strong bridge over the first small river, and smoothed out the would-be lawn in front of the Epulu River by chopping down shrubs. The place was known officially as "Hackers' Camp," but the prince, who had seen the Camp Putnam sign, sent greetings to Abanzima and the men in charge and made it known that he wanted Patrick Putnam told that the royal party had stayed *chez vous.*[1]

By April 14, 1933, Putnam had been assured that the concession would be his for five years, with renewal likely. He signed the lease and sailed for New York. One month later, on May 15, 1933, Patrick Tracy Lowell Putnam and Mary Farlow Linder were married.

Mary Linder was tall (5'8" to Putnam's 6'1"), slender, and pretty in a conventional way with brilliant blue eyes and light brown hair. "At any Boston party there would be a dozen girls present who looked like her," one friend remembers.[2] Friends and family members consistently describe her as "very sweet." She was also capable, talented, and unflappable.

Born on September 1, 1905, Mary was twenty-eight years old and Patrick was twenty-nine when they were married. She had spent her childhood in the New England countryside, surrounded by brothers, animals, and plants. The Linder home in the rural town of Canton, Massachusetts, had a conservatory, a greenhouse, extensive flower and vegetable gardens, and acres of wild and cultivated shrubs and trees.[3] John Linder, Mary's father, was a chemist and businessman. His real love was horticulture, but a strong family tradition insisted that plants were not a good way to make a living. (John Linder's uncle, William Gilson Farlow, was a professor of botany at Harvard, yet he had earned an M.D. degree just in case.) By Mary's generation, however, botany had become an acceptable profession. David Linder, one of her three older brothers, was a specialist in mycology (mushrooms) and curator of the Farlow Herbarium and Library at Harvard founded by his great-uncle. Mary was graduated from Smith College and then studied at the Cambridge School of Landscape Architecture (later absorbed by Harvard). There she met Patrick Putnam, just back from his first expedition to Africa and rooming temporarily in Cambridge with a friend of one of her brothers.[4]

Sometime after Patrick's return to Africa to live with Abanzima, Mary took a job with an architectural firm in New York. The Putnam family continued to see her; Patrick's brothers Russell and Sebastian helped her move into an apartment, and Angelica Putnam invited her and her roommates to suburban Bedford for weekends. One of Angelica's fears about Patrick's escapades in Africa was that if he took African wives no "decent" girl would ever have him. But Mary Farlow

Linder was tougher than Angelica Putnam knew. Mary succumbed to Patrick's charm, as did everyone who knew him, but she was aware of what she was in for. Patrick had delegated to Emily Hahn the task of telling Mary about the African wives. Mary's quiet response, according to Hahn, was, "Well, I can see that I would have to give him a lot of love."[5]

Behind Mary Linder's willingness to marry Patrick Putnam and go to Africa with him was not only Putnam's persuasiveness but also the fact that the Belgian Congo held no terrors for her or her family. Her brother David had been a member of the first Harvard African Expedition, a biological and medical survey, which crossed Africa from west to east in 1926–27—one year before Wulsin and Putnam were sent out by Hooton. The eight men on the earlier expedition had spent much of their time in the Belgian Congo. They had traveled on foot along trails and the uncompleted road through the eastern part of the Ituri Forest until they reached Irumu, very near Patrick Putnam's future site at Epulu. David Linder collected hundreds of plant specimens. His colleagues photographed pygmies and, with their help, tracked and shot a gorilla, which they brought back to the Museum of Comparative Zoology at Harvard.

One purpose of that first Harvard expedition had been to demonstrate that it was possible to travel in Africa without succumbing to disease. The men took quinine regularly and reported no dysentery or diarrhea or serious illnesses and only a few fevers.[6] The Linder family was therefore not unduly worried about Mary's living in Africa. She was going to familiar territory, to a place where her brother had recently traveled.

Patrick and Mary had a honeymoon in Florida and made a last round of visits to family and friends. One cousin remembers Pat suddenly turning up with a full red beard, driving a fancy new car—an open phaeton—with a beautiful blonde woman at his side, and a monkey (Chimpo) sitting on his shoulder.[7] Pat and Mary stopped in

8.–9. Passport photos. Mary Linder Putnam and Patrick T. L. Putnam. 1933. By permission of the Houghton Library, Harvard University.

Washington to see Milton Katz and his wife, Vivian, and Pat reported that the sands on Daytona Beach were non-skid—he knew this because he and Mary had driven their car ninety miles an hour on them and then stopped suddenly, in order to test them. He was as foolhardy as ever. The next morning Mary appeared in Milton Katz's office. "Could you cash a check for us?" she asked apologetically. "We don't have any money."[8]

In late summer of 1933, a few months after they were married, Pat and Mary sailed for Africa. In Marseille they joined Carleton Coon and his wife, also named Mary, who were on their way to do fieldwork in Ethiopia. Walking along the quays, the Putnams were especially interested in the shellfish—sea cucumbers, sea urchins, mussels of all sizes, and crayfish—and Pat insisted on sampling them all. On board ship he created an uproar when the purser tried to put him in a cabin with other men and Mary in a female cabin. "Shaking his beard angrily as he towered over the uniformed official, he won," Coon wrote. Coon remembered another typical Putnam exploit: "In the Suez Canal, while the ship was tied up to let the northbound traffic through, Pat

10. *Patrick Putnam. Taken by Mary Linder Putnam in Kenya on the way to Epulu, 1936–37. Courtesy of Anna Lowell Tomlinson.*

11. *Patrick Putnam and Mary Linder Putnam at the Epulu River. Courtesy of Anna Lowell Tomlinson.*

12. The "Palais" at Epulu, exterior view. Courtesy of Anna Lowell Tomlinson.

13. Living room at Epulu with the fireplace in the center of the room. Photograph by Leon Mondron. Courtesy of Josephine Baca.

created a diversion by leaping naked into the canal. He swam to the east bank and back, while the whistle blew. Emerging dripping at the head of the pilot's ladder, he shook himself and said, 'The water is too warm.'"[9] In the mornings on board ship Pat gave Mary lessons in KiNgwana and was soon conducting a regular class with several young English officers and administrators also attending.

Dr. Putnam sent them fatherly advice: "I hope that you are getting a good rest on the voyage and lots of fun. Do not try to reform each other. Nobody ever changes (by conversion) in politics or religion or *anything else*. It is all a matter of adjustments." He signed himself "an old friend and colleague of Mary's (if she will accept the assumption) in the garden and of yours [Pat's] in the study of tropical medicine."[10]

At Epulu, one of the loveliest spots in the Ituri Forest, Patrick intended to run a medical clinic, as well as the small hotel that would help to pay expenses and would bring them interesting guests. The altitude was 2,500 feet, so the nights were cool even though Epulu was only two degrees north of the equator. Patrick's chosen site was a plateau crossed by small streams at a point where the Epulu River channel narrows to a small gorge that looks as if it has cut its way through the tall forest looming up on either side. Along much of its course through the forest the Epulu River is wide and slow. At Camp Putnam it is narrow, swift, and powerful, breaking into rapids and channels flowing around small rocky islands. The clearing along the bank of the river in the deep forest is lovely in its own right, and this loveliness is heightened by the rushing noise of the water, which cuts the spot off from the rest of the world, transforming it into a secret paradise.[11] "Orchids gleam in the forest recesses, and huge macrolobium trees, the branches weighted down with luxuriant creepers, reach to great heights, towering over the almost impassable woods beneath," one visitor wrote.[12] Epulu was the name given to the place where the main road crossed the Epulu River. There was nothing there other than Camp Putnam, a half-mile off the main road, and a ferry poled by local men.

It consisted of five large canoes lashed together with boards placed on top, on which vehicles could be carried across the river.

The house they built in this private paradise was designed by Mary with the help of a Rhode Island architectural firm. Called affectionately *le Palais*, the palace, it was a larger version of a typical native house, made of mud and thatch but with a concrete floor. It had a large main room (25 by 40 feet) with a central fireplace—a wooden box filled with bricks on which a log fire burned every evening—around which four deep armchairs were set. In the south wall a large window looked out over an area cleared of undergrowth all the way to the rapids in the Epulu River. Besides additional windows, doors, and bookshelves, the other walls were decorated with dance masks, bows and arrows, shields, bark cloth, and woven raffia platters. Antelope skins and fiber mats with beautiful designs served as rugs, and Mary kept vases around the room filled with tropical flowers, usually frangipani or hibiscus.[13] All the windows were open with no screens or glass, but there were wooden shutters. The Palais also had a bedroom, bath, and two studies or offices, one for Patrick and one for Mary. Meals were served on a table laid with damask and the old New England family silver in an open-sided dining room next to the kitchen. The original two-room house that Patrick had built at Epulu became a guest house, slightly to the west. East of the Palais they eventually added two small round huts with thatched roofs to accommodate more visitors.

Around the compound the canopy of tall trees was so dense that little sunlight reached the ground. Patrick had been careful in laying out the site to cut down very few trees so that there would not be the usual bulldozed effect of European settlements in the forest. They lived in the dim light of the tropical rain forest; only out on the river could clouds, blue sky, birds, the sunset, and the solid green wall of trees across the water be seen. But eighty miles to the east of Camp Putnam the forest ended abruptly, and the road led out onto rolling grassy hills looking toward the Ruwenzori Mountains, which marked the Congo-Uganda border, far in the distance. Toward the west the road led 285 miles through the forest to Stanleyville, their shopping center. The nearest town with any other European residents was the tiny, dusty village of Mambasa, forty-two miles to the east, founded by Arab slave and ivory traders and named by the local Bila people "Mambaisa" ("meeting place"). Camp Putnam had no electricity or running water, no radio, no telephone. Water for baths was heated in an oil drum over an open fire. Once a week there was a mail truck from Stanleyville, and every morning around eight o'clock gasoline trucks came through on their way to the mines. The Putnams knew all the drivers and could flag them down when they needed something. These drivers and the occasional passersby who stopped in were their only contacts with the outside world.

Twenty to forty workmen, houseboys, and medical aides lived with their wives and children in a village of mud huts a three-minute walk from the Palais through the forest. Several of the workmen had come with Putnam from Penge, including Alfani, one of the BaNguana (Muslim descendants of the slave traders) who was a trained hospital worker, and Ageronga, a member of the Budu a prosperous tribe related to the Mangbetus. Ageronga had been a policeman at Penge. He came to Epulu as a gardener and worked his way up to chief of staff and Putnam's most trusted employee. Large and dignified, he exerted great authority without ever raising his voice or losing his temper. He taught himself to read and write KiNgwana and would send Patrick reports. In his later years he became a Christian and conducted weekly worship services at Epulu.[14] Other workers at Camp Putnam came from local Bila or Lese villages, usually in flight either from colonial law or from witchcraft trials. If they were in trouble with the law for illegal hunting or unpaid taxes or other such misdemeanors, Putnam interceded when he could or employed them after they had served their prison terms. If they had been driven out of their villages on witchcraft charges, Putnam took them in when no one else would.

Epulu happened to be located at the conjunction of several different tribal areas, those of the Lese (who were Sudanic) and the Bila and Ndaka (who were Bantu and looked down on the Lese, regarding them as poor, shiftless, and undeveloped). There were also a few Mboli-Mamvu and BaNguana in the vicinity. Consequently, the population of Camp Putnam was usually diverse for a small African village. The Putnams created an international community at Epulu, a mix of Europeans (all white persons in Africa were considered Europeans) and Africans and also a multitribal, multiethnic village in which Patrick Putnam functioned as village chief.

And then there were the pygmies. At least one pygmy family had followed Putnam on his trek from Penge to Epulu. Others soon came, drawn by Putnam's reputation as a giver of "strong medicine"—they called him "Totorido," their word for iodine.[15] Eventually, two bands of pygmies—about fifteen families, seventy-five people in all—attached themselves in more or less regular fashion to Camp Putnam by attaching themselves to one or another of the workmen. The pygmies brought meat and honey from the forest and expected in return to receive an ample supply of plantains, the mainstay of the native diet. The pygmies considered themselves as belonging to Camp Putnam in the same way that other bands of pygmies were affiliated with neighboring villages. They moved at will, rather like gypsies, back and forth between their camps at Epulu and temporary camps in the forest. The pygmies were alert, quick, and mischievous, dissolving into laughter at the slightest provocation. They were connoisseurs of pleasure, wild mushrooms, wild honey, marijuana, and the joys of yodeling, tracking, and hunting in the forest.[16]

The regular working day at Camp Putnam began with roll call at seven o'clock and continued until two o'clock, except for the hotel workers, who had shifts throughout the day and evening. Tuesday was hospital day, when Putnam gave injections for yaws and syphilis. Friday was payday and market day, which became a big event. Putnam started the local market as a way of getting supplies and encouraging local crafts. People came from surrounding small villages, sometimes from fifteen miles away, bringing rice, eggs, chickens, ducks, goats, tomatoes, spinach, corn, eggplant, and manioc, as well as animals to sell to Putnam for his growing zoo. The pygmies brought bark cloth, sleeping mats, and sometimes pottery or plantains they got from their village masters. The Putnams or their houseboys sold palm oil, soap, salt, cigarettes, pencils, stamps, notebooks, and sometimes cloth at cost.[17]

To encourage pygmies and villagers in the area to come to the medical clinic, Putnam gave a cigarette to each one on every visit. Soon they began to bring in friends for a cigarette, and as a result Putnam was sometimes able to spot a treatable disease in early stages. He cooperated with witch doctors, out of both tolerance and curiosity. Gradually the word spread that "Totorido" at Camp Putnam was not interested in collecting taxes or recruiting workers for the mines and rubber plantations, nor was he trying to persuade people to adopt the white man's religion. He would simply try to make you well if you were sick.[18]

Putnam ran his clinic for the first year with money and medicines sent by his father. In 1935 the Belgian colonial government designated his clinic as an official dispensary, to which it provided medicine and supplies. The clinic at Camp Putnam was never as large or as famous as Albert Schweitzer's hospital and leper colony at Lambaréné in French Equatorial Africa, 1,200 miles west of Epulu, although a few name-conscious tourists made a point of stopping at both of them. Patrick Putnam never claimed to be doing anything comparable to what was being done at Lambaréné. He was not a medical doctor; at best he offered injections, treatment of minor wounds, and emergency care for the seriously ill or wounded until he could send them on to the nearest hospital, at Mambasa. But he did take pride in the atmosphere he created at Epulu, an atmosphere markedly different from that at Schweitzer's hospital. Some travelers described Lambaréné as a dour and dirty place where employees were harassed and overworked, Europeans were ordered to wear sun helmets whenever they stepped outside, and everything—medicines, supplies, even food—was kept tightly locked up.[19] Albert Schweitzer, famous Swiss organist and Bach expert, medical doctor, and biblical scholar who spent fifty years at Lambaréné, lived and understood his life in religious terms as one of service and atonement. He made the African bush a place of sober penance. To Patrick Putnam, Africa was not a purgatory but a virtual paradise. His Africa was not the low, hot coastlands where Lambaréné was located but the astonishly beautiful world of the Ituri Forest, where the local people, when they were not harassed by outsiders, lived relaxed and even indolent lives. It was the one place on earth where he wanted to live. Patrick and Mary Putnam ate local food. They were interested in and respected local customs. They tried to create a community where truthfulness and general good will were the norms, where trust and mutual respect made locks and keys unnecessary. There were no locks on doors or windows at Camp Putnam.

To encourage guests, Pat and Mary published and distributed a thirteen-page illustrated booklet titled *Our Camp on the Epulu in the Belgian Congo*. Readers were offered accommodations in "untouched country." "The pigmies often roam the forest around our place," Pat wrote, "and our BaNguana neighbors are great elephant hunters."[20] The booklet stressed how easy and safe the journey to Africa could be. Mary drew two maps for it, one showing the roads and settlements around Epulu, the other showing routes to Epulu from Europe, Asia, and several points on the African coast. Visitors were offered the use of a darkroom and scientific laboratory, a library with a unique collection of books on the Congo, a tennis court, and swimming in a deep still pool in the Epulu River. "We run a sort of 'dude-plantation,'" Pat wrote to the tourist agency Thomas Cook & Sons in 1935. They were trying to catch another okapi, that seldom-seen animal of the Ituri Forest, to replace one that just died, and, Putnam boasted, "Our pigmy show cannot be duplicated anywhere else."[21]

It was these two rarities, the pygmies and the okapis, that made Camp Putnam famous. Of the two, the "pygmy show" was easier to manage. For an ample gift of salt or other payment, some fifty to seventy-five pygmies would demonstrate how they build their tiny round huts out of sticks and leaves, how they climbed trees to get wild honey, how they hunted elephants and chimpanzees. They would also dance for the benefit of tourist curiosity and tourist cameras. For a larger payment the pygmies would work as actors for a movie director or one of the several film companies that came to Camp Putnam. They became so experienced at this that they knew exactly what to do (what scenes would be wanted) and what not to do (such as look directly at the camera). Generally they enjoyed it, for they were irrepressible mimics and liked to outperform one another. Innumerable photographs and hundreds of feet of film were taken of the Camp Putnam pygmies over the next two decades by everyone from the Vanderbilt Expedition of the Philadelphia Museum of Natural History in 1934 to film companies to single tourists clutching Brownie cameras. Some anthropologists would later charge that the Camp Putnam pygmies were so tainted by contact with European civilization that they could not be considered typical of Ituri Forest pygmies. But in fact there *were* no "typical" Ituri Forest pygmies; like all the other groups in the forest, they had adapted over and over again to changing situations. Camp Putnam was simply one more ecological niche into which some bands of pygmies had succeeded in fitting themselves.

The okapis were another matter; they had to be captured. The okapi, relative of the longer-necked giraffe, has a velvety dark purple skin, white stripes on its legs, and a long sinuous tongue. One of the last large mammals to be discovered by Western scientists, the okapi was first described in 1901 by Sir Harry Johnston, an English artist and traveler who had been appointed Special Commissioner for Uganda by the British government in 1900. Okapis are elusive. In all his years in the Ituri Forest, Patrick Putnam saw one in the wild only three times, yet they were common in the forest. Putnam liked to compare them to rats in New York City: plentiful but seldom visible.

The Belgian government had given the okapi protected-animal status and made hunting them illegal, but Putnam was given a special permit to pen them up for study. He became something of a specialist in capturing okapis and keeping them in captivity in good health— neither one an easy task. To capture one, he and his workmen dug pits along okapi trails in the forest and covered them over with branches and leaves. When an okapi fell into one of these traps, they would build a box over the pit, shovel dirt down around the animal until they raised it to ground level, and then move it, surrounded by the box, through the forest to Camp Putnam. Another way was to chloroform the okapi, pull it out of the pit, tie it to a stretcher, and have twenty men carry it to the enclosure built for it at Camp Putnam.

It was more difficult still to keep an okapi alive in captivity, for when confined to a pen it tended to become reinfected with intestinal parasites from its own droppings until the level of worm infestation became so high that the animal died. Putnam worked out a system of almost hospital-level cleanliness for the okapis and sent his employees into the forest to gather the leaves they liked to eat. By mid-1937 he had managed to keep two okapis alive in captivity for several months. When he and Mary left for a brief visit to their families in the United States, he promised the three keepers money enough to buy a wife apiece if both animals were still alive when they returned.[22]

Okapis and pygmies made Epulu famous, but Patrick and Mary Putnam themselves gave Epulu its special charm. That such a talented young couple with illustrious backgrounds would choose to make their permanent home in this remote and primitive spot was considered remarkable and romantic. Patrick and Mary were devoted to each other and ran Camp Putnam together as a team of equals, both of nearly unfailing good humor. Mary loved the animals and gardening and was well liked by the native workers and the pygmies. She kept the books, wrote most of the letters, and was a gracious hostess even in chaotic situations when unexpected guests arrived and food supplies ran out. Patrick was a near-ideal host, for he combined a vast store of practical knowledge about Africa with an eagerness to learn and an interest in people that made him an appreciative listener even to the dullest bore. He was also the center of constant activity as he directed building construction and automobile repair, examined and treated a steady flow of native patients, thought up new projects, and received visitors. Nearby chiefs came to see him, sometimes to enlist his aid in a quarrel with the local administrator. Truck drivers, colonial administrators, merchants, and missionaries stopped at Epulu. Hotel guests began to arrive, usually several every week. Among those signing the school notebook that served as the hotel register in 1934 were Professor of Anthropology Martin Gusinde from Austria, George Vanderbilt from New York, the Duc de Rochefoucauld from Paris, and professional hunters Donald Ker and Baron Bror von Blixen.[23]

On "vacations"—brief journeys away from Epulu, sometimes as guide for a hunting party—Patrick continued to see his African wives. Mary knew about this, for Patrick insisted on being honest and aboveboard in everything he did. Before he was married, he had asked Emily Hahn to tell Mary about his African wives, and he had written Abanzima to explain to her what he was contemplating. He sent the letter through Hubert Smet, elephant hunter and storekeeper in Mambasa, who read it to Abanzima, and she sent word back via Smet that she was very *satisfait*.[24]

Many letters flowed between Camp Putnam and families and friends in America. "Mary sends her best," Putnam wrote to James Chapin in 1935. "If we were millionaires, we'd be home often on vacation, but she agrees with me that the tropics are the best place for home. And under her guidance it is getting to be such a home, if not a mud-palace, that an old bush-man like me hardly recognizes it, although he likes it."[25] And in one letter to Patrick, Dr. Putnam wrote, "One of the things you said that stuck best in my memory, and that finally had some good result was, 'I hope I shall never be as busy as you think you are.' You and Mary will have to remember that, and take time out to live."[26]

Dr. and Mrs. Putnam planned a visit to Epulu in the fall of 1936. When Charles's health became a problem, Angelica went alone to visit her "dear children." She disembarked from the Nile steamer at Juba and waited, sitting on her suitcase, until Patrick arrived to pick her up—one day late. After the long journey to Epulu, she stayed only for a weekend, not willing to tolerate conditions she considered very primitive. The workers and pygmies were fascinated by her white hair, and she let them touch it. As she was leaving, however, when Patrick said, "Now, Mother, you must shake hands with all the boys," she did as she was told but washed her hands immediately afterward.[27] "Mother's weekend in Africa" became a family joke, in contrast to Dr. Putnam's months-long stays and his reluctant departures.

In 1936 Florence Lowther, a zoology professor at Barnard College, spent several weeks at Camp Putnam. She enjoyed the "two beautiful okapis" and the chimpanzee family. Pat's Chimpo had died in the early 1930s and had been replaced by Mr. Fataki. Mr. Fataki had a mate, Madame Fataki, and a baby named Mugwump. They had the run of Camp Putnam, and Mugwump, who had taken a liking to Florence Lowther, clung to her leg when she went for walks and insisted on having a cup of coffee or tea whenever she did. Mary Putnam took Professor Lowther on a two-week trip in a motor truck, accompanied by a black chauffeur and a pygmy boy, the latter dressed for the first time in his life in a white shirt, black and white striped shorts, and sneakers, of which he was very proud. They visited all the chiefs within

14. *Mary with chimpanzee Mugwump at Epulu. By permission of the Houghton Library, Harvard University.*

a radius of 500 miles. The chiefs received them formally and called out their wives to be introduced. One chief had fifty.[28]

The stream of visitors kept Patrick informed on colonial activities in the Congo. To find out what was happening locally and when important ceremonies were taking place in nearby native villages, he worked out another system. On any visit to a native village he liberally handed out salt, tobacco, or palm oil. This made his presence a welcome and much-sought addition to most village events.

In 1934 a new governor general of the Belgian Congo, Pierre Ryckmans, issued new regulations that allowed some previously protected animals to be hunted, but only if the hunter purchased an expensive permit. Patrick thought the new laws discriminated unfairly against native hunters and wrote an angry first draft of a letter to the governor general. But then he rethought the problem and reworked the draft until he had changed its tone completely. Instead of attacking the government, he made respectful, if slightly wry, suggestions as to how the officials might better accomplish their goals. These he defined as allowing the natives to continue to hunt by the methods used by their ancestors, conserving game, and attracting tourist hunters for the revenues to be derived from their hunting permits and other expenditures. The letter that Putnam finally sent was four and a half singlespaced typed pages, and it showed how well he knew the Ituri Forest and its animals. He went through the list of protected animals, commenting on each. The elephant deserved absolute protection, he agreed, although something ought to be done in those "certain regions where it makes frightful havoc on the gardens of the natives." As for the dwarf elephant, "of whom I strongly doubt the existence, I would propose, for whoever would kill one, a decoration and not a fine." He agreed that the rhinoceros and the giraffe, found only in the border areas of the Congo, deserved absolute protection. But for all the other mammals on the list he thought absolute protection was "ridiculously superfluous." Gorillas were sufficiently numerous in the Parc National Albert as well as in several river valleys that resident and nonresident hunting permits might well be sold, for a high fee, to take one adult male. The same was true of chimpanzees and other monkeys. Elands, kudus, klipspringers, pangolins, and yellow-backed duikers were all sufficiently numerous that the holders of hunting permits ought to be allowed two or three adult males.

As for the okapi, Putnam wrote, the conservation measures are much more severe than necessary. On the basis of his own observations of their trails in the forest around Beni, Mambasa, Gombari, Penge, and Buta, he estimated that the total number of okapis was greater than 15,000 and that the natives killed annually perhaps a tenth of these—the pygmies by hunting with a bow and arrow, the villagers by setting traps. The natives needed this meat, Putnam suggested, and they should be allowed to have it legally. In addition, why not agree to fifty permits for Europeans a year, at 5,000 francs per permit? This would draw many tourist hunters away from Kenya and pose slight risk to the okapis, for hunting them with a gun is so difficult that most of the permit holders would leave the Congo without having killed even one. "As proof," he wrote, "I cite the Vanderbilt Mission, holder of a special permit, which came through in 1934, of which the two professional hunters did not succeed, after a month of effort, in killing an okapi."

Though Putnam thought most of the hunting laws were too severe, particularly because they created unnecessary hardships for the Africans, he noted some "astonishing" omissions. The bongo, a beautiful large forest antelope, and the chevretain, a forest ungulate, were both very rare yet not protected at all.

Putnam's letter, with its shrewd appeal to both altruism and self-interest, was well received. Governor General Ryckmans replied personally, thanking him for his "very interesting" communication and his "excellent" ideas, and a year later the director of agriculture and colonization for the Congo sent Putnam his proposed new hunting and fishing regulations and asked for his comments.[29]

Among Patrick Putnam's papers is a quotation he attributed to Giacomo Leopardi, the Italian poet, which he copied: "The human race is divided into two parts: some use oppressive power, others suffer it. Since neither law nor any force, nor progress or philosophy or civilization can prevent any man born or yet to be born from belonging to one or the other party, it remains for him who can choose to choose. Not all, it is true, can choose, nor at all times."[30] Putnam was choosing, insofar as possible in a colonial world, to be neither oppressed nor oppressor but to live as an equal among his fellow human beings, in a situation of mutual benefit and mutual good will.

With all the other demands of Camp Putnam, Patrick had little time for anthropology. In the Harvard Class Reports for 1931 and 1935 he listed his occupation as "Explorer."[31] In the fall of 1937 E. A. Hooton wrote to a friend, "Pat Putnam turned up here a week or two ago equipped with two live pottos. They are the first I have ever seen and they are extraordinarily interesting animals. We are going to try to have some moving pictures taken of them since their gait is a very primitive sprawling sort of lizard-like walk. I gather that Pat's dude ranch business in Africa has prospered considerably. I also gather that he has done no scientific work of any sort and is not likely to do any."[32]

Hooton's correspondent was George Schwab, a Presbyterian missionary in Cameroun. Hooton was discovering that it was sometimes easier to get fieldwork done by missionaries than by would-be anthropologists.

Emilie

In the late summer of 1937 Patrick and Mary Putnam buried the family silver at Epulu and returned to the United States to visit their families, leaving their employees in charge of the hotel. They took with them two pet loris (Hooton's "pottos," the scientific name being *Perodicticus potto*), which were destined for an American zoo. Small, brown, nocturnal animals, they could crawl but not jump. In lieu of a cage the Putnams kept them on a pedestal table with a forked tree limb in the center, which the loris would climb into to sleep.

Putnam told a local reporter who interviewed them on Martha's Vineyard that "dude ranching in the Belgian Congo" was his occupation. "Don't mention science, exploring, or jungle in connection with me," he begged. "None of them applies."[1] Instead, he talked about his camp, the forty African workmen he employed, and the pygmies who had adopted them. He stressed how safe Africa was "in so far as natives and wild animals are concerned." He did not mention illness.

Mary had a mild case of bilharziasis, a disease caused by a parasitic fluke that travels around the body through the bloodstream and can sometimes be seen where the blood vessels are near the skin at the temples and wrists.[2] It is difficult to get rid of without a strong course of medication, but she apparently did not worry about it. In the end it was not an African disease but a disease of the Western Hemisphere that took her life. As they were about to return to Africa, Mary Putnam became ill with viral pneumonia from a strain of the virus found only in the West.[3] She died five days later, on December 18, 1937.

Patrick Putnam was devastated by her death. Among his papers there is a scrap in his handwriting that reads, "one I'd loved and never hoped to have, but had and loved, and lost."[4] He refused to attend her burial, a brief ceremony before a small number of family and friends in the old Indian burial ground on the Putnam estate on Martha's Vineyard, near Sebastian's grave. Friends were so alarmed by his behavior that they insisted he should not be allowed to return to New York by himself, and Aunt Elsie, his favorite relative, was commissioned to go with him.[5]

Putnam went into a moody depression, began to drink heavily, and seemed to friends and members of his family to become a different person.[6] His despair was almost more than he could cope with. In this mood, he wrote to Emily Hahn:

Bedford, N.Y.

21st Jany. 1938

Mickey,

Mary died on the fifth day of pneumonia. You may have heard of this. You once tried to kill yourself, I think. I wanted to, but didn't try. Very selfish, still, I remain. But not quite selfish enough to give my silly doting parents such a pain as that.

Selfish enough to not want to live here close to them, doing God knows what.

Not selfish enough (now, at least) to think of asking some "innocent" woman to marry me, expecting me to find her all I wanted, and not think of Mary whom I had for 4 years, wanted ever since I met her 10 years ago, and will always want.

From creature habit more "at home" in Africa than here. From silly, but sincere, sentiment, not being able to bear the thought of selling, or letting rot, that beautiful place that Mary built.

15. Patrick Putnam and Emilie Baca Putnam, 1938. Courtesy of Josephine Baca.

Patrick Putnam went on to ask Emily Hahn to come and live in Africa with him, preferably as his wife. He wrote, "Mickey, for once in my life, I could write reams, but I won't. I ask you to send me a telegraphic answer, either 'NO', or 'NO THANKS' or 'YES AWAITING DETAILS.'"[7]

Emily Hahn declined this proposal—but Emilie Baca, another old friend of Patrick's from his New York days, did not. Emilie Baca was a small and strikingly attractive woman, with dark hair and eyes. She was a member of an old and prominent Spanish-French family in New Mexico, where she had grown up on a vast ranch in the Rociada Valley, ninety miles north of Santa Fe. Her father, Don José Baca, had been a lieutenant governor of the state of New Mexico and was being spoken of as a likely candidate for governor when he died suddenly of pneumonia in the early 1920s. Emilie's mother, Doña Marguerite Pendaries Baca, and her brother ran the ranch until the agricultural depression of the late 1920s, when they lost it and moved to Santa Fe. Marguerite Baca was later elected secretary of state in New Mexico.

Emilie studied journalism at the University of Missouri, traveled in Europe and the Far East, and then became a social worker in New York. She met Patrick Putnam there through his college friend Tom Scudder, whom she had known when he was living as a would-be artist in Santa Fe.

In contrast to Mary Linder Putnam's modest and unassuming nature, Emilie Baca's demeanor was that of a rather grand Spanish lady. When Mary died, Emilie was particularly emphathetic, for she had apparently experienced a recent tragedy of some kind in her own life.[8] On April 20, 1938, Patrick Putnam and Emilie Baca were married in New York. Six months later they returned to Epulu. When Angelica Putnam discovered two days before they sailed from New York that they had taken a cabin on D deck, she immediately went down to the docks, paid more money, and got them one of the best cabins in the ship.[9]

Angelica had misgivings about the marriage because she thought Emilie would not like Epulu. She was right. Nor did going back to Epulu ease Patrick's pain and torment. Their return almost coincided with the visit of a reporter for the *Reader's Digest*, Jerome Beatty, who had followed them across Africa and arrived at Epulu only two weeks after they did. Putnam had been away for a year and a half, and although the workers and pygmies were still around, to his eyes Camp Putnam had degenerated sadly. He worked to get the Palais, the guest houses, the dining facilities, and the pygmy show back in order, while recreating for Jerome Beatty—with the help of Mary's diaries—his vision of what Camp Putnam had been.

Beatty wrote an enthusiastic report on Camp Putnam, "Dude Rancher in the Congo," for the *Reader's Digest*, but Putnam was furious when it appeared because it did not distinguish between the wife who was there with him at the time and the wife who had helped to build Camp Putnam. "In spite of my expressed desires and his promises, he ignored the existence of my late wife, Mary Farlow Linder,"

Putnam complained. He considered the omission especially unfortu-
nate because "it was largely by her charm and hospitality" that Camp
Putnam became a home people felt privileged to visit.[10] Putnam vowed
to have nothing to do ever again with anyone representing the *Reader's Digest*. He was enraged all over again when he discovered that a
slightly longer version of the same article had been published in the
American Magazine, titled "Great White Chief of the Congo," and he
threatened a lawsuit if that title were used again.[11] The Patrick Putnam
who had told Emily Hahn he did not care what she wrote about him
(although he let his father censor it) suddenly minded intensely the
distortions of publicity, the convenient but jarring ellipses, the atten-
tion-grabbing headlines that could haunt him for years after, as "Great
White Chief of the Congo" was to do.

At Epulu, Emilie Baca Putnam was immediately and almost constantly ill with malaria. She was also moody and depressed, symptoms
linked to her illness but also to her isolation. Their Belgian visitors
spoke French, and the workers at Camp Putnam spoke KiNgwana,
neither of which Emilie understood, although Patrick immediately
began to give her lessons in both languages. Patrick found himself virtually a prisoner at Camp Putnam, for to leave, even to go a hundred
miles to Irumu or forty-two to Mambasa, the nearest towns, meant
leaving Emilie at home ill and unable to communicate with anyone
around her.

Emilie prided herself on being a good businesswoman and household manager, but transferred to Epulu, these skills turned her into the
household scold, complaining constantly about the workers being
slipshod and indolent and about Patrick's lack of business sense.[12] She
also found the dense forest hard to get used to. "You have no idea what
an intensity of green it is here," she wrote her family. "I feel sometimes
that I'm hedged in by three impenetrable green walls—fortunately
the expanse of the river is before us. . . . and yet there is a real beauty
to it with trees so tall they seem to hold up the clouds by day and brush

the stars at night."[13] It was, she admitted, an "easy, pleasant life." They lived surrounded by servants, who for less than $2.00 a month would do their every bidding, from an early morning wake-up call and coffee in bed to the last drink at night. Emilie Baca Putnam wrote her mother after six months at Epulu, "It is so easy to get into the habit of being waited on that I am getting very spoiled."[14]

Patrick Putnam alternated between periods of black despair and frantic attempts to get out of himself and reach out to others in forced cheerfulness and binges of letter writing. In this crisis he reevaluated his life, including not only his previous seeking of publicity but, far more profoundly, his relation to Africa. On December 20, 1938, he revealed some of what he was thinking to a Belgian friend, a Mr. de Bergyck, who had written seeking advice. He had been back at Epulu only a month, Patrick Putnam wrote de Bergyck, and he was having money troubles, for the allowance from his family had been eaten up by his and Emilie's travel expenses. "Our camp," he wrote, "is actually very little visited," and he feared that "it will never attract numerous tourists, thanks to the absence of the charming host that Mary was."

> I remain here and I work here, and exactly why I do not know, a little from sentiment and a little because I am less unhappy here than in America or Europe, . . . [but] from a "business" point of view there is absolutely nothing to do here.
>
> I have very much lost my previous childish point of view. Even if I had Mary—and we were so happy here together—I would hesitate to remain in Africa. For, when one does not limit one's thoughts to the well-being of the present day, and when one thinks of the morrow, one realizes that the colonial course is one which will end fatally with a settling of old scores.
>
> In the long run, one finds that life in Africa lacks much—and more, much more, in the spiritual than in the material. One returns [to Europe or the United States] and one finds that one's friends—

faithful friends always—are separated by the fact that you no longer share their interests.

So, dear friend, take my advice and abandon the idea that you will install yourself in Africa. Write me your news and excuse my hesitation and slowness in responding to you. They were because of the spiritual confusion which while making my life disagreeable, has opened more clearly my eyes on life in general, and in particular on the supposed merit of the colonial life.[15]

Putnam had changed, but Africa too was changing. During the year and a half that he had been away from Epulu, leopard men were reported to be active in the area. These were members of a secret society who dressed in the skins of leopards, or cloth painted with dots, and wore iron claws with which they mauled and killed their victims. The society was originally a group of old men who tried to renew their strength through ritual cannibalism, believing that eating the raw flesh of young victims would restore their youth and vigor. But it soon became associated with revenge and sorcery. Young men were said to be tricked into joining the society by being given human flesh to eat unknowingly. When the source of the powerful medicine they had just taken was revealed to them, an oath of secrecy on pain of death was demanded of them, and they were required to produce the body of a relative for the next sacrifice and the renewing of the medicine.[16] The district commissioner stopped in at Epulu shortly after Patrick's return with Emilie and reported that thirty-four leopard men, thought to be responsible for ninety murders in that part of the Congo in the past year, had been hanged. The commissioner said they had the leopard men under control for the moment, but it was not encouraging news.[17]

The official purpose of the district commissioner's visit was to arrest Putnam's number one "boy," not for anything as serious as leopard-man activities but for violating the colonial hunting laws. The previous summer, while Pat was away, the man had killed an elephant that was looting Putnam's oil palm groves. He subsequently sold some of the elephant meat to white people, which was against the law. Putnam watched helplessly as his employee was ordered to pack up his things and prepare to walk twenty-five miles to the nearest native court, where his penalty was a week of hard labor.[18] Putnam had always defended the colonial powers in Africa, but he was beginning to revise that opinion.

Emilie Baca Putnam was to live at Epulu for less than a year. In the spring of 1939 Angelica Putnam was operated on for cancer. She continued to send Patrick and Emilie cheerful letters, but there was an unmistakable undercurrent in them. "I have revolted [from the care of all the doctors] and have got back the upper hand," she wrote in July, adding, "So many people are talking about your American article. . . . Well! I wish I were going to live forever for life gets more and more interesting." In the same letter she wrote that she was going to the Vineyard to put gravestones for Mary and Sebastian on "that beautiful hill" overlooking Vineyard Sound. "Papa was going, but he got so worried about it and about my going that he got sick. He gets so excited and upset about any changes."[19] Dr. Putnam knew that it could not be long before a third grave was dug on "that beautiful hill."

Sensing the severity of his mother's condition, Patrick packed up at Epulu and hurried back with Emilie to the United States. They arrived in New York in December. Mrs. Putnam was very ill, and from then on Patrick scarcely left the house, wanting to be near whenever she called for him. "I've really seldom known anyone with more courage and will to live than she has," Emilie Putnam wrote her own mother. "Since we've returned her mind has been so active, too active much of the time, . . . she thinks of everything even planning most of our meals and yet she herself can't eat, and is in constant pain. . . . She hates to have to go and has told me several times how hard it is to die. I hope when my time comes I'll go without being aware of it before time. I know I will not have her courage."[20] Emilie had worried from afar about Dr. Putnam, thinking that he would hardly be able to survive his wife's death. "He is completely wrapped up in her, and she dominates his life completely," was Emilie's analysis.[21] But Dr. Putnam was keeping busy, and he too had great reserves of courage.

Angelica Putnam died in January 1940. Although she was formally a Presbyterian, a nurse told the family that she had become a Roman Catholic before she died.[22] The convent education, against which she had rebelled all her life, never left her.

Patrick remained in America for a year afterward, wanting to be near his father. In April he went (without Emilie) to Hollywood, where he took a job with Metro-Goldwyn-Mayer. MGM was considering sending a film crew to Africa to make a bigger and better Tarzan picture, and "leading that crew around" was to be Putnam's job.[23] But first he had to convince them to do it. The Tarzan films were based on the wildly popular novels by Edgar Rice Burroughs, the first of which appeared in 1912 with successors following at regular intervals for the next thirty years. They told a saga of a baby who had been raised by apes in Africa after his British aristocrat-explorer parents died. For a would-be anthropologist to end up making Tarzan films may appear startlingly incongruous, but Patrick Putnam was not simply desperate for something to do or eager to experience Hollywood. The Tarzan saga was close enough to the myth he had tried to live in his own life to attract him.

Literary critics during the Tarzan revival in the 1960s tended to interpret the Tarzan books as escapist reading for people who felt trapped in contemporary Western society and wanted to get away, but it is also possible to read them as an account of how an "innate gentleman," an orphan of good breeding (such as might be imagined by Charles Dickens) would go about recreating civilization if he suddenly found himself alone in the jungle.[24] Tarzan is raised by anthropoid apes; he teaches himself to read English through children's books left by his parents; and he eventually rescues Jane, a white woman who has been abducted by a rebel ape. He falls in with a dignified tribe of African warriors who make him their king, and they all live together on an African estate that Tarzan creates for himself and Jane, a paradise carved out of the forest and clearly separated from European settlements. The African warriors do the work of cooking, cleaning, and gardening and are intensely loyal to their white Bwana. In a situation similar to Putnam's in his camp on the Epulu River, Tarzan imposes order on the jungle by creating and ruling his own private kingdom. In the MGM films Johnny Weismuller played Tarzan as a semiliterate man who communicated his wants largely through monosyllables, but in Burroughs's books—particularly the early ones before the author was influenced by the films—Tarzan is eloquent, very intelligent, and a superb linguist.[25] Burroughs's harsh criticisms of the atrocities of King Leopold II's rule in the Congo would not have displeased Putnam, who increasingly wanted to distance himself from the Belgian colonial administrators who were Leopold II's successors.

Putnam's ostensible goal was to help MGM make more accurate pictures of Africa. In screening the first four Tarzan films—*Tarzan, the Ape Man* (1933), *Tarzan and his Mate* (1935), *Tarzan Escapes* (1938), and *Tarzan Finds a Son* (1941)—Putnam discovered that none of them had more than five minutes of genuine African footage. *Tarzan and His Mate* had only about six seconds from Africa: one shot of a crocodile with some native chanting on the sound track. He was most surprised to find, halfway through *Tarzan Finds a Son,* a ten- or fifteen-second shot of his own okapi inside the fence at Epulu (the fence carefully hidden by bushes) and to learn that MGM had paid an itinerant photographer $2,000 for those few seconds of footage.

Putnam urged MGM to make a whole series of films in the Congo. Until then the only films shot on location there had been *Dark Rapture,* (made by Armand Denis for Universal Studios) and *Saunders of the River* (United Artists). Putnam suggested sending Johnny Weismuller to the Congo to be filmed with the giant Watusi for one movie, with the long-headed Mangbetu and the pygmy BaMbuti for another, and in swimming sequences with the Congo River Wagenya for a third.[26] Another idea was a film about the explorer Henry Morton Stanley with Lionel Barrymore. "The title will be *Emin Pacha* [*sic*] and the story would deal with Stanley's very thrilling march through the Ituri Forest to rescue the little German Jew doctor, George Schnitzer, who had become Emin Pacha, governor of Equatoria under Chinese Gordon," Putnam wrote in an interoffice memo. He added, "On this march Stanley passed within ten miles of my camp at Epulu."[27]

Putnam asked the Los Angeles Public Library to send him a list of books on central Africa and had the story department at MGM send him its synopses of novels set in Africa. Of eighty-seven stories he selected eleven that he thought had possibilities.[28] One of these was Emily Hahn's novel, *With Naked Foot*, loosely based on what she had observed at Penge. Putnam had suggested that for the film on Henry Morton Stanley they find one of Stanley's young officers and get this man to play himself in the film. It must also have occurred to Putnam that he could play the young American teacher, a version of himself, in a film based on Emily Hahn's novel.

All these pleasant and rather fanciful Hollywood prospects ended abruptly when German troops invaded Belgium and France in May and June of 1940. There could be no filming in their African colonies in the foreseeable future. Patrick spent the summer and fall marking time on Martha's Vineyard. In February 1941 he set out alone for Africa, leaving Emilie behind in his father's care.

His departure was almost as abrupt as his running away from home at age sixteen: he virtually vanished. The long letters Emilie wrote him nearly every day went unanswered. Packages his father mailed him went unacknowledged. "You are so completely gone that it is hard to believe that you were so much in my life for a whole year after Jan. 1940," his father wrote him in April.[29] On Martha's Vineyard Dr. Putnam nursed Emilie back to health and equanimity. "Your father is the kindest, the most unselfish of men,"[30] Emilie wrote Pat, and she chided him for his own lack of gratitude and his abandonment of her: "I stood by that first year and a half when it was imperative that someone stand by, even though I was taking a terrific beating. One which your family, my family, your friends and my friends recognized."[31] To her plaints and those of his father, Putnam's response was silence.

Although Putnam was intent on returning to Africa, he had no notion of what he would do there; there could be no tourists at Epulu for the duration of the war. Putnam thought of becoming a freelance African reporter and made tentative arrangements to send articles by mail and cable to *Fortune, PM*, the North American Newspaper Alliance, and *Newsweek*. He did publish one article on Africa as a possible source of raw materials for Germany (in the *Los Angeles News*), but nothing further developed. He began an essay comparing British colonialism with that of the Belgians and the French. "This discourse," he wrote, "begins on whisky, continues on more whisky."[32] The essay continued for a paragraph or two and then ended abruptly.

Nor was he sure how much longer he would be welcome at Epulu. To the author of a recent book on Africa, he wrote:

> There is a line from Hilaire Belloc that I love to quote:
>
> > Whatever happens we have got
> >
> > The maxim Gun, and they have not.
>
> You are quite right in saying that to the average native a white man is nothing more nor less than a white man, whether he be British, French, or German. I think I'm fairly well liked by my black neighbors, but I wouldn't give a nickel for my life in case of a general uprising. Look what happened to Emin Pasha.[33]

He was referring to the death of Emin Pasha, who was having coffee after dinner one evening in 1892 when several of his Zanzibar Arab friends showed him a letter from a deputy of the notorious slave trader Tippu-Tib instructing them to kill him—which they did. It was the beginning of the final round of the bitter war between Arab slave traders and European colonists.

In order to see more of Africa, Putnam took a different route to Epulu, disembarking at Accra in the Gold Coast (today's Ghana) and driving through Nigeria, Cameroun, and the French Congo to the Belgian Congo. He was held up unexpectedly for three months in the Gold Coast, and only later did he learn the reason. Emilie's letters to him had contained long discussions of the war and awed evaluations of Germany's military strength, and they had been intercepted by military intelligence in the Gold Coast.[34] Putnam was finally able to convince the authorities there that he was not a German sympathizer, and he was allowed to continue on his way to Epulu.

He still fancied that he might make a contribution in anthropology. In a rare letter to Emilie he wrote that he wanted to establish the fact that pygmies are defined in Africa not by size but by mode of life: "Our pigmies are called Batwa [the Bantu word] not because they are small, but because they live in and on the bush, never doing today what will benefit them in the far-distant future of tomorrow."[35]

When Pearl Harbor brought the United States into the war, Patrick asked his father to go to Washington to see if there was some job he might do that would make use of his knowledge of Africa. The result was a flurry of interest at first but then silence from the State Department. Patrick interpreted this, probably rightly, as meaning that the strong recommendation his friends had given him in Washington had been undercut by word from Africa that he was a maverick and not completely to be trusted.[36]

Meanwhile, he visited his Portuguese friend Hubert Smet, who had moved from being a merchant at Mambasa to managing a rubber plantation. Putnam became interested in the problems of rubber production and offered his services to the Stanleyville Provincial Agricultural Service. He was hired immediately, and he cabled home in June 1942 to say that he had a government job. Emilie eventually left the Vineyard to work with the Red Cross in Australia and New Guinea. Meanwhile, in Africa, Pat was thinking about rubber. Wild rubber—how to make it better, faster, and more efficiently—was the subject that would occupy nearly his every waking moment for the next two and a half years.

War and Rubber

Patrick's years with Mary at Epulu in the mid-1930s were his happiest, but the years during World War II were those of his most satisfying work. His wartime activities combined all the aspects of Congo life that he loved: economics, anthropology, biology, chemistry. It was practical work with a valuable end product. It allowed him to travel throughout the forest. He was his own boss, paid by the day at his own request, and although officially he was employed by the Province of Stanleyville in its Agricultural Service, in fact he could go directly, when he needed to, to the governor general of the Belgian Congo, Pierre Ryckmans, whom he had known for a decade and who respected his knowledge of the Ituri Forest. "This war is a war of production," Governor Ryckmans told the colonists in a radio talk in 1942.[1] The Belgian Congo could help the Allied cause by increasing the production of raw materials, particularly rubber.

For two and a half years Patrick Putnam thought of rubber, talked of rubber, dreamed of rubber. It was a way of losing himself in work. Since Mary's death in 1937 he had been haunted, he admitted in a rare letter to his father, by "a morbid fear, where loved ones are concerned," of "other such damnable sudden calamities."[2] To cut off all contact, to rid himself of human attachments, was his way of trying to avoid being hurt again.

So all-consuming did Putnam make his immediate work that the Allied cause hardly engaged him. Isolated as he was in the Ituri Forest, where colonial questions were more real than German expansionism and where mail often did not reach him for six months because he was constantly on the move, he was indifferent to the Allied war effort. "I am more of a world citizen—'mundotic,' shall we call it—than ever before," he wrote in that same letter to his father in late 1942, "and I distrust an American or English peace only less than I trust a Hitler peace. That is no frame of mind with which to get along in the Western Hemisphere nowadays; and I'm far better off here getting the natives to get a better price by preparing better rubber; which—incidentally so far as I'm concerned—helps the manufacturers of arms for the United Nations."

That became his cause—to help the Africans get the best possible price for work they were required to perform for Belgium. With his usual intensity, Putnam threw himself into the question of how the Africans could make the best possible rubber in the most efficient manner. He read everything he could find on rubber production, talked to everyone from Belgian agronomists to local chiefs who might know something about rubber, and then began his own experiments.

Rubber gathering had a short but notorious history in the Congo. Four hundred species of plants can yield a rubberlike substance, but the best source of natural rubber is the rubber tree (*Hevea brasiliensis*), which is native to South America. Rubber from that tree had been known in Europe since the voyages of Columbus, but for three hundred years it was used largely for toys (rubber balls) and writing aids (erasers). It was the discovery of vulcanization in the mid-nineteenth century—treating crude rubber with heat and sulfur compounds in order to increase its stability, elasticity, and strength—that gave commercial importance to rubber. The European nations began a search for regions in the equatorial zone where rubber trees flourished best and where they could establish rubber plantations. Britain, France, and the Netherlands chose Southeast Asia, where they all had colonies or special trading relationships. The United States looked to Liberia. After 1885 Belgium turned to the Congo. In that year an international conference in Berlin had rewarded King Leopold II of Belgium for his long-standing interest in central Africa by giving him the Congo Free State, an area eighty times the size of Belgium, to be ruled as his personal property.

Leopold II and his agents decided not to establish plantations with imported rubber trees from Brazil but instead to require the Africans to collect wild rubber from a tree that had come originally from Southeast Asia (*Funtumia elastica*) and from several species of vines indigenous to Africa.[3] In 1890 they instituted a labor tax in the Congo Free State which required the Africans to collect rubber and ivory for King Leopold without pay. When uncooperative villages did not meet their quotas, their leaders were punished with beatings, executions, or the cutting off of hands, which were taken back to headquarters to show how discipline was being enforced. This was the world portrayed by Joseph Conrad in "Heart of Darkness," a fictionalized depiction of his journey by steamer up the Congo River to Stanleyville in 1890. In 1903 the British Foreign Office decided to make public its files on abuses of power and conditions of servitude in the Congo Free State. The result was an international outcry—not all of it disinterested, for the other Western nations resented the Belgian monopoly of wild rubber. A Congo Reform Association was organized in 1904, the Hearst press took up the campaign, and several prominent writers joined in, including Mark Twain (*King Leopold's Soliloquy,* 1905), Richard Harding Davis (*The Congo and the Coasts of Africa,* 1907), and A. Conan Doyle (*The Crime of the Congo,* 1909). In 1906 the labor tax in the Congo Free State was limited, officially at least, to forty hours per month. With the pressure of world opinion building against him, King Leopold went to the Belgian Senate to request an enormous personal loan to cover his expenses in developing the Congo. The Belgian Congress acquiesced but only with the stipulation that he cede control of the Congo to the Belgian nation, which he did in 1908. In 1910, upon Leopold II's death, the Congo Free State was formally annexed by Belgium and renamed the Belgian Congo. The scandal of rubber gathering had forced the Belgian monarch to give up what he considered his personal property.[4]

Although the people of the Congo were thereafter governed by colonial administrators rather than by personal agents of the king, they continued to be exploited. Africans were recruited to work on food plantations, in mines, and at road building by methods that differed little from forced labor. But they were no longer required to gather wild rubber, for in 1912 its price on the world market suddenly dropped. The reason was simple: the plantations in Southeast Asia were proving to be phenomenally productive. Southeast Asia produced four tons of rubber in 1900. By 1910 it was producing 50,000 tons, half of the world's supply. With the coming of automobiles the demand for rubber increased dramatically, but so did output in Southeast Asia until it held a near monopoly, producing 90 percent of the world total of 400,000 tons in 1920, and by 1940, 97 percent of world annual production of more than 1.5 million tons of natural rubber.[5]

Then came the Japanese invasion of Southeast Asia in World War II. As the rubber plantations on which the Western world depended fell to the Japanese, the Allied nations intensified their search for a synthetic rubber and also turned back to their own long-abandoned sources of natural rubber. The colonial government in the Belgian Congo undertook an emergency program to gather wild rubber for the Allies. It also encouraged the establishing of rubber plantations, although this was a long-term measure, for Brazilian rubber trees did not produce good rubber until they were six or seven years old. Patrick Putnam returned from America to find his old friend Hubert Smet running a rubber plantation. Intrigued, Putnam signed on to head the wild rubber production project in Stanleyville Province.

African wild rubber was potentially of good quality but had never brought high prices on the world market because it was prepared so casually that it was generally impure and discolored. Putnam wanted to replace the "more or less bad mixtures resulting from various concoctions" with uniform rubber of the highest possible industrial value for which the African workers could get the highest possible prices.[6] He took thirty African men with him into the forest and set up a rubber-making camp. While they tapped trees and vines and collected the liquid, he experimented with different species and different coagulants and methods, comparing indigenous methods with those recommended by Europeans.[7] The workers were gathering two kinds of latex, which they coagulated by pouring it slowly into great quantities of boiling water. Putnam wanted to find a coagulant to make the process easier. He decided that ideally the coagulant would come from some plant readily available in the forest at all seasons. The plant should contain so little of it that it would be nearly impossible to make it too strong and thus ruin the rubber, and it should contain no tanning material.

As soon as he understood what was needed, Putnam made some experiments in the laboratory of a veterinarian in Stanleyville. Then he went again into the nearby forest, this time taking with him a Belgian army officer who was a botanist. In the first village they came to they found several old men who knew about rubber making. The men told them to use as a coagulant a tea ("tisane") made of the scraped bark of a tree which the botanist identified as belonging to the genus *Chrysophyllum*. They also met in the same village a former chief of the region, an old BaNguana man named Ngoma. Ngoma began to tell them in detail about rubber making, and it was obvious that he knew the trade well. He mentioned the leaf of a particular shrub and sent a child some yards off to bring back leaves, which the botanist recognized immediately as a member of the cola family. This shrub, the "dwarf cola," turned out to have the qualities Putnam was looking for.[8]

In October 1942 Putnam published an article on the making of rubber in *Le Courrier Agricole d'Afrique*. Three species of plants in the Congo give rubber, he wrote—*Funtumia elastica, Clitandra elastica,* and *Landolphia* vines—but, he added, "If there are three species of rubber in the forest, there are 36 ways of harvesting and treating it."[9] He described what he had found to be the superior way.

Putnam became so knowledgeable about rubber making that he began to be consulted on the public relations aspects of rubber gathering as well as on scientific questions. In the spring of 1944 two South Africans criticized rubber gathering in equatorial Africa, raising again the question of "bloodstained" rubber in the Congo. The charge was first made by L. Silverman, professor at the University of Witwaterstand, in a Johannesberg newspaper. It was repeated in Philadelphia by W. J. De Vries, a secretary of the South African Trades and Labour Council, and picked up by Reuter News Service.

Governor General Ryckmans sent the articles to Patrick Putnam, who responded to the charges but urged that they not be given wide publicity. "What ought to be given wide publicity is an objective and popular description of the collecting of wild rubber, making an allusion to de Vries's and Silberman's [*sic*] claims discreetly in the text," he suggested, adding, "It was Bismarck, perhaps, who said 'Credence can not be placed in the truth of a report until it has been officially denied.'"[10] Putnam wrote press releases, including one answering the South Africans' charges, and a radio script for use in the United States, South Africa, and Great Britain. He sent the whole package to Governor Ryckmans, who liked it so much that he wrote "*d'accord*" (agreed) in the margin of Putnam's letter and "excellent! R/" (his initial) at the end.

Putnam's press releases and the radio script about wild rubber are curious documents, for although ostensibly he was defending the colonial government that was employing him, it does not take much reading between the lines to find criticism of that same colonial regime. His defense of rubber making was that it was better than the other occupations forced on the Africans by the Belgians, for it at least allowed them to spend time in their hunting camps, an activity the government had been discouraging. To the charge by Silverman that the rubber gatherers had to go far into the forest and stay for weeks and months in makeshift camps, where they were exposed to diseases and lacked medical attention and adequate food, Putnam replied that they did this no more than on their voluntary hunting expeditions. They are urged, he said, to spend four to six weeks in rubber-making camps two or three times a year.

To the charge that all administration officials hated the very word "rubber," Putnam replied, "Yes, they do hate the word, not because they feel it is a hardship for their charges but for two reasons. A. Because it interferes with the more civilized economy of growing crops for export, an economy which for years administrators have been at great pains to inculcate, and B. Already understaffed, because so many of their young assistants have been drafted to the Belgian Army, rubber gathering gives administrative officials considerable extra work, in checking up to see that each able-bodied native makes the amount prescribed by war-effort legislation, and in supervising rubber markets to see that the native is not shortweighted by the trader."

To the charge that rubber was "bloodstained," Putnam replied, "This is a lie . . . occasionally a rubber gatherer is hurt or killed by a falling rubber vine. The Congo Government pays an indemnity in such cases. It may also be pointed out that native children, who always climb to the tops of the vines to get their delicious sweet fruit, which they like to eat, also occasionally fall." He concluded:

> All in all, rubber gathering in the Congo may be described in a very few words. For twenty years, the gathering of wild rubber [has] been discouraged in the Belgian Congo, the policy being rather to intro-

duce large scale production of cultivated crops for export. Busy with these occupations, the natives have not had as much time as they would have liked to spend in forest hunting-camps.

Now that wild rubber is urgently needed, the Government, at great sacrifice of the export-crop production, has in effect said to the natives: We allow you, now, to go and make forest hunting camps. Hunt all you like. But for each week you spend in camp, each man must make such and such a quantity of rubber. The required quantity is never excessive, and varies with the richness of any particular forest in rubber vines.

He ended with a typical and wry Putnam touch: "The saddest thing in rubber gathering is what happens to the man who doesn't give enough of his rubber earnings to his wife for her new cloth."[11]

In the news releases he prepared (he called them *entrefillet,* "filler" for newspapers and magazines) Putnam was eloquent in describing, not rubber gathering but life in traditional villager hunting camps in the Ituri Forest, camps that through the pressure of world events had become, temporarily, rubber-gathering camps.

The life these rubber gatherers lead would seem pretty tough to us. But these natives born and brought up in Africa's jungles don't mind it . . . glad of a chance to get out and camp for a few weeks two or three days march from their village. For game is plentiful out there, antelopes, wild pig, and the succulent porcupine. The rubber gatherers take with them their spears and bows and arrows, and hunting nets and hunting dogs, and rubber gathering is most judiciously combined with the hunting which they love so much and have missed in these late years since they have been so busy cultivating cotton and other crops the white man has brought in.

A rubber camp at close of day is a pleasant scene. Far out in the forest some old-style hunting shacks have sprung up. Between them the evening fires are beginning to glow, the men are cooking their rubber sap, the women are cooking the supper, and the children are enjoying themselves playing or squabbling. Grandfather, who has managed to hobble out to the rubber camp so as not to miss his share in the feasts of antelope steak, tells of what huge quantities of rubber *he* used to make when *he* was a young man.[12]

Camp Putnam at Epulu remained Patrick Putnam's home base during the war years. At least one of his African wives, Mada, had moved back there to be with him; in 1943 he made some notes on treating her wounds.[13] But for weeks at a time he was in the forest, going from one rubber camp to another, driving the Plymouth roadster he had brought back with him when there was anything resembling a road, and walking where there was not. Putnam's rubber gatherers were not the pygmies, whom the Belgian administrators had never been able to tax or even to count, but he encountered them frequently in the forest, and he noticed again that they were always associated with villagers. Never did he find pygmies who did not have "masters."[14] The pygmies said that he was better at walking in the forest than any other white man they had ever known. Putnam's knowledge of the Ituri Forest, its people, its animals, and its plants, came to be phenomenal. Later, whenever his third American wife, Anne Eisner, asked any Belgian agricultural officer a question about the forest, she would invariably be told, "Only your husband knows the answer to that."[15]

Putnam's health continued to be poor, and he grew more isolated and lonely. The work chart he kept in 1943 shows him "sick" through all of August, all of September, and nearly all of October. Later he thought he might have had Malta fever. And one day he experienced a new symptom. He was carrying "Putnam sheets," rubber made according to his instructions, to his temporary campsite when he noticed for the first time a peculiar shortness of breath.[16]

Leery of human attachments, Putnam had one constant companion that had been with him for eleven years. It was Mr. Fataki, the chimpanzee that had been Mary's favorite at Epulu. Mr. Fataki was well trained, ate at a table with Putnam, drank beer with him, and twice traveled with him to the United States. But he was getting old and irritable, and the Africans in the rubber camps who did not know him teased him so much that he began to attack in turn and finally put two of them in the hospital. Putnam knew he could no longer keep the animal, but neither could he send him to a zoo where he would be miserable, or to the wild where he would no longer be able to defend himself. Putnam decided he would have to kill the chimp, though he told a friend it was like killing a brother. He would not let anyone else do it. The two of them had a last meal together, with Mr. Fataki's favorite foods and lots of beer, and then Putnam put one hand on the chimp's shoulder and with the other put a bullet through Mr. Fataki's head. After this he refused to have a chimpanzee as a pet.[17]

In March 1944 Governor General Felix Eboué of French Equatorial Africa, with his wife and daughter, made an official visit to Camp Putnam, to see the pygmies and a demonstration on the preparation of wild rubber. The visit was arranged by the provincial commissioner. Two agricultural agents helped the pygmies build a pygmy camp "in a very picturesque place near a little stream of water in the forest about 600 yards from my house," Putnam reported later to the commissioner. "Monsieur and Madame Eboué seemed to find very interesting the different songs, dances, and animal imitations of the pygmies." The party had arrived late, in midafternoon, so they decided not to spend the night as originally planned. The daughter went to the pygmy camp in a tepoy, and pygmies were brought to the house for her parents to see. They invited Patrick Putnam to have dinner with them in Mambasa, but he declined, explaining to the commissioner that "they were tired and Monsieur's auditory apparatus wasn't working." He went on: "After their departure, I expected interesting comments from my men who generally speak to me very freely. I was deceived. They limited themselves to admiring the beauty of Mademoiselle Eboué and giving the opinion that in this world the child always resembles its father. I thank you Monsieur for having given me this very interesting mission."[18]

What the report to the Belgian commissioner reveals is not only Putnam's tone of slight condescension toward an African head of state but also his surprise that his employees would not gossip with him after the visit. He tried to ignore the fact that he was a white man living in black Africa, but they never did. It was one more hint to him that however much be himself might identify with Africa, the identification was not reciprocated.

The emergency wartime program of rubber production in the Belgian Congo was so successful (exports jumped from 300 tons in 1942 to 6,000 tons in 1943) that by mid-1944 Governor General Ryckmans was praising Patrick Putnam publicly in speeches in the United States.[19] At the same time, back in the Congo, Putnam was warning that production could not continue at the same rate. Two things were necessary for the production of wild rubber, a willing labor force and a sufficient supply of lianas or vines, but the Ituri Forest had an uneven distribution of both. Putnam had learned during the war years how heterogeneous the Ituri Forest was. The human population varied from place to place, in density as well as in tribal composition. The animal and plant population varied throughout the forest, owing to human actions, natural disasters, and changes in altitude and rainfall.

Late in 1944 Putnam wrote the governor of Stanleyville Province and sent an additional personal note to Governor General Ryckmans describing this situation and its policy implications. He warned the two colonial officers that the road from Stanleyville to Irumu, which began in savanna and ran through the Ituri Forest, gave officials who traveled on it a completely erroneous idea of population distribution. The savannas seemed unpopulated along the road, Putnam noted, but off the road there were many people, so many that it was impossible to go more than two or three kilometers without encountering a human settlement. In these areas the nearby forests were exhausted of rubber, for tapping a liana to extract the rubber sap killed it. These villagers simply could not continue to gather rubber at the same rate unless they turned to a different plant such as *Ficus vogelii*, which gave a product that had to be sent to England to be deresined. Deep within the Ituri Forest, on the other hand, the problem was usually not lack of rubber lianas but lack of people to harvest them. Within the forest the people lived along the road, giving the appearance of a large population. But appearances were deceptive, he pointed out, for away from the road there was *"no one"*: the forest was "an immense green desert!"[20]

What Putnam was trying to tell them was that Stanleyville Province could not be considered a homogeneous rubber-producing unit. Rather, there were three areas: the left bank of the Congo and the Ituri-Aruwini basin, which had a very low population density and the "uninterrupted immensity of the forest," where one man could easily gather enough rubber to earn double the normal wage; the basin of the Mbomu in the territories of Bondo and Ango, where there was savanna often interrupted by trees and some forest galleries, a "possibly rich" area; and the basin of the Uele River, treeless savannas with a very dense population. This third area, because of its large population, had contributed one-third of all the rubber produced in Stanleyville Province, but the men could meet their quotas only by working four times as hard as men in the first area. Putnam reasoned that if their contribution was considered absolutely necessary for the Allied war effort, they ought to be paid four times as much as people were being paid elsewhere.[21]

Putnam did an unplanned feasibility test on the production of rubber from the heretofore unused *Ficus vogelii*. He had set up an isolated camp deep in the Ituri Forest at Nembambada (in Circonscription Azanga, Territoire de Paulis), in a vast primary forest in the northeastern part of the district, hoping to find there living lianas of good rubber plants—*Landolphia, Clitandra,* and *Funtumia*—or at least dead

lianas with which to experiment by beating the bark. To his surprise
he found no lianas of any kind. Rather than return empty-handed, he
decided to experiment with another plant common in the forest, *Ficus
vogelii*. Fifteen men were with him, all of them eager to return to their
villages. Promising them that each would be free to do so when he had
produced a half-kilogram of *Ficus* rubber, Putnam put them to work
searching for rubber and preparing it in sheets according to a process
he had developed with them previously. The men made their alloted
half-kilogram of rubber in four to five days. Putnam was then able to
calculate how much *Ficus* rubber could be made per man per day and
what the rate of pay should be, given the going price for rubber of
seven francs per kilogram. He concluded that the pay was much too
low when compared with the wages paid conscripts in the army. *Ficus*
rubber should he harvested only if there was no better rubber around,
he concluded, and the government should pay at least fifteen francs
per kilogram.[22]

Putnam was so valuable as adviser to the government on rubber
that the chief of agriforests consulted him on the possibility of finding
in the Ituri Forest a substitute for chicle. Belgian officials were thinking ahead to postwar world markets and hoping to compete with Central America for the vast chewing gum market in the United States,
where about 4,000 tons of chicle gum were purchased annually. Putnam replied that he was flattered to have been thought of, was interested in the problem, and had tried some experiments.[23] The question
was deferred for the time being, but it prompted Putnam to begin
thinking about a future in the exporting business, over which he was
to expend much fruitless energy in the next several years.

Putnam's rubber work came to an abrupt end in December 1944,
when he learned that his father was ill and was to be operated on for
gallstones. He asked for a leave of absence from the Agricultural Service and flew to New York to be with him.[24] His well-worn Plymouth
roadster he left with a grateful Congo friend, Father Longo, the much

beloved Roman Catholic missionary at Nduye. Father Longo, like Putnam, was a skilled mechanic and loved to tinker with automobiles. He took out the rumble seat to make the car into a pickup truck and, because of the gas shortage, converted the engine to a charcoal burner. After the war, when he heard that Putnam was returning, he converted it all back again.[25]

Writing about the Pygmies

The last months of World War II were a watershed in Patrick Putnam's life, although at the time it must simply have seemed to him that he was stalling, waiting first for his father's recovery and then for the end of the war, wondering along with everyone else what the postwar world would be like and what his place in it might be. He was drifting in the spring and summer of 1945. But in these months he met the woman who was to become his next wife, and he made one last try at anthropology.

When he was satisfied that his father was recovering from surgery, Patrick Putnam went to Washington for two months in the spring of 1945 to try to sell rubber for the Belgians. He looked up Vivian Katz, whose husband, Milton, was overseas with the oss (Office of Strategic Services) and soon had established himself in a sleeping bag in her living room. Putnam's disdain for personal hygiene was as strong as ever, and he disliked wearing his eight-tooth partial denture. Vivian Katz told him that if he would wear his false teeth and clean up, he could go to a party with her. The transformation startled her, because the scruffy-looking man suddenly "was absolutely wonderful looking, and he collected *all* the women at every party we went to."[1] Putnam was articulate and engaging, and people were eager to talk to him about Africa. After every such gathering Vivian Katz felt that she had brought the star of the evening.

He was equally fascinating to children. One day he took the two young Katzes and his godchild, the daughter of Harvard friend Gordon Browne, to the Washington Zoo. They were gone all day, and as it grew late the parents became very worried. Then the children came home "with stars in their eyes." Dr. William Mann, director of the Washington Zoo and an old friend of Putnam's, had taken them all on a private tour of the back rooms and let them hold the baby animals. Putnam was as excited as the children.[2] He was not selling much rubber, but he was enjoying himself, living, as he would always live, in the moment.

Sometime in the spring of 1945 Putnam made a visit to Cambridge and the Peabody Museum at Harvard. There he was introduced to Dr. George W. Harley, a Methodist medical missionary in Liberia who was spending his year of leave at the Peabody Museum as a protégé of Earnest Hooton. The unlikely conjunction of Hooton and missionaries had begun thirty years before when George H. Schwab called at the Peabody Museum. "He looked like a retired football guard," Hooton wrote, "but he said he was a missionary." At the time, Hooton added, "my conception of a missionary was the wet cartoonist's idea of a prohibitionist."[3] But Hooton soon found that George Schwab not only had an irrepressible and puckish sense of humor but could talk knowledgeably about pygmies, gorillas, and West African ethnology. In 1917–18 Schwab and Hooton worked on a map of Africa for the United States delegation to use at the peace conference. Then Schwab returned to his mission station in the Cameroun and began sending artifacts back to Harvard.

Ten years later, when Harvey Firestone of the Firestone Rubber Company offered to support an anthropological expedition to Liberia, where his company had rubber plantations, Hooton thought of George Schwab. The Presbyterian Board of Foreign Missions granted Schwab and his wife an eight-month leave of absence, and in January 1928 they headed for Liberia. There, at one of their first stops, the mission outpost at Ganta in northeast Liberia, they met George W. Harley, M.D., and his wife, Winifred. From Schwab, Harley learned about Earnest Hooton at Harvard and his interest in African anthropology. in 1930–31 George Harley enrolled in graduate courses at Harvard in anthropology and tropical medicine, and both he and Schwab were named Research Associates in African Ethnology at the Peabody Museum. Every seven years thereafter, as steady and methodical in this as he was in every other aspect of his life, Harley returned to Cambridge to spend his sabbatical year at the Peabody Museum. In 1937–38 he completed his book *Native African Medicine,* a study of two hundred medicinal plants. In 1945, when Patrick Putnam met him, Harley was studying the large collection of masks he had brought from Liberia, about which he would write two seminal monographs, "Notes on the Poro" and "Masks as Agents of Social Control in Northeast Liberia." He was also editing for publication the voluminous notes from Schwab's 1928 expedition in Liberia, which Schwab—like Patrick Putnam in this respect—had never quite gotten around to publishing.[4] Hooton was so impressed by Harley that in 1942 he wrote: "As an anthropologist, I have completely reversed my judgment of missionaries. These men and women have contributed more to our knowledge of peoples of the world than have the entire ruck of professional travelers and explorers. They may have done more than the anthropologists themselves. Missionaries are men and women of character and they tell the truth. Some may be bigoted but most are not! Harvard U. has a steady clientele of missionaries who are research associates in anthropology, doing splendid investigations as a sideline of their regular duties. I am for missionaries."[5]

The key to George Harley's success as an anthropologist was not only his methodical nature. In early midlife, with an M.D. degree from Yale University, he was willing to become a student again, to learn a new field and learn how to keep up to date in it. This was something that Patrick Putnam was never willing to do. He liked to drop in at the Peabody Museum and regale his friends with stories about Africa, but he would not give up his stance as visiting expert, home from the field. He was too proud to go back as a student when his friend and classmate, Carleton Coon, was a professor.

Patrick Putnam could not, nor would he have wanted to, model himself on Dr. George W. Harley, a rather dour, quick-tempered man, devoted to duty, and a severe judge of himself and others. Harley was a missionary of the old school, one who would suffer for others but preferred not to mix too closely with them. Winifred Harley admitted in her memoirs that although they lived at Ganta for thirty-four years (1926–60) and built a large mission and school complex there, neither she nor her husband ever learned the native language of their area, Mano. They could count to ten and give simple instructions, such as "come" and "go," but for all else, including the questioning of patients and of vendors of masks, they had to rely on an interpreter.[6] This was not Putnam's style of anthropology. Still he could not help but notice how pleased Hooton was with Harley's work and how disappointing his own career appeared in comparison.

In the late spring of 1945 Putnam went to Martha's Vineyard, to the family farm. There all summer long he played host to an ongoing house party. His divorce from Emilie Baca became final in June. In July at King's Beach, a nude beach near Chilmark, he met Anne Eisner, a New York painter. In August in a letter to her parents Anne described the man with whom she had fallen in love virtually at their first encounter. She wrote:

> Dearest family, Aug. 13, 1945,
>
> I feel very apolegetic for not having written sooner but life has been exciting, hectic, and fun.
>
> Frieda Utley was up on the Vineyard for about ten days visiting Pat Putnam. A most interesting and charming guy who has lived in

the Belgian Congo for the past 15 years. He's supposed to be the greatest authority on the pigmy tribes.

The household is the wachyest I've ever incounted. Among his guests are Emily Hahn who wrote "China to Me." Her daughter Carola who she's always writing about in the New Yorker who is a little older than Christie Anne [Anne's niece]. An anthropologist by the name of Carl Coon who teaches at Harvard and is an authority on Morocco etc. His new young society wife who has the perfect cocktail voice and is always trying to clean up the place, two million children ranging from Carola, Emily Hahn's daughter, pats newphews and nieces, friends of Pats children. 4 or 5 goats keep strolling through the house at will. A couple of dogs and cats and any stray person who is so included from any place ranging from Africa to me who feel very dull and out of the picture not having dropped from Mars or something.

Its really much coo-cooer than anything in You can't Take it with you!

Frieda is English you know and quite deaf and very political. So everyone's been yelling for ten days all about their interests. Frieda wants everybody to be polotical every second. Since Pat wont write his own book about the Congo, Coon the anthropologists made a list of 30 pages of questions that he'd keep asking Pat so that he could write the book or at least a pamphlet. Some minor castastrophe is always happening among the children with wild yells for Uncle Pat every other second while everybody waits for everyone else to do the chores and Micky Emily Hahn swipes the typewriter which everybody else in the house needs equally badly.

Mickey went back to New York for a couple of days and brought back her cook who was a Dutch sailor with his monkey. He got sea sick on the way over, drove out to the farm in the truck, made a mad dash for the telephone, called a taxi to take him back to Vineyard Haven where he took the next boat back to New York.

As you probably gathered I have been haunting the place.

When Pat and Coon did really get down to the questions and answers about the Congo it was most exciting things i've ever seen or heard. Because as they got going, Pat would begin to describe in detail and suddenly jump up and illustrate the things and in a few minutes pigmy life seemed no stranger than Linville Falls or sword fishing. Then Carl would begin the describe the customs with other tribes and I've never been so excited.

It takes a few minutes to get used to Pat's looks as he's very tall and has a terrific beard. He looks quite like something out of a bizantine painting or one of the early Greek paintings. At first look you expect him to be some kind of a phony. But in a few minutes you realize he's one of the realest people you've ever met.

Sister says he's supposed to be a Lowell so in some respects hes very much the Harvard gentleman. He says his father who was a surgeon has retired from painting and is studying at the [Art Students] League.

I'm going to do a painting of him next week. I'm going to do a langscape with him in the foreground. It should be an interesting problem. I hope I do a good job. . . . Write soon.

Loads of love, Anne[7]

Anne Eisner's zest for life, her forthrightness, and her notoriously bad spelling are all much in evidence in this letter. Wartime rationing of gas soon gave her an excuse to join the house party. When September came, she stayed on at the Putnam farm, returning to New York only for a few days at Christmas. By spring she and Patrick were making plans for her to accompany him back to Africa.

What Patrick Putnam loved about Anne Eisner is not hard to see. She was in her mid-thirties but moved in a gawky, awkward, adolescent way, and she looked African with hair pulled back from her sculptural features. Putnam's first American wife had been a pretty blonde from New England and his second an elegant, dark-haired

Spanish-American from New Mexico. The woman who would become his third was equally distinctive. Anne Eisner was of German Jewish background, intense, explosive, indifferent to personal appearance. She was honest, direct, and without any pretenses—the qualities that Putnam had loved in Abanzima—and frank and vivid in expressing herself, not least in expressing her delight in him. Finally, that she was an artist and quite well known in New York as a painter added to her appeal. With her there was no competition, as increasingly there was on several levels with Emily Hahn, for the typewriter.

Emily Hahn and Patrick Putnam had renewed their friendship since Patrick's return from Africa and her return from China and had even made a try at being a couple. But Hahn was a dedicated professional writer, a member of the *New Yorker* staff and already the author of several books. Her productivity and commitment to her career increasingly annoyed Putnam, who did not like to be shown up in any area and who tended to assume rather as a matter of course that everyone else's life would revolve around his. When an admiring, even adoring woman showed up who was a painter, not a writer, he swiftly transferred his interest.

Carleton Coon, recognizing that Patrick Putnam was wooing Anne Eisner and was going to tell her about the pygmies, decided to make use of the situation. He suggested that he and Putnam collaborate on a work about pygmies as one way to get some of what Patrick Putnam knew into print. Putnam agreed enthusiastically, perhaps thinking the plan analogous to the situation he had observed at the Peabody Museum where George W. Harley was editing the notes made in Liberia by George Schwab. Coon gave him a list of ethnographic topics, and for several days Putnam talked and energetically acted out events in pygmy culture. Coon took all this down in longhand and typed it. Then he cut it up into topics, added information from Paul Schebesta (an acknowledged expert on the pygmies of the Ituri Forest), and wrote some interlinking commentary. The result was a 130-page manuscript that he titled "Pygmies of Africa" and bylined "Carleton S. Coon and Patrick Putnam." Coon sent it off to Patrick for approval.[8]

Putnam, predictably, did not like it. He thought it hastily and sloppily done; he feared that its publication would preempt a book of his own, which he still intended to write; and he did not want his work merged with Schebesta's. He sent Coon a detailed criticism of a single chapter, "The Use of Drugs," going through it sentence by sentence, objecting to generalizations and amplifying them with long paragraphs of additional details. Then he wrote:

> Well, Carl, I hope I have made my point clear. It would take some time to get through your 53 chapter headings with such a fine-toothed and critical comb. What about it. We could:
>
> 1. Give the whole thing up.
>
> 2. Go through it chapter by chapter in this way and have it ready months from now.
>
> 3. Publish it without my name as collaborator, and citing me *only for specific sentences,* which sentences I could mark for you and get back to you in a couple of weeks.
>
> Think it over, and let me know your decision.[9]

Coon immediately chose neither option 1 nor (as Putnam may have hoped) option 2, but option 3. He offered to publish under his own name a carefully edited version in which "facts stated and endorsed by Putnam," "statements quoted from Schebesta," and "connective material and deductions made by Coon" would each be clearly indicated.[10]

But Putnam could not agree to having his material published in a book written by a friend. The result was a stalemate, with Coon wanting to publish the manuscript and Putnam not answering his letters. "Shall I say, 'Published over the dead body of Patrick Putnam' or 'Published with Putnam's begrudging consent' or what is the least repulsive thing I can say that satisfied your scruples? PLEASE GIVE ME AN ANSWER," Coon wrote him in February 1946.[11] Putnam did not reply.

Nearly a year went by, and Coon tried again. He was editing a new sourcebook of anthropology for colleges, to be published by Henry Holt, and he begged to be allowed to use the pygmy manuscript because "it is the only thing in existence that gives a clear picture of a symbiotic life between forest hunters and agriculturalists."[12] Coon promised to remove anything that Putnam considered controversial and to make it clear that this was only a sample of a large monograph to follow.

Putnam, en route back to the Congo, finally agreed: "As to the pigmy business, ca. 3000–4000 words for Henry Holt: my first tendency is to shout 'No.' But I am really getting slightly wiser as I get rapidly older (and may be wise enough to write by the time I'm sixty), and so I say 'Go ahead,'—give you carte blanche, in fact, and add only that if you think wise you might say 'by C. S. Coon, based on conversations with Patrick Putnam, who many years ago had anthropological training at Harvard and who has spent most of the last 20 years at his place at Epulu in the Stanleyville Province of the Belgian Congo—that is to say, in almost daily contact with the teeming pigmy population of the Ituri Forest.' But if you don't like this, omit it, and, as I say, go ahead in any way you think best."[13]

With this grudging carte blanche in hand, Coon in turn was magnanimous. He removed most—but not all—of what he had added to his original transcriptions of what Putnam had told him on Martha's Vineyard and published the remainder as "The Pigmies of the Ituri Forest" with Patrick Putnam named as the sole author, and this disclaimer in a footnote: "Putnam has been living with the people of whom he spoke for nearly two decades. He dictated to me a somewhat longer story of pygmy life, which I have condensed to its present compass. He went over the copy carefully and made corrections. He is not satisfied with it, and has gone back to learn more. Meanwhile he is willing to let you read what follows. This material has never before been published."[14]

Thus Carleton Coon had dragged Patrick Putnam willy-nilly into print. "The Pygmies of the Ituri Forest" was to be Putnam's only publication on the pygmies. He never liked it, for reasons that are understandable if one compares it with the original typescript. The twenty-page published essay was a matter-of-fact, nonromantic, but rather charming and appreciative account of a rigorous way of life. It described how pygmy men climb a hundred feet up trees to get honey and to gather bark for cloth. Falling from high trees and being hit by falling tree trunks in a storm were among the major causes of death among pygmies, Putnam said, along with diseases such as pneumonia and dysentery. Unlike the villagers, who bathed often, pygmies disliked water and were usually dirty and full of lice. They were fond of smoking hashish, and some were addicted to it. They were skilled at stalking game in the forest but not good marksmen, at least the net hunters were not. According to Putnam, pygmy camps usually consisted of about twenty-five people and were governed by two factors: respect for older people, and the right of every man in the camp to state his views on any subject, with the "pungent remarks" of the women also having considerable influence.[15]

Putnam suggested that it was unlikely that the pygmies had ever lived alone in the forest. He doubted that they could survive there without the iron-tipped arrows and hunting nets, as well as the plantains and other vegetable food, that they got from the villagers, although they did eat many products of the forest, including ibambi fruits and baselli nuts (which ripened in January and February), wild vegetable foods, mushrooms, and "slow game"—small animals that do not move rapidly and can be caught by a woman or child, tossed in a back basket, and carried home. Putnam asserted that the traditional role of the pygmies had been to serve the villagers as scouts, intelligence agents, and soldiers in the forest; in return the villagers provided them with plantains, their major food, and with manufactured goods. The relationship was an ethnic caste system; the pygmies were "a genetically and occupationally segregated segment of a larger economic entity."[16] Since the Belgians had brought peace to the forest, the pygmies had only part of their bargain left to fulfill, the bringing of meat and honey from the forest, while the villagers continued to carry out all their traditional obligations. Thus Putnam thought that what looked like a bad bargain for the villagers was the result of a changed historical situation.

Coon kept in the published piece the historical changes in elephant hunting noted by Putnam: that it was incidental in the Ituri Forest until the traders began demanding ivory at the turn of the century, at which time some pygmy hunters developed elephant hunting as a specialty in order to please their village masters. But Coon omitted the more recent historical changes in the forest that Putnam had noted. One was a falling birth rate among the villagers because of venereal disease, which may have made village men more eager to take pygmy wives. Another was the effort by Catholic priests to get pygmies to purchase wives in lieu of their traditional system of sister exchange, because in the latter, if one couple broke up, the other one had to as well. Another was the pygmy preference for the BaNguana, descendants of the Zanzibar Arabs who moved into the interior in the slave and ivory trade, over their earlier Bantu or Sudanic masters. Putnam had said, "For some reason these Banguana Moslems have a great attraction for pygmies. Band after band of pygmies has abandoned its pagan negro hosts and gone to work for the Moslems." Putnam had also noted a tendency in areas strongly under Belgian control for the traditional and hereditary individual relationship between a village man and his pygmy to be replaced by a relation between village chief and a "chief" of the pygmies who supposedly spoke for his group—this because the Belgian government liked to have a single official to deal with.[17] Coon's version gave a timeless quality to the life of contemporary pygmies, instead of the ever changing historical situation Putnam had described.

Even more serious than his omissions were Coon's added summary statements and irrelevant editorial comments. At the beginning of the section on villager-pygmy relations, Coon inserted one sentence: "This forest is inhabited by two kinds of people, Negroes and pygmies, who maintain an almost symbiotic relationship, based on trade."[18] This is the only mention in the text of "symbiosis," a term that Putnam had long since rejected as misleading because it implied that the relationship was advantageous to both sides. Putnam believed the villagers could get along very well without the pygmies and would someday realize this and stop supporting them. A generation of American students, however, would use Coon's *Reader in General Anthropology* and pick up the term "symbiotic" as an apt description of the supposedly mutually dependent and timeless relation between African villagers and pygmies.

Other misleading additions follow Putnam's statement that the pygmies remain in one camp for two or three months, "until the game is scarce, the fruit gone, the camp ringed by high refuse heaps and pungent with the smell of rotting food and human refuse. Or they will perhaps move on a little earlier if someone dies and is buried there." To this Coon added, "They do not count time; they simply respond to the practical needs of the moment, the way lower organisms respond automatically to changes in intensity of light." Putnam's next statement was, "Moreover, they will never go back to exactly the same place [camp]. One reason for this may be the presence of funeral remains; but there may be other reasons." Here Coon added: "The pygmies do not say why, and probably do not know."[19] The effect such interpolations was to denigrate the pygmies' intelligence, even to make them seem less than human, which was obviously contrary to Putnam's beliefs and intent. These sentences would later be singled out by Putnam's critics.[20]

In a final note at the end, Coon remarked on the paucity of "religious" phenomena in pygmy culture. In this he was true to Putnam—

but exactly contrary to what Putnam's contemporary and rival in pygmy studies, Paul Schebesta, would spend a lifetime trying to show.

Schebesta was a blunt, good-hearted, hard-working Roman Catholic missionary priest. He was born in 1887 in a small Moravian community in Silesia, a part of Prussia. In his youth he joined the missionary order of the Society of the Divine Word. He would spend the rest of his life with this order as a missionary, ethnographer, and professor. By 1945 the Reverend Dr. Paul J. Schebesta had been making field trips to the Ituri Forest for more than fifteen years, longer than Putnam had lived there. He and Putnam were the world's two leading experts on the pygmies of the Ituri Forest. But there the similarities ended.

Patrick Putnam and Paul Schebesta came from markedly different anthropological traditions, Putnam from the Harvard tradition of biological anthropology, Schebesta from the Vienna school of ethnohistory. They had very different fieldwork styles and goals. Putnam settled at one place, a particularly beautiful place, in the Ituri Forest, made it his headquarters for fourteen years, and intended to spend the rest of his life there. Schebesta came to the Ituri on research expeditions lasting from six to twenty months. He traveled throughout the forest, rarely spending more than a few weeks with any single group of pygmies, then retreated to his study at the seminary outside Vienna to write up what he had learned. Putnam had to be coerced into print, whereas Schebesta published extensively: three popular travel books, a four-volume scholarly monograph, and a hundred articles. Putnam felt he could not write until he knew everything. Schebesta wrote as he went along, revised his views frequently, and did not let the contradictions bother him. When he died in 1967 after forty years of writing about the pygmies, he was preparing a final volume in which he planned to rethink his whole approach in the light of criticism and his most recent investigations.[21]

Schebesta himself was not a theorist, but he was a student of one of the great ethnographic theorists and system builders of Europe in his time, Wilhelm Schmidt, the founder of the Vienna school of ethnology. Schmidt was a member of Schebesta's religious order and taught at its seminary, St. Gabriel, at Mödling near Vienna, as well as at the University of Vienna. In 1906 he founded the anthropological journal *Anthropos*, which Schebesta helped to edit for many years.

Wilhelm Schmidt, S.V.D. (Societas Verbi Divini), left his mark in three massive scholarly projects. In linguistics he was the first to demonstrate the connection between languages spoken in southeast Asia and in the South Seas, a discovery comparable in importance to showing the relationship among the Indo-European languages.[22] He followed this with a systematization of all the languages of the world. In ethnology he is best known for an elaborate theory of spreading cultural complexes ("cultural circles" or *Kulturkreiselehre*) by which he explained the entire early history of human culture. Schmidt hypothesized that an original primitive culture, similar to that of the contemporary pygmies, had split eventually into three primary cultures: the patriarchal hunting culture, the matriarchal hoe culture, and a shepherd-nomad culture. The intermixing of these three in turn gave rise to more advanced cultures.[23] The theory was a true house of cards, an elaborate and fanciful construction on a precarious base, and has long since collapsed, but for a time it had a considerable following in the German-speaking ethnographic world. Simultaneously, Schmidt worked on a multivolume compendium on primitive religion, *The Origin of the Idea of God*, in which he argued (with Andrew Lang and against the British evolutionists) that animism and magic were not necessarily the first stages in the evolution of religion and that the idea of a high god was far older than was usually assumed.[24]

In searching for the origins of monotheism, Schmidt turned, as he had in his search for the origins of culture, to the pygmies. They lived in the most primitive fashion known, by hunting and gathering, and they were thought to be among the oldest of contemporary peoples. In studying their culture, he believed, one might catch a glimpse of the mind of the original primitive human being. In 1910 Schmidt wrote, "It is my firm conviction that the study of the pygmies constitutes one of the most important and most urgent, if not the most important and urgent [problem] in ethnology and anthropology."[25]

World War I and, two decades later, World War II interrupted his work. But in the 1920s, with the financial support of the Vatican and various scientific societies, Schmidt sent his students to study pygmies, generally defined as hunter-gatherers of short stature. Paul Schebesta was sent to the Semangs of Malacca on the Malay Peninsula (for which work he received a Ph.D. from the University of Vienna in 1926) and then went to the Belgian Congo.[26]

Schebesta made his first survey trip in the Ituri Forest for seventeen months in 1929–30, a journey he described in two books, *Among Congo Pygmies* and *My Pygmy and Negro Hosts*. Both are fascinating books with little theory and much loving detail, mostly day-by-day accounts of where he went and what he encountered in the Ituri Forest, in nearby Ruanda to the east, and in the Equatorial Province of the Belgian Congo to the west. At first, he despaired of his goal of finding evidence of a belief in a god among the pygmies; he even wrote in a letter that he had apparently discovered a people who had "no god."[27] But Schebesta did not give up easily. He noticed that in distributing a carcass, the pygmies cut a fragment from the heart and threw it into the forest. When he made inquiries, he was told that they always sacrificed the first fruits of their labor to their god. He heard some pygmy women on a difficult march singing a song to "Asobe" and was told that they were asking their god to protect them and see them home.[28] Eventually, he became convinced that the pygmies had a definite idea of a powerful being associated with the rainbow, lightning, thunder, and snakes.

Schebesta's preparation for departure from Africa in 1930 coincided with Patrick Putnam's return as an employee of the Belgian Red Cross, and Putnam made a special trip to see him. It was the only time they ever met.[29] Four years later, on his second expedition through the Ituri, Schebesta reached the banks of the Epulu River near Camp Putnam and must have known that the young American he had met on his previous trip was living there, but he did not stop in. Schebesta's indifference over the years to Putnam's presence in the Congo bothered the latter, and he was pleased when near the end of his life he finally received a letter from Schebesta.

On that second trip Schebesta traveled for eight months with another anthropologist, Martin Gusinde, and a medical doctor, Jean Jadin (who studied blood groups and pathology among the pygmies), then went on by himself for six months. On his return to Europe in 1935, Schebesta wrote another popular book, *Revisiting My Pygmy Hosts,* and began work on his multivolume scholarly work, *Die Bambuti-Pygmäen von Ituri,* the first part of which was published in 1938, with subsequent volumes in 1941, 1948, and 1950. Schebesta was by then certain that the pygmies had a belief in a creator god who was called by various names, including "father" and "grandfather." This was a storm and rain god who took the form of lightning, thunder, and the rainbow and was also called a snake. Behind these various manifestations Schebesta saw a single powerful deity who was the final cause of all things. Schebesta had no ready answer as to the source of his very non-African belief in a single all-powerful god, but he suggested that it might have come from rational thinking on the part of the pygmies or, alternatively, that it was implanted in their subconscious.[30] He contrasted the pygmies attitude toward their deities, which he called one of childlike trust and simplicity, with the religious outlook of the villagers, who lived in constant fear of spirits and unknown powers.

On Martha's Vineyard in 1945, when Patrick Putnam and Carleton Coon discussed Schebesta's work (mainly his popular travel books, which had been translated into English), Putnam accepted the description of pygmy material culture but took issue with Schebesta at several other points. The first was language. Schebesta thought that the pygmies had at one time had their own language and perhaps still did.[31] He was to hold to this position with increasing tenacity, eventually going so far as to suggest that the pygmy language was the fundamental one out of which the Bantu and Sudanese languages had developed.[32] Putnam was sure, on the contrary, that the pygmies did not have their own language. They spoke the language of their present hosts and sometimes in camp among themselves the language of their former hosts. Putnam's position at the end of his life, as reported by Anne Eisner to Colin Turnbull, was that the pygmies probably had had a language at one time but that it was lost except for a few pygmy names.[33]

Putnam also questioned the validity of Schebesta's division of the pygmies into three groups whom he called the Efe, the Aka, and the Bambuti or Basua, distinctions based on geography, language, and the different groups of villagers who were their patrons. Putnam thought it was much more useful to divide the pygmies into net hunters and non–net hunters. Net hunting was a communal activity that required pygmy bands of a certain minimum size, whereas non–net hunters depended on individual stalking of game with bow and arrow. Again, as with language, it depended on what their village patrons had, for the pygmies got nets or arrow tips from them. But for Putnam, who questioned everything, even this distinction was not universally valid. On his way back to Epulu in 1947 he met some pygmies at Libenge living in conjunction with a Mavo-speaking people. He found that these pygmies, like their hosts, used neither hunting nets *nor* bows and arrows. "What will pigmy culture be reduced to?!!" he wrote Carleton Coon.[34]

But the point on which he disagreed most vehemently with Schebesta was pygmy cosmology. Putnam accepted Schebesta's description of rituals but not the meaning he attributed to them. Where Schebesta described pygmy women carrying bananas and singing a song begging Asobe (god) to see them safely home, Putnam commented to

Coon that he would like to know the exact local meaning of Asobe, for it was a common first name, and the whole chant might be only a Bantu subjunctive meaning "May we get home safely" without reference to any deity, or it might possibly be an invocation of an ancestor.[35]

When Coon pointed to Schebesta's insistence that some pygmies believe in a soul (some of which is carried to the sky after death and some to a local spirit place to become part of a totemic ancestral spirit) and Schebesta's description of a class of forest spirits that play tricks on people and take game away from hunters, Putnam admitted that there was some evidence of pygmy belief in spirits. The pygmies he knew refused to go near certain rocky hills where there were dense thickets; they would say, "That hill is full of *sitana"*—a KiNgwana equivalent for the Arabic word *shaitan* (plural *shayatin*), which means devil or fallen angel. Putnam saw in this sign of Arab influence.[36]

In his conversations with Coon, Putnam discounted any evidence of a concept of god or soul among the native peoples in the Ituri Forest, villagers as well as pygmies, and aligned himself with what he called the "Franco-Belgian school of 'dynamism.'"[37] He was alluding to the theory of Arnold van Gennep (a French anthropologist often misidentified as Belgian) who in his well-known book *Les rites de passage* (1909) insisted that not all primitive people believe in personalized spirits. Some of them, van Gennep wrote, have a concept of an impersonal, indefinite force active in the universe, a theory which he and others called "dynamism" in contrast with "animism."[38] Putnam insisted that the natives of the Ituri Forest were "dynamists" who believed only in direct cause and effect in their magic, which he compared to the American ritual of knocking on wood; Coon called it "the old Frazerian principle of sympathetic magic."[39] Putnam maintained that this was the only kind of magic practiced by either pygmies or villagers in the Ituri Forest and that neither group had any gods. He contrasted the Ituri Forest people with the grassland people, such as the

Azande, whom he called "animists" because they believed in gods and spirits who could be appealed to.

Putnam could agree with Schebesta on the material culture of the pygmies and even on the forms of ritual. But about the meaning of those rituals he could not agree for each anthropologist looked at the people of the Ituri Forest and saw himself. Putnam identified with both villagers and pygmies and denied that either one had any concept of god. He himself had none. Sex is my god, he would later tell Anne Eisner. In the Ituri Forest he would acknowledge only the same sort of half-serious sympathetic magic that was practiced by his American friends when they refused to walk under a ladder or let a black cat cross their path. He looked at the pygmies and saw a clever, skeptical, insouciant people who loved life as it is, who repeated a few formulas to allay their anxieties, but who in general could not be bothered with speculations about the unknowable. He looked at the pygmies and saw not only himself but his father, who shared his agnosticism.

Schebesta likewise identified with the pygmies but in *his* own way. He saw them as the oppressed minority in the Ituri Forest, just as in childhood he had been a member of an oppressed minority, the Moravian community, within the Prussian state. In his popular books he used the feudalistic terms "lords" and "vassals" to describe the relationship between the villagers and the pygmies. He contrasted the superstitious villagers, the "lords," with the pygmies, the "vassals," a simple and untutored people who nevertheless lived (as he did) with a confident trust in a divine being and struggled to express in various ways the universal religious truth embedded deeply within them.

Putnam's eagerness to be recognized as an expert on the pygmies had led him to cooperate with Carleton Coon. He knew that alone he would not write the great book he envisioned. Perhaps he knew that alone he *could* not do it. He was floundering in data and was so far removed from the academic world that he no longer knew, if he had ever known, what questions he should ask. But he had grown increasingly dubious about the collaboration with Coon and displeased with the result. Meanwhile, he watched a hard-working German-Austrian scholar, missionary, and priest solidify his position as expert on the pygmies of the Ituri Forest.

Around this time Putnam did write a ten-page personal manifesto, which seems to have been provoked by his renewed contact with his anthropologist friends and professors. In it he evoked the Harvard motto *Veritas* but used it to defend himself as a dilettante. Describing his personal philosophy as "veritas, and away with hypocritical camouflage," he continued:

> Many years ago, when I went out to Central Africa as a young assistant on an anthropological expedition, I found the country pleasant and decided to stay there. I do not choose to speculate on the type of neurosis which made Central Africa seem to me pleasanter than the country where I was born and brought up. Once settled there, I have never stopped examining my environment. I have learned to speak one of the many native languages well; I have conversed with my native employees; I have had various native women as acting wives, relationships which have sometimes engendered considerable mutual affection. I have struck up friendships with Europeans of the most diverse occupations, doctors, Belgian district commissioners, Greek retail traders, German Catholic missionaries, Scottish Protestant missionaries, and many other varieties of resident white-men. With my late wife, Mary Linder, I built and operated a tourist camp, on one of the main automobile roads but fifty-miles from the nearest white-man's residence, and there as paying guests have had Belgian financiers, globe trotting retired American whiskey manufacturers, German spies disguised as movie crews, an ex-English governor of the Punjab, etc. etc.
>
> In the United States, each time I have revisited it I have spent considerable time in looking up the complementary knowledge which can be found in books, whether on early Portuguese explora-

tion of the Guinea Coast or on the interlocking directorates of huge diamond and palm-oil concerns which, between them, are the masters of the whole mid-continent.

After fifteen years I have learned how little I know, and wonder if my personal satisfaction would have been greater if I had become a world-recognized authority on some reasonably limited subject such as the subjunctive infixes in Bantu languages.

However, on the whole, I think I am glad that I have remained a dilettante. Again in an attempt to understand better the place where I have my home I have made each return journey to it by a different route. Thus I have gone to Alexandria and up the Nile through Egypt and the Anglo-Egyptian Sudan; and by Dakar in French West Africa, then stopping at various French, British, and ex-German ports down along the Guinea coast, disembarking at Matadi, the seaport of the Belgian Congo, and from there by river steamer up the Congo; another time, I landed a car at Mombasa on the East Coast and drove up through Kenya, Tanganyika, and Uganda; in 1941, I landed a car at Lagos, on the "slave Coast," and drove from there across Nigeria, and then across the interior of the Cameroun, and French Equatorial Africa, during that curious period when the French residents were being forced to spontaneously acclaim de Gaulle. So that, altogether, I have seen a good bit of Central Africa. On the other hand, there are many regions of the Belgian Congo into which I have never set foot.[40]

Patrick Putnam's renewed contact with his anthropological friends and former professor, after the wartime years of isolation in Africa, had not been easy. He found himself having to scale down his dreams and his self-image. The manifesto he wrote set forth the new persona he was trying to develop and be content with: the dilettante who was an all-around practical Africa expert.

Anne

In May 1946, Patrick Putnam and his new companion, Anne Eisner, boarded a freighter in New York. That night, while the ship was still in the New York harbor, Patrick became very ill with pneumonia; he was carried off the boat on a stretcher and taken to the Brooklyn Hospital, where he was treated with oxygen and penicillin.[1] He recovered, and they sailed ten weeks later. But for Anne it was a foretaste of the serious illnesses that would increasingly plague him—and terrify her.

Patrick had already been given the diagnosis of the disease that would end his life. He was walking down a street in New York with a friend when the friend noticed that Putnam was breathing oddly. Patrick went immediately to his father and announced, "Gordon [Browne] says I'm wheezing." His father sent him to a lung specialist, whose diagnosis was emphysema. Putnam was told that as the loss of elasticity in his lungs increased, a walk of ten meters would leave him gasping for breath as if he had run five kilometers. The prognosis was that he would spend the last years of his life in a wheelchair. At the time Putnam thought the doctors were describing a condition that was decades away.[2]

The Belgian who had been Putnam's boss during the war wrote him in 1947: "If you knew how often I have envied you, you who travel so freely through the world, content to know human stupidities without having it affect your good humor. Unhappily, one does not meet every day a spirit like yours, but always and everywhere now anxious faces, discontented, envious, and contemptuous."[3]

This blithe image continued to be Patrick's face to the world. Privately, however, he felt a growing desperation. The issue was money. Wanting to be fair to Emilie, he had signed over to her in separation and divorce settlements $1,200 per year for life, which was virtually all of his annual trust fund income.[4] Dr. Putnam continued to send his son an allowance of $2,000 a year, but the extra funds beyond the allowance that he had always been willing to provide vanished when on March 2, 1946, the seventy-eight-year-old Charles Putnam married again. The bride was Margaret (Margo) Kreuder, forty years old and a friend of his daughter Marley. Margo Putnam had worked in advertising on the staff of J. Walter Thompson before her marriage.[5] She doted on Dr. Putnam, babied him and ordered him around, and he loved it. She also soon became a firm voice in family financial matters.

For the first time in his life Patrick Putnam felt desperately short of money. The hotel business at Epulu did not pay for itself, let alone provide any surplus for the trips back to America that he liked to make. He wanted to live in Africa, but an essential part of his way of life had been the possibility of frequent visits home to New York and Boston and Martha's Vineyard. How was he going to keep all this going?

He decided to try to become an exporter of African raw materials and curios. While still in New York he contacted various importers and planned a route back to Epulu "hell bent on trade," as he wrote Carleton Coon.[6] He would look for derris root, an ingredient in insecticide; for piassava, a palm fiber used in making brooms; for rattan; for gangi, a substitute for chicle in chewing gum; for copal, an ingredient in varnishes and assorted leather goods; for snake skins, crocodile skins, and leopard hides; for arabica and robusta coffee.[7] He wanted to buy masks, for he intended to open a museum and a shop with masks and

curios at Camp Putnam and also sell his best masks through the Knoedler Gallery in New York. He thought he might try again to write travel
accounts for the popular press, and he asked Carl Coon if he would
peddle them in New York.[8]

With failing health and a thin wallet, Putnam set out with Anne
Eisner from New York. He knew that for the first time in his life he was
going to have to use whatever resources he had, of knowledge or influence, for his own benefit. If he were to continue living in Africa, he
would have to exploit it in some way. He could no longer choose to be
above the fray, neither taking nor giving orders, as he had once expressed it. Patrick Putnam returned to the Congo in 1947 knowing sin,
recognizing that he with his white skin and European connections
was among the powerful in Africa, and that by his very presence there
he was a beneficiary of colonialism. He had lost his innocence. He no
longer thought he could live outside of history.

He saw the colonial situation ever more clearly as he became increasingly disillusioned with the United States and its Western allies.
In Washington and elsewhere in the United States in 1945–46, Putnam was appalled at the discrimination directed against blacks and
Jews. In lecture notes he prepared around this time, he wrote, "In all
these years in Central Africa, two things have been most distasteful to
me, one is Forced labor. [The other is] the Colour Bar." Forced labor
he called "a subject with which I've had only too much contact during
my African years," and on the color bar, "Social discrimination seems
to me to be a worse thing for the happiness of the worlds people than
political . . . " and here his writing becomes illegible. His notes go on
to say that he "went out there long ago with the feeling that natives are
natives and in all these years have learned one big thing and that is
that they are people differently brought up from us, to be sure, but
nevertheless people. . . . Africa a wonderful place for thinking object[ively] and for seeing soc. ineq. and miserable bitterness it eng[en-

16. *Patrick Putnam and Anne Eisner en route to Africa, 1946. By permission of the Houghton Library, Harvard University.*

ders]."[9] The "miserable bitterness" he had observed in Africa was a product of the same social prejudice he had found in the United States.

The arrangement that Patrick Putnam had made with Anne Eisner was carefully casual. She was to travel to the Congo with him in order to make paintings of the Ituri Forest and to see whether she liked living in Africa. Anne paid for her passage by offering sales in advance of the paintings she would do there, mostly to family and friends, although a columnist in *Art Digest* mentioned her project and urged prospective buyers to contact her at her studio.[10] With the $1,000 she collected for ten promised paintings plus a steady $100 per month allowance from her father, who had a waxed paper factory in New Jersey, she was on her way.

They left New York on July 28, 1946, aboard the tramp steamer, *M. V. Freetown,* on which they spent nine weeks. On board ship Patrick gave Anne French lessons, as he had done with Emilie. Anne wrote in her journal, "Pat has a talent for setting up offices all over the boat. He takes the folding table, chairs, and tarpolin and makes wonderful little nitches."[11] They were together so constantly that the other passengers teased him about not being able to escape from her.[12] They disembarked for brief stops at Las Palmas in the Canary Islands, at Dakar in French West Africa, at Freetown in Sierra Leone, and at Monrovia and the Firestone Plantation in Liberia. They wanted to go to Ganta, Liberia, to visit Dr. George W. Harley, whom Patrick had met at the Peabody Museum the previous winter, but the motor road ended eighty miles inland, and they learned that from there it was a two-day walk to the missionary compound. Instead they bought "at white man's prices" some superb masks that Harley had collected and had left with a government agent.[13] After another brief stop at Takoradi in the Gold Coast (today Ghana), they left the ship at Port Harcourt, Nigeria. From there they set out in Anne's 1938 Chevrolet coupe for the overland trip to Camp Putnam.

They had left New York with different expectations. Anne was following the man she loved; she would have gone anywhere with him. That it was the Ituri Forest toward which they were heading was irrelevant. She had been promised a marvelous sightseeing trip across Africa along the way, and to her it was almost a honeymoon. With a last-minute gift from her parents of $1,000, they planned to buy African art en route.

Patrick, on the other hand, was heading back to Camp Putnam, which he knew he could no longer afford to support and where, unknown to Anne, he had an African wife (Mada) waiting for him. For

him the trip across Africa was not just a sightseeing and art-buying so-
journ but also a business trip on which he hoped to establish trade relations with producers of agricultural products and manufacturers of
African goods. Anne was a timid traveler and disliked being left alone
even for an hour or two. When Patrick returned from an appointment,
distracted with business worries that he did not particularly want to
share, she would chide him for being moody. To add to their difficulties, they were both frequently ill, Anne experiencing her first African infections, and Patrick having recurrences of old and serious illnesses. Their six-month journey across Africa stretched into a year. At
every stop Patrick gathered information on importing and exporting.
Anne wrote to her parents, "He's pretty good at it I must say though he
takes it for granted that the only reason these people exist is to spend
their life giving him the necessary information and gets quite griped if
they don't know everything or happen to have another appointment."[14]

They moved through several worlds, from the court of an African
Muslim ruler, to villagers dancing in the bush, to English and Scottish
colonels drinking gin on a hotel terrace. Anne soon became surfeited
with the colonial custom of drinking for several hours and dining finally at 11 P.M., and she wrote a friend, "I don't think I'll ever make a
good colonel as I can't get the necessary nasty voice involved in calling
"Boy."[15] Patrick had little patience with the pomp and protocol of local
rulers, and in an audience before the Oba in Benin he did all the talking (the obverse of the usual procedure) and declined brusquely an offer to be shown the shrine to the Oba's ancestors, saying he did not
have time.[16] His disdain for authority included black rulers as well as
white.

They had stopped at a rest house in Nigeria, near Ikot Ekpene, and
left a basket of curios on the veranda. The next morning Ibibio people
began to appear with masks to sell and kept coming, day after day. For
ten days Patrick Putnam and Anne Eisner had a daily private market
and spent most of their money in an orgy of buying, acquiring some

seventy masks and wood carvings. Their stay lengthened to three weeks, for after buying all the masks, they had to find a way to carry them. They were in the main raffia-weaving district, and Patrick hit on the idea of buying baskets, into which they would pack the masks.[17] They finally managed to get everything in the car and headed off again. But the heavy load meant more delays, for at every border they were questioned and cross-questioned about their cargo.[18] Putnam had written to the governor of Nigeria asking permission to export the masks, but they left without receiving an answer, and the British later complained that they had taken masks out of Nigeria without a permit.[19]

Meanwhile, still in Nigeria, they stayed in a rest house in Kano for more than a month. Patrick talked to everyone and, according to Anne, made "hundreds of acquaintances," including all the good chess players.[20] "Pat and I continued our rounds of visiting various traders looking for pocketbooks, grips, and other gift shop items," she wrote her family.[21]

In February, on the border of the Belgian Congo, they discovered that Patrick's passport had expired and were forced to wait in Libenge for months until a new one arrived. To pass the time they made frequent visits to a nearby pygmy village, and they were there during a three-minute eclipse of the sun. Putnam had told the pygmies that the sun was going to be sick, hinting that it was because they were not bringing him enough meat. The pygmies watched disbelieving as it got dark. As it began to get light again, Putnam stood up and walked away in triumph. It was the sort of dramatic performance he loved, where he could pretend to be an all-knowing and all-powerful person, Patrick Putnam, King of the World, as he had written long ago in his geography text on Martha's Vineyard.[22] It did not matter that his kingdom was only one small pygmy village and one admiring American woman.

Once across the border it was a four-day drive to Stanleyville, where they picked up the car Patrick had lent to Father Longo. Their two-car caravan drove into Epulu on the evening of August 23, 1947. Patrick had been away from Camp Putnam for almost three years, since December 1944, when he had been called home by his father's illness.

He wanted Anne to see the local pygmies immediately, for it was his friendship with them that had made him famous. The first morning at Camp Putnam they had themselves carried out to the pygmy village in tepoys decorated with leaf fans and hibiscus flowers and in a procession with drums and rattles beating time as the bearers sang. The African workers and tepoy bearers had replaced their assorted Western clothes with brightly colored lengths of cloth tied around their loins, and they wore basketlike caps decorated with feathers. "Putunami" was back. It seemed to Anne that everyone—villagers and pygmies alike—adored him.[23] In typical Putnam fashion he turned his homecoming into a gala performance and a party for all. But the procession of tepoys had a darker side. It masked the fact that his health had worsened and that it was difficult for him to walk even the few kilometers to the pygmy village. In earlier days he would have scorned to be carried.

They settled in at Camp Putnam. During the war Patrick had trained several of his trusted employees to run the hotel as a cooperative, dividing the profits among themselves after paying him a certain percentage for maintenance. He continued this system after his return. The employees continued to run the hotel, and he and Anne paid for the meals that the two of them ate.[24] Anne wrote to one friend, "The place is just magnificent, my idea of Paradise, except for the biting ants."[25] To another friend she complained, "This place is magnificent and Pat is in his element bossing fifty people around. He's also so busy I hardly ever see him, a [in] fact I miss him, after being with him almost every minute for the last two years."[26]

Then the reason for some of his absences appeared: his African wife. There was turmoil at Camp Putnam as Mada Gobaneka returned to live there, and Patrick began publicly to show his affection for her. Mada was thirty-two years old. She had joined Patrick Putnam's household when she was fifteen, while he was still at Penge.[27] Patrick was back in his African world, his African kingdom, where he was virtually chief of an African village and had an African wife. Anne found herself being treated as a casual acquaintance, a European guest at Camp Putnam.

She was torn apart in anger, indignation, and embarrassment and was no longer sure she was even welcome at Epulu. Was she just a summer romance who had hung on too long and was now spoiling his life? But she had not come all this way simply to turn around and leave. What ought she to do? Should she travel on through Africa, perhaps to Ruanda, by herself? Should she head back home? Or should she stay? Too embarrassed to return immediately to New York but too timid to travel on by herself, Anne decided to stay for a few months and do the paintings she had been commissioned to do. But she could not continue to live at Camp Putnam. Never one to hide her feelings, she directed acid barbs at Pat and at Mada. Camp Putnam, which had seemed Paradise, became the scene of constant unhappiness and tension. She had no friends among the colonials to whom she could turn—they were all Pat's friends. But she could go into the forest with the pygmies, and that is what she did.

In January 1948, Anne Eisner headed off into the forest with the official Camp Putnam band of pygmies. In a clearing they built her a hut of leaves that was slightly larger than the huts they built for themselves. The group was led by Faizi, a quietly authoritative man about thirty-seven years old who loved dancing. It included Andonata, short, funny, and vulgar; his outspoken wife Bassalinde; and their two children, an older daughter and a son, Teliabo Kenge, who was eight or nine years of age and the leader of the children. It also included Herafu, whom Anne called the most sensitive and graceful of the pygmies.[28] Herafu had a motheaten notebook that he had bought at the market and carried around with him, often upside down. One day in camp after much vacillation he brought it over to Anne, who wondered what philosophical thoughts she might be asked to write down. Herafu pulled his chair up next to hers and, looking very serious, said in KiNgwana (which she was just beginning to understand), "Madami, will you please write in my book that each time a white man takes my picture I want one franc."[29]

When Faizi's band of pygmies returned after a month (their usual stay in the forest), Anne went off with a second group, Cefu's band, which belonged officially to a nearby Bira (Bantu) village on the other side of the Epulu River whose chief was Saboni. They preferred Camp Putnam, however, and eventually moved in and built themselves a mud village next to Faizi's.[30] A month later, around the first of March, Anne returned to find that Patrick had gone to Stanleyville on business for an indefinite period.

With Patrick away, Anne lingered at Camp Putnam, uncertain what to do next. She studied KiNgwana and practiced with the workers: Ageronga, the head man; André One, the cook; André Two, his son, the gardener; Ibrahemu, the hotel boy; Abanzinga, the animal man; Paul, the carpenter; and others.[31] Several groups of expected visitors came for extended stays, among them a British duke and duchess, a French film crew, and Alfred Emerson, a termite specialist from the University of Chicago, and his wife. Emerson discovered many new species of termites and named two of them for Anne (*Odontotermes annae*) and the absent Patrick (*Microtermes putnami*).[32] Anne wrote Patrick cool letters; he wrote her warm, affectionate ones, encouraging her to serve as hostess at the hotel and trying to make everything all right between them. He had moved on from Stanleyville to Leopoldville, to look into the possibility of exporting derris root (for insecticides) and arabica coffee. He was not sure when he would return to Epulu. "I can't face it, I can't face it, I can't face it," he admitted. "For, except for those wonderful first three weeks or so, our time together at the Epulu has been, shall we say, not very pleasant,—or, shall we say, Hell."[33]

Finally, in an unusually crisp and cool letter after he had been away for three months, Patrick offered resolution: he invited Anne to fly to Leopoldville, where he would marry her on the condition that she accept the situation at Epulu.[34] Anne agreed ecstatically in a letter addressed to "Dearest, dearest Pat."[35] At Epulu she and Mada drank a glass of beer together, pledged to cease quarreling, and arranged to share Patrick equally—one week with one, one week with the other. With this understanding, Anne Eisner flew to Leopoldville. On July 26, 1948, the anniversary of the date they had met in 1945 and of the date they had finally sailed for Africa in 1946, she and Patrick Putnam were married in the office of the mayor. One of the two witnesses was Patrick's old boss during the war.[36]

Camp Putnam now became Anne's home. She had her own separate house there, as did Mada; the Palais was used as a hotel. Anne threw herself into life of the community. She was incessantly curious about the people and their lives, and she loved to argue with them. She learned KiNgwana, but she always spoke it badly. Gradually a few of her linguistic errors crept into the general parlance at Camp Putnam; for example, everybody began to adopt a double negative that she used.[37] The Africans called her Madami ya Kaleli, which means the lady of lots of noise.[38] The nickname may just have been a reference to her exuberant spirit, but more likely it was an amused comment on her first months at Camp Putnam, for one African expression for the situation of a woman discovering her husband's infidelity is "a lot of noise."

The pygmies remained Anne's special interest, as they had been from her first days there. In Leopoldville after their marriage, Pat quizzed her at length about her experiences in pygmy camps, and he had his temporary secretary, a Gold Coast clerk, type up some notes she had taken. From the library he got for her Schebesta's two books in

17. *Anne Eisner Putnam and Patrick Putnam with Mbuti pygmies at Epulu. By permission of the Houghton Library, Harvard University.*

English, and as a wedding present they bought themselves the first two volumes of Schebesta's major work on the pygmies, which was in German. Patrick read parts of it to Anne, and they compared her experiences with what Schebesta described.[39] Patrick Putnam could be selfish, but he could also be generous, and he wanted his new wife to love Africa as much as he did. He began to speak of her as a pygmy expert, and the pygmy camps in the forest continued to be her refuge—a place to go whenever life at Camp Putnam got to be too much for her.

At Home at Epulu

After their marriage in Leopoldville, Patrick and Anne went on a six-month art-buying and sightseeing tour of what Pat called the "least-developed" corner of the Congo, along the border of Portuguese Angola, across the Kwango, the Kasai, the Sankuru, the Tchuwapa, to Poala and Stanleyville.[1] They were in one of the best art-collecting regions in the Congo, unlike the area around the Epulu, where little art was produced. The Putnams bought twenty-five masks from the BaYaka people, who lived on both sides of the middle reaches of the Kwango River, the boundary between the Congo and Angola.[2]

But the trip was a terrible strain on him. Putnam was frequently ill and spent about half the time in bed. His old Plymouth broke down constantly; just outside Leopoldville they had spent three months waiting for a gearbox to be repaired. Meanwhile Ageronga, the head man at Camp Putnam, sent letters in KiNgwana to Patrick from Epulu reporting that Mada was "sad" and was threatening to leave if Putunami did not come back quickly.[3]

Patrick and Anne returned to Epulu to find that some of the most treasured African objects they had left behind were gone, sold by mistake for very low prices. An unscrupulous visitor had persuaded the staff that they were supposed to sell the objects on exhibit in the hotel and those put away in the storeroom. The theft, for such it was, prompted Putnam to send out an "Explanatory Note" to would-be purchasers. He wrote:

> The things we sell are divided into three quite distinct categories:
>
> 1. Ebony and ivory junk as is widely made in the Congo specifically for sale to whites, and in no way resembling anything the natives used to make in the past for themselves. These we sell at the prices prevailing in hotels throughout the Congo.
>
> 2. Things made by the tribes living in the neighborhood of the Epulu,—the ba-Bira, the ba-Lese, the ba-Ndaka, the baNguana and the pigmies, specifically for us, but in imitation of the things they used to make for themselves before the invasion of enamelware and cotton prints. These we sell for a profit, but very cheap. (Items such as Babira pipes, ivory hammers for beating bark cloth, mandolins, wooden spoons, baskets)
>
> 3. Real museum pieces, which we have collected at great expenditure of time, trouble, and money, during our journeys to various out of the way parts of Central Africa. These we sell here at high prices, but which are only about half the prices we ask for them when we send them on approval to America. (Items such as Ibibio tribe masks, a crocodile shaped paddle from the Ijaw tribe, wooden balls, statuettes, a Ngombe shield)[4]

Even after the theft the Putnam collection of African art was impressive and became quite well known. Laurance Rockefeller and Janet Gaynor with her husband Gilbert Adrian were among the people who came to make purchases. Putnam encouraged the production of crafts immediately at Epulu. One of his employees, Pascal, made ivory carvings, mostly statues and chesspieces, for sale to visitors, and a forger (ironworker) settled at Epulu and made knives and arrow points.[5]

Putnam's attempts to export African goods and products fizzled completely. The American market for African raw materials was a seller's market in 1945, but prices dropped as soon as the war was over and supplies of rubber, derris root, and plant fibers again became available from the Far East. Putnam was operating in a wide-open frontier where the winners were those who were swift, single-minded, and competitive, and he was none of those things. Importers in New York who had expected to hear from him in Stanleyville in six months lost interest when he did not write them for a year. Putnam spread himself too thin and at the same time, with his usual passion for thoroughness, probed too deeply, trying to master all the intricacies of growing and marketing five or six different crops.[6] Meanwhile more experienced entrepreneurs simply leased plantations, bought up available supplies, and established a monopoly over a product, leaving the details of production to others.

Putnam tried exporting African handcrafts such as masks, ivory and ebony statuettes, woven raffia table mats, and small musical instruments. But each piece had to be bargained for individually, for he could not find a reliable supplier of large quantities of high-quality goods, and his shipping was amateurish. One dealer complained that two packages arrived but without an invoice, so the dealer did not know what to charge.[7]

He had similar difficulties when he tried to export animals, live ones to zoos and dead ones and skeletons to scientific researchers. He got a list from his friends of zoos that might be clients, studied government quarantine rules and restrictions on shipping wild animals, and made arrangements with an international airline. As a trial run he shipped two boxes of live chameleons to the San Diego Zoo, but they got caught in the Christmas rush in America, were inadvertently shipped by rail instead of plane, and were dead on arrival. He sent a water cobra to the New York Zoological Society, but it, too, arrived dead, and the zoo officials told him they already had a capable collector in the Congo.[8] In any case, Putnam could have provided only small animals, snakes, and birds, for the government of the Belgian Congo kept for itself a monopoly on the export of all protected animals, from gorillas, okapis, and pangolins to the blind fish of Thysville caverns.

As for research specimens, he discussed with Sherwood Washburn, anthropologist at the University of Chicago, the possibility of sending twenty to forty pottos preserved in alcohol. The payment was to be $100 to Putnam for his efforts and $5.00 per potto. "This kind of a job is something that I have been wanting to get for years and seldom got," he wrote Washburn. "For example, our good friend, James Chapin, is always wanting to get to study the lyre-tailed honey-bird but he never mentions the possibility of his rather rich museum's paying a penny for the job."[9]

Putnam was torn between his need to earn money and his desire to be a colleague, generous host, and friend. When Sherwood Washburn talked about visiting Camp Putnam, Patrick wrote him, "My place is run as a hotel with the usual Congo hotel rates. However, if you are trying to do the trip economically and have camping equipment, you could hire a cook and boy and you would be welcome to camp 'in my woods' as long as you liked. I have pigmies and full-sized negroes that are good cooks and good hunters with guns."[10] Patrick Putnam would let impecunious travelers who interested him live at Epulu for weeks and sometimes months for the cost of their food. He wanted to sell masks to museums or to Knoedler's, but he could not resist sending one of his best BaYaka ones as a gift to the Peabody Museum in 1948 in honor of his friend J. O. Brew's appointment as director of the museum. "It will make an interesting contrast with the beautiful set of masks brought from Liberia by Harley," he wrote Brew.[11] He was trying to be an entrepreneur, but he could not make it work because what he really wanted to be was a respected colleague.

Another possibility he hoped for was that Camp Putnam might be made a branch of IRSAC (Institute pour la Recherche Scientifique en Afrique Centrale), a research station at Costermansville founded in 1947 and funded by Belgian and American interests.[12] But in typical Putnam fashion, he wanted this to happen without having his own freedom in any way compromised. He wrote Louis Van den Berghe, director of IRSAC, in September 1948: "Of course, I never give up hope that you may be able to appoint Camp Putnam at Epulu as a sub-station, and also hope that although I would be left free to travel to America or elsewhere as I please, the fact of my place, which runs perfectly even during my absence being a sub-station, would bring me some financial return. Since I am, thanks to my father's generosity, a 'petit rentier' [recipient of an annual unearned income], and since the purchasing value of even the dollar is getting so low, I must get, in order to continue living at the Epulu, some extra income."[13]

The bureaucracy moved slowly, but after some natives brought Putnam a newborn okapi, which he raised successfully with great quantities of powdered milk, Camp Putnam was made an official *Deport d'Animaux* for IRSAC, and an official IRSAC sign was posted on the premises. Putnam was given permission to acquire and hold for IRSAC okapis and several other kinds of animals.[14] A young male okapi named Lelo remained a pet at Camp Putnam for nearly two years.

Patrick's father urged him to stay home and save money instead of spending a fortune traveling around trying to make money, and Patrick finally acceded to the wisdom of this view. He had gone to Leopoldville in 1948 expecting to make a fortune exporting *Urene lobata* (for billiard balls), he admitted to friends, but instead spent every cent he had. He also knew that the days of his grand journeys through parts of Africa or anywhere else, for that matter, were over. In December 1948, while still on his wedding trip with Anne, Putnam wrote to his African friends Agnes and Alobe, whom he had not seen since the war years, to bring them up to date on what had been happening to him.

After describing his divorce from Emilie and his recent travels with Anne, he wrote:

I will not make many more of these voyages: My health is terrible. Right after I left you at Busu Djansa I was in a rubber camp experimenting with rubber that I created in the territory of Poko under the auspices of de Breuls de Tiecken. They made good "Putnam sheets" in the bush and when I took a pile of them to my gite, I was astonished to find myself out of breath. This breathlessness slowly increased, and in America I consulted a doctor and then others. Diagnosis: emphysema—beautiful Greek word that Alobe will know is only one of these medical superwords meaning simply "difficult breathing," or more simply, "poumons foutus." Case—unknown. No germ, tuberculosis or other, was responsible. Treatment: none. And what prognosis, I asked the doctor. "Ah, you will no doubt spend the last 5 years of your life in a wheel-chair." The impression the doctor's answer gave me was that, many, many years from now, in the far distant future, when I was 70 years old or so, I might need a wheel chair. That news didn't sound so bad. But, alas, watching the disease progress in myself, I note that it is unpleasantly rapid, and am afraid that in about 2 years I will need that wheel-chair, and then be able to use it for only about 2 years until I die of suffocation. My present state is that I can drive a car all right, but *have difficulty walking ten meters, or even getting up from a chair.* Rather a change of mode of life is necessary for your friend Putunami, who used to get around quite a bit and scorned tepoys. My muscles are still all right, and I forget sometimes, and move suddenly, and then almost faint from lack of breath. My symptoms, to the non-medical, are something like those of someone suffering from a very bad heard, and, to simplify and avoid long explanations, I often tell people that that's my trouble. . . . Well, now you won't be surprised when you see me, which I hope will be soon.[15]

Putnam's self-prognosis was not far off the mark. He would live for five more years—one more than he had predicted.

Putnam alternated between accepting the prevailing medical verdict, that there was no treatment for what ailed him, and hoping against hope that somehow, somewhere, he could find a cure for it. In October 1949 he and Anne spent $300 from their dwindling resources to seek medical aid in the Congo. They traveled several hundred miles in one direction, to Kilo, to consult a Belgian doctor who worked for the mines, and then several hundred miles in the other direction, toward Beni, to see an American doctor. Neither could do anything for him. At various times it was suggested that his problem was related to Malta fever, which he might have had during the war; to an outbreak of brucellosis among the farm animals on Martha's Vineyard in 1945; or to the gonorrhea of his youth which had perhaps never been completely cured. In each case he was treated accordingly, but nothing stopped the rapid progression of the disease.[16]

Their financial situation became increasingly dire. Dr. Putnam was no longer willing to send the extra money he had always contributed; he even asked to have the two-hundred-acre farm on Martha's Vineyard, which he had put in Patrick's name, deeded back to him. Patrick agreed, having no alternative, for he had little hope of going there and could not afford the taxes and upkeep. "The graves on the hill top are, to me, as they say 'no object,' for I share your opinion on the worthlessness of our physical remains (as well as your doubt as to the existence of any other kind of remains)," he wrote his father.[17] Neither of them mentioned the implicit reason for the transfer, which was Dr. Putnam's wish that the farm go eventually to his second wife, Margo, rather than to Anne Eisner Putnam.

The farm in Massachusetts no longer his, nor was the name Epulu any longer entirely his. After World War II the territories of the Belgian Congo were reorganized, and the old Territoire de Mambasa became Territoire de l'Epulu. Patrick confessed to his father that the change "makes me mad, because heretofore 'epulu' has been an absolutely exclusive address for me."[18] It was a hint of what was to come.

Although to his father Patrick affirmed his agnosticism, the thought of death turned him back inquiringly to his mother's religion. Around the time that the hopeless prognosis of his disease was confirmed, he bought a Bible in French from some Protestant missionaries and inquired about getting a Catholic one in French or English.[19] He and Anne occasionally read it, along with the fiction, scientific books, and works on Africa in their large library and the out-of-date newspapers and old *New Yorkers* and mystery novels that their families sent them.

As Putnam's illness progressed, he ironically found himself doing more and more hospital work. This, finally, was the source of additional income. A government medical mission visited Camp Putnam in 1949 and, liking what they saw, offered to make it an official dispensary under the Congo's new Ten Year (health) Plan. Putnam was supplied with medicines and paid medical aides and given a stipend of $40 a month. The money was welcome, but the official status and abundant medicines meant an ever increasing load of patients. The staff were soon giving a hundred injections a day, mostly for gonorrhea, syphilis, and yaws, all very common in the area. They also treated sleeping sickness, bilharziasis, trachoma, typhoid, and paratyphoid.

The infirmary—or hospital, as it was sometimes rather grandly called—was a large rambling mud and thatch hut with fifteen beds and a tiny laboratory and pharmacy. Behind the infirmary was a colony of native huts for relatives and those not so ill. In front, a broad veranda served as waiting room, consulting room, and operating theater. Every morning a long line of villagers and pygmies queued up on the veranda. They were seen first by an African medical aide sitting at a table, who listened to each complaint. Those with simple ailments were sent inside to be treated, while puzzling or difficult cases were sent to Putnam for examination. Frequently the aide would go to Putnam's nearby hut to get instructions.[20]

The hotel, averaging about two guests per day, continued to bring in some money—mostly for the workers who ran it, with a small amount going to the Putnams for maintenance—but business was very uneven. Anne served as hostess at the hotel, but Patrick was the authority. That was always his role at Camp Putnam. "Pat was like the Dutchess in Alice in Wonderland today and chopped off a lot of heads," Anne wrote her family in December 1949, "as he fired the hotel cook and he demoted Herafu as chief of the pigmies, because he said the pigmies hadn't brought in any meat or roofing leaves the way he had requested. If a chief couldn't make his people mind then he wasn't a good head. Herafu was very broken up. Pat then held a conference to find out from the pigmies who should be their chief. All decide that Faizi should. He does have the most influence anyway."[21]

Increasingly, Putnam was called upon to arbitrate disputes among the people at Epulu and the surrounding area. He had a fair knowledge of the local languages, KiBila, KiNdaka, KiLese, and KiMbo, as well as excellent KiNgwana, and he understood the varying customs of the different peoples and could decide what was fair. They came too to talk to him about government directives. Should they plant more cotton, as they were being told to do? Putnam would set out the pros and cons as he saw them, so they could make up their own minds. The local Belgian administrators were not always comfortable either with his popularity or with his free-thinking.[22]

Putnam started a school for the village children at Epulu. The girls refused to attend, but the boys came and learned to count and to read and write in KiNgwana. Classes were held at the hotel or outside under a tree, and the teacher was Lukamba, a mission-trained employee. The boys had slates, and Lukamba used chalk on a blackboard made from a hammered-out gasoline drum. He and Putnam had long arguments on whether learning by rote (which he favored) or by doing (which Putnam favored) was the better way. Lukamba was also put in charge of a *hotel des chauffeurs* that Patrick had his workmen build. It was a simple affair—two rooms, a veranda, and a cookhouse across from an old garage—but it provided a place where the native drivers who accompanied tourists could sleep and eat.[23]

Another project was the zoo. Putnam offered good prices for animals that people brought him from the forest, paying half on arrival with a chit promising the remainder in two weeks if the animal were still alive. It was his way of ensuring that the animals would be brought to him in good condition. He took the temperature, weight, and measurements of each one, then had the carpenter build cages for them, which he labeled with scientific and popular names and descriptions that in pithiness and interest were worthy of a world-class zoo. Here is a sample:

> *Potto* (Perodicticus potto)
>
> This lemur, by the slowness of its movements and its nocturnal habit, is known to most Europeans as "parasseux." But a true parasseux is a South American animal belonging to a completely different animal family, and it is fortunate that the name "potto" is spreading.
>
> When the keeper lets this animal out of its cage, you will see that one of its toes is provided with a claw entirely different from the perfect little nails on the other toes and on its fingers. In touching its nape you will feel the curious prolongation of its cervical vertebrae in a true dorsal spine, of which we don't know the use. Pay attention to its sharp teeth for it likes nothing better than to bite your finger.
>
> The potto eats with pleasure fruits but dies eventually if its food does not contain enough protein, such as milk or eggs. In the wild it probably eats many insects and eggs and perhaps even young birds when it finds them in their nests.
>
> It moves at night and little during the day but in between likes to get up into trees, its favorite resting place. Like monkeys, it does not have a home but makes a nest of leaves in the crook of a branch of a tree. When it rains it is protected only by hiding under a branch.
>
> The family comes one at a time. It does not have a loud cry and contrary to what most Europeans think it is not this animal which

possesses the piercing and mournful sound often heard in the night by travelers, in the rest-houses in villages throughout the forest. That cry, which is unmistakable, is emitted by the *daman* (hydrax) of which a specimen is found in another cage.[24]

Putnam's zoo in August 1951 included two okapis, several giant rats, a brown mongoose, horned vipers, Gabon vipers, cobras, and other venomous snakes, in addition to the potto and the hydrax. He kept records of what the animals ate, studied their food preferences, and procured special foods when necessary. Animal babies were bottle-fed. When an animal died, Putnam directed one of his workers or visitors in doing an autopsy.

The forest world often created its own excitement. Although attacks by wild animals were rare, in January 1950 a pygmy woman in a village three kilometers from Camp Putnam was attacked by a leopard and her neck was broken. Putnam cleaned her wounds, sprinkled them with sulfa powder, and gave her intravenous saline infusions and injections of morphine, but he could not save her; she died the next day. Several days later three pygmies killed the leopard with spears and steel-tipped arrows and brought it back to Camp Putnam for a victory dance. The leopard was gibbeted on the lawn, and that night as the drumming began, the pygmies, some of them daubed with paint to look like leopards and wearing clothing made of leopard skin, danced around its body, stalking, taunting, and spearing it. Putnam, watching from his chair, had Ageronga bring out palm wine for everyone, observers and participants alike.[25]

Later that year Faizi killed an elephant, an unusual event because the Camp Putnam pygmies were net hunters. None of them were elephant-hunting specialists, who were usually trained from childhood. For a week the pygmies gorged on elephant meat in the forest. Then for another week they held wild celebratory dances, for three days at Camp Putnam and four more days at Kopo's village, where Faizi's official master Ngoma lived. The Putnams had no meat until the celebration had run its course; thereafter, the pygmies became "normal" once again and went off net hunting in the forest.[26]

Putnam's control over the pygmies was no greater than that of any of their other patrons. The pygmies went back and forth, playing their masters off against one another. When they tired of entertaining visitors at Camp Putnam, they would go visit Ngoma and Pakalili in Kopo's village until those two patrons got tired of feeding them. Then they would return to Camp Putnam. They brought meat when it suited them. For a time when Moke was serving as the leader of a pygmy camp, he turned against the Europeans and for weeks refused to bring the Putnams any meat from the forest.

When nothing much else was happening, Putnam would create excitement. He had an old bicycle fixed up, and dozens of people at Camp Putnam learned how to ride, with roars of laughter every time anyone fell and with many requests for bandages and iodine. He sent to the United States for balls, bats, and mitts and, when they arrived, spent one Sunday afternoon teaching the men at Camp Putnam to play softball. His employees seemed to enjoy it, but at the end of the afternoon they wanted to be paid for a half-day's work.[27] It was 1950, and the colonial world in Africa was coming to an end much more rapidly than anyone, including Putnam, realized.

In January 1951, when Putnam learned that the international Algiers to Cape Town auto race was going through the Ituri Forest and would pass by Camp Putnam, he had the pygmies set up a roadside stand. Whenever they heard an automobile coming, they rushed out with bows and arrows and spears and pretended to be attacking. Most of the drivers stopped and stayed for a cup of coffee and talk with Patrick Putnam, for whom it was a way of making contact with the outside world. With the arrival of forty-six drivers spread out over twelve days, however, the pygmies soon lost interest and returned to the village. But Putnam stayed on at the stand to the end.[28]

In the spring of 1950 Anne went back to the United States alone to visit her family. Patrick wanted to go with her, to attend the twenty-fifth reunion of his Harvard class, but he could no longer do much walking. There would be steps to climb and much drinking. He would need a taxi as constantly at his command as the tepoy at Epulu, and that he could not afford. "I think that if I went to 1925's Twenty-fifth reunion I would drop dead in the middle of it," he wrote to his father.[29]

In November 1950 the area around Epulu was hit with epidemics of paratyphoid and influenza. The Putnams turned their camp into one large isolation ward, and for several weeks they and three medical aides worked twenty hours a day treating two to three hundred patients daily and inoculating all the people in nearby villages.[30] Not long afterward they were given three babies to raise whose mothers had died in childbirth. The first to come, in February 1951, was Kokoyoo—or William J., as Anne and Patrick called him in honor of her father—a half-pygmy baby eight days old. The father (a Bila) and the pygmy grandmother brought the baby wrapped in a square of bark cloth and indicated their intention to leave him with the Putnams. Anne fed the infant Carnation canned milk and made diapers out of torn curtains. For some weeks all Patrick's scientific passion was focused on this baby as he kept detailed charts of temperature, feedings, stools, and weight.[31] For a time William J. even slept in Patrick and Anne's bed, between them. They raised him as their own for nearly two years until they realized that he had to learn how to live as a pygmy.

Next to come was a premature baby, Katchalewa Lengana, also half pygmy and half Bila, who weighed slightly over two pounds. No one—not even the father, Mundufu, who was a local Bila medicine man—expected the child to live, but it thrived. Then a pygmy infant named Ndeku was brought to Camp Putnam. Patrick, who was interested in native medicines and very good at ferreting out bits of secret knowledge, had been told that a certain flowering plant rubbed on the breast can produce milk in a woman who has had a child. He asked Mundufu about this, and the medicine man, eager to help because

Putnam had saved his child, provided some of that plant. They gave it to Ndeku's aunt, Myuma, whose youngest child was five years old. For a week nothing happened, and Anne fed the baby canned milk. On about the tenth day Myuma started having a little milk, and it increased daily until she had enough to give the baby half of its supply, which Anne supplemented with two bottles a day. They learned that in a similar case at Camp Putnam, with medicine obtained from a BaNguana medicine man, an old grandmother who had not had a child for twenty years was able to nurse a baby whose mother had died. The father was Alfani, a BaNguana and a longtime worker at Camp Putnam. Putnam was told that the cost of the medicine depended on the relationship of the woman to the child.[32]

Anne was involved in virtually every aspect of Camp Putnam, but her presence was felt most strongly in the art activity at Epulu, the planning and service of the hotel meals, and the pygmy shows, which became her particular specialty. Anne had instigated much of the Putnams' collecting of African art, and gradually the second room of her house, originally her studio, was transformed into a museum. After they had seen her painting and sketching, the pygmies took greater care with the paintings on their bark cloth, and the villagers began to carve figures and decorate their pipes. All this was new at Epulu.[33]

Guests at the hotel commented on the excellent and imaginative table that Anne set. First came drinks in the living room around the central fireplace, and then dinner in the open dining room overlooking the river. Dinner might be chicken broth, freshly caught fish, antelope stew with wine, boiled and riced manioc, hearts of palm salad, local coffee, and pineapple, papaya, and passion fruit. One of her specialties was a whiskey–hot pepper sauce made from the Duchess de Ligne's recipe. For hot baths she provided an Abercrombie and Fitch canvas shower bucket donated by Prince Ferdinand of Liechtenstein: the canvas bucket with a shower head on the bottom, filled with warm water and suspended from the sapling frame of a mongongo leaf enclosure, offered an excellent shower.[34]

But Anne's greatest contribution to Camp Putnam was her discovery of the special pygmy world in the forest. Feeling abandoned and humiliated after her arrival at Camp Putnam, for two months she had lived in the forest with the pygmies, and in so doing she experienced the pygmy world in a way that Patrick Putnam never had. He readily admitted as much. In 1949 he wrote to a would-be visitor: "I have lived in the Ituri forest a long time, and liked it, but have found so many things of interest in it that I have never become an authority on any one of them. My present wife, in a stay of a year, saw more of the pigmies 'at home' than I have in twenty years." Putnam urged his potential guest to follow her example: "If you want the pigmies called in, that is perfectly feasible, but rather dull. If you want to go out to their camp and accompany them on one of their net-hunts, that is much better. Best of all is to take the folding beds and other equipment, and go out and sleep for a night or two in the pigmy encampment."[35]

When visitors chose, as most of them did, simply to observe the pygmy demonstration and perhaps also to go net hunting, Anne took charge. In a clearing down along the Epulu River the pygmies demonstrated the building of their leaf huts, setting up camp, making bark cloth, and tree climbing. In the evening there were songs and dancing, and the next day they went net hunting. To see it all required a stay of two full days and three nights, and some advance notice, "as quite often my pygmies are far off in the forest and have to be called in," Anne wrote one tourist agency.[36]

Anne also organized a special group of singers whom she called *Ndege*, ("birds"). They imitated the calls of various birds of the forest and then did a rollicking medley of parrots, hornbills, and plantain-eaters in full cry. They would conclude by imitating animals, one little boy climbing a tree like a chimpanzee, making chimp noises, and showing how a chimp builds a nest in a tree. James Chapin, who saw one of these performances, called it "unforgettable." He was also impressed by how the supposedly elusive pygmies had the run of the Putnam home and showed "not the slightest trace of shyness."[37]

The pygmies were sensitive to an audience's reactions and varied their performances accordingly, so that no two shows were ever the same. It was amusing for them and for Anne, as well as for the visitors. They tried to outdo one another, and they were wonderful mimics. After some visitors from Argentina had been at Camp Putnam, the pygmies added the samba to their dances. But Anne insisted, as Patrick always had, on as much authenticity as possible in the pygmy shows. Armand Denis, a commercial filmmaker and photographer, had photographed pygmies at Camp Putnam putting up a bridge of lianas across the river in accord with his instructions, though that was not something they ordinarily did. After his film was released commercially, visitors to Camp Putnam would frequently ask to photograph pygmies on a liana bridge. Neither Anne nor Patrick would cooperate with this request, but it was usually possible for tourists to hire the pygmies to do it anyway, and some of them did.[38]

In 1950 Merlyn Severn, an English journalist, was on her way to Mambasa with her driver and a servant when they were delayed by rain. Severn "remembered hearing about an eccentric American couple who conducted a holiday camp in the depths of the forest somewhere along this road," and when she saw the Camp Putnam sign, they turned in. She found Patrick Putnam reclining in a lounge chair beside the fire in the living room of his house, "the living image, I thought, of D. H. Lawrence, . . . emaciated, bearded, blue-eyed." His greeting was kindly but vague, and he immediately went back to the animated conversation he had been having with several Africans in their language. When Patrick Putnam was not interested in a visitor or had other things on his mind, he could be the most distant of human beings. Eventually, Severn was rescued by Anne Putnam, who made her feel welcome and offered to show her around.[39]

As the two women set off for the pygmy village with their pockets full of cigarettes to ensure their welcome, Anne explained that the pygmies were living in mud huts: "Of course, that's all wrong really—not pygmy style at all; but since they adopted us they've taken to imitating a lot of things they see our house-boys do. We don't interfere at all: we just leave them alone and watch to see what they will do."[40]

Anne told Severn that the recent well-known photographs of pygmies building a bridge of lianas over the river were fake because the photographer had told the pygmies what to do. She recounted other frustrations with visitors. A university professor wanted to study "the African woman's emotional reaction to childbirth" and was particularly interested in the pygmies, but he thought it would take too much time to find out for himself, so he gave Anne a list of eleven questions and wanted her to get a yes or no answer for each. Later that night Anne Putnam urged Severn to stay for a few days, to go into the forest with the pygmies, live with them in a traditional leaf hut, and photograph their hunting and cooking. "Nobody who has come here has bothered to do that: they all want something exciting and dramatic, but quite untrue to life, like that bridge-building. Honestly, their ordinary day-to-day living is like all the fairy-stories in the world come true."[41]

Merlyn Severn declined this suggestion, but Colin Turnbull, who arrived at Camp Putnam shortly thereafter, did go into the forest to live with the pygmies, and he wrote a best-selling book about them.

Colin Turnbull

Colin M. Turnbull first arrived at Camp Putnam in April 1951. He was twenty-seven years old and on his way home to Scotland from India, where he had spent two years studying Indian music and philosophy. He was traveling with Newton Beal, a young musician and music teacher from Ohio. They took deck passage on a boat from Bombay to Mombasa, where they were met by Sir Charles Markham, the local agent of the international accounting firm for which Turnbull's father worked.[1] Markham advised them to get out of Kenya because of the Mau Mau unrest. He bought Turnbull new clothes, lent him money to buy a motorcycle, and suggested that in the Congo they look up a man he had known when he went hunting there: "His name's Putnam. He's your kind of a person. He likes the natives."[2]

Crossing Africa on their motorcycle, Colin Turnbull and Newton Beal saw the Camp Putnam sign on the road through the Ituri Forest and turned off, intending merely to spend the night. They pulled up in front of the large thatched mud house that was the hotel and suddenly found themselves surrounded by pygmies who were pointing at the motorcycle, talking, and laughing. The two travelers were startled, not by the pygmies' small size, for that they scarcely noticed at first, but by their large bright eyes looking directly into the visitors' faces as they talked and by their serious demeanor alternating with shrieks of laughter. Turnbull and Beal stood there uncomfortably until Anne Putnam came out of the house to welcome them, happy to have visitors to talk to.

By 1951 Patrick Putnam was no longer the enthusiastic hunter he once had been. When he learned that Turnbull, although having come at the suggestion of a big-game hunter, was himself a student of Indian philosophy and vegetarian, he was interested and opened up immediately. To Turnbull and Beal it was a startling experience to meet Patrick Putnam in the depths of the Ituri Forest. He seemed the prototypical proper Bostonian, still young looking but immobile in his chair. They were interrogated politely and then welcomed as academic peers and given glimpses of his intellect and his ideas. They immediately got into a discussion of Indian philosophy and then music. Putnam said, "Oh, you've got to stay here. There's some of the richest music here, and no one has done any work on it." He offered to let the two young men live free in one of the small circular huts near the hotel and buy their food at cost.

Putnam talked first about village music, explaining the different styles of the Lese, the Bila, the Nguana, and the other tribal peoples who made up Camp Putnam, and what kinds of stringed instruments they had. Then he said, "The pygmy music is something totally different. I personally think you'll find it much more interesting." Pygmy music in the forest, he said, was very different from what it was in the village. The pygmies agreed: after Turnbull had filled a notebook and a half with transcriptions of the songs they sang around Camp Putnam, they announced that that was not their real music. They told him that if he wanted to hear their real music, he would have to go into the forest with them.

Putnam had made the same suggestion offhandedly: "I can't get back into the forest anymore, and you know if you want to go in," he told them. It was what Anne had urged much more overtly on Merlyn

Severn. Newton Beal declined, but Colin Turnbull did go into the forest to a pygmy camp, and he was overwhelmed by the experience: "The first night out my mind was blown by what I heard! The comparison that came to my mind was some of the really great organ music that you hear in some of the better cathedrals in England." Turnbull was eventually able to distinguish four pitch collections used by the pygmies. He also found that they sing in parallel seconds and in hocket, where a melodic line is divided up so that each singer has only one note. Then they sing the same as a canon that overlaps so that everyone has two notes. They exchange notes by eye contact, saying in effect, as they look across at someone and blink their eyelids, "You take my note, I'll take yours." He found the pygmies' music spatially and structurally as complex as the forest itself.

Music had been Colin Turnbull's first choice as a profession. He studied organ at Worcester cathedral while still in boarding school, but at an early date he decided that he was not good enough to have a satisfying career as a musician. At Oxford he concentrated on politics, economics, and philosophy. Then he went to Benares University on a two-year fellowship to study Hindu and Buddhist philosophy, for which the study of Indian music was a prerequisite. In heading home through Africa it was his stay at Camp Putnam, and particularly what Patrick Putnam told him about pygmy music, that started him on his career as an anthropologist.

The residents at Camp Putnam were as taken with Turnbull as he was with them. "Pat and I [are] both really loving Colin and liking Newton," Anne wrote to her parents in her weekly letter, adding, "But Colin is a rare person."[3] In many ways Turnbull seemed to be a twenty-years-younger version of Patrick Putnam. He was tall and thin, with a reddish beard and an engaging, outgoing personality of great charm. Behind that lay a quick, inquiring mind and something of a rebel spirit. That he was well educated they discerned immediately from his interests and his careful and precise use of language. He was also good with his hands and liked to tinker with cars, as did Putnam. And he was adventurous. He went often into the forest with the pygmies, and this became a special bond between him and Patrick Putnam, who, no longer able to go himself, wanted Turnbull to give him an exact description after each visit of everything he had seen, heard, or found. Sometimes Putnam would ask Turnbull to look in the forest for a particular kind of mushroom or plant that he was curious about.

Colin and Newton were supposed to have their own meals cooked for them, but Patrick invited them to dinner so often that it became a habit. He would grandly produce a bottle of whiskey or some imported Swiss cheese, items that Anne would hint they could ill afford. Then, after Turnbull and Beal had been there for several weeks and had exhausted their funds, Putnam told them that he wanted to build a dam across the Nepusi River. He offered to hire them for an African wage, enough to buy food, if they would supervise the construction. They accepted. Not until several years later did Colin learn from Anne that the dam had been pretext, a spur-of-the-moment inspiration, because Patrick liked having the young men there and wanted to keep them around as long as possible.

The Nepusi was the small stream that ran between the hotel and the infirmary. Putnam had been having his employees carry him across the stream every day, stepping from one boulder in the riverbed to another. His excuse for the dam was that it would be safer to cross on a high dry bank. Once the dam was built and the water behind it had reached a level he liked, Putnam decided to try a hydroelectric project. He had the young men make a sluice gate in the dam, and he and Turnbull invented a kind of paddlewheel and rigged it up to a generator found on an old bicycle and a three-volt light bulb. Putnam loved mechanical projects like these that required a certain logic and inventiveness. In great triumph they got the flow of water to produce a glow in the light bulb.

To celebrate their success, Putnam gave a party. He bought cases of beer, invited people from neighboring villages, and invented games. One was a contest to see who could build the best boat or amphibious machine. Two men tried an old wheelbarrow with some tin cans stuck on the side, which floated for a time and then sank slowly, to gleeful applause from the riverbank. Putnam had a case of beer dropped into the river and held a diving contest to see who could retrieve it. He was encouraging his friends to enjoy themselves, but at the same time, Turnbull noticed, he was learning, watching, taking notes. Even at his most expansive he was somewhat removed, separate, apart.

After the dam was finished, Putnam invented another project. Anne's old Chevy coupe had broken down and been abandoned in Stanleyville several years before. Putnam asked Turnbull if he would go to Stanleyville, try to repair it, and drive it back. Turnbull hitched a ride to Stanleyville on a passing truck. There he found the old car, put in a new battery and a few other parts, and got it going again.

In Stanleyville, Turnbull happened to meet a then relatively unknown post office employee named Patrice Lumumba. Turnbull had gone into an African bar and ordered a drink. When he was told they could not serve him, someone in the room called out, "*Give* him a drink," implying that though it was illegal to sell him a drink, it was not illegal to give him one. Glass in hand, Turnbull sat down next to a man playing a *mekembi* (thumb piano). The African noticed that he was listening intently and asked him in KiNgwana if he could play it. Turnbull replied, "Yes, but not the way you've tuned it." The African handed it over, and when Turnbull had returned it and started playing, he burst into guffaws of laughter. "That's how the pygmies play it!" he roared. He took it back and retuned it. "This is how the Tetela tune it. Now isn't that better?" Turnbull disagreed, and they argued back and forth for a few minutes. Then Patrice Lumumba introduced himself. He had seen Turnbull at the post office in Stanleyville, where he worked as a clerk, and he knew that Turnbull was staying out at

Camp Putnam, because that was where his mail was being sent. Lumumba indicated approval and respect for Putnam, implying that he was one of the few Europeans around who cared about Africans.

On the final day of their visit, which had stretched into two months, Turnbull and Beal got ready to take off again on their motorcycle. Patrick, at work at the hospital across the Nepusi, where he directed the activities of his aides from his chair, challenged Turnbull to drive his motorcycle across the narrow dam they had built. Turnbull had misgivings, but he made it across. When he got to the hospital, Putnam stood up (the first time Turnbull had ever seen him standing), took four steps to the motorcycle, climbed on, and, gasping for breath from this exertion, told Turnbull to drive him back over the dam. Turnbull did so, to the great jubilation of the villagers who had gathered. Putnam's aides came running across the dam with his chair, and he collapsed into it on the other side, as Turnbull and Beal drove off. It was the kind of performance Putnam loved: a celebration of their visit, a triumphal farewell, and a way of avoiding sentiment.

Colin Turnbull and Newton Beal, along with two other young Americans who were soon to visit Camp Putnam, saw Patrick Putnam at the height of his greatness. He was no longer the cocksure but appealing vulnerable young man whose wealth, family position, charm, and talents all seemed to set him apart from the rest of the world. Accidents of fate from Mary's death to his own illness and the frightening struggle to breathe, the withdrawal of his father's unstinting support, and his increasingly ambiguous position in a colonized continent on the eve of revolt had nearly crushed him. But Putnam was surviving all this, adapting to it, devoting himself to hospital work in the infirmary, managing the community he had created, which was, as Turnbull would later write back to him, "more efficient and happy than most in that part of the world."[4] But if Turnbull, Beal, and the others saw him in his greatness, it was in part because their presence called out the greatness in him. In them he had the admiring audience he always wanted, witnesses of the world he had created, and witnesses of the way he was coping with the downward turn in his fate. He was following the gentleman's imperative to be manly, to meet whatever life dealt him in style, without complaint.

When Colin Turnbull left, it was understood that he would be back. Only later did he begin to think about the significance of the dam they had built. More and more Putnam had been withdrawing across the Nepusi River to his own hut near the hospital. Although it was only a quarter-mile from the hotel, psychologically it was very removed and totally African, unlike the main compound with its tourists and visitors and his American wife. Building the dam across the Nepusi had been a way of keeping the two young men whose company he enjoyed at Epulu, but Putnam was also breaking down the barrier he had made of that small stream, for the dam was a bridge too. Though Putnam was becoming more and more isolated in the Ituri Forest, the dam for a brief time connected him with Europe and America. It was a bridge to the world he had left but still yearned for.

Thirty-five years later, Turnbull reflected on Patrick Putnam: "One of the best things that he's done . . . was simply as a foreigner in the forest, living all those years there, making a better name for us [Europeans] than any colonial administrator ever could." Turnbull added, "I mean that man was just so loved in the forest. And because of him, I was accepted."

Withdrawal, Illness, and Death

After Colin Turnbull and Newton Beal left Epulu, Patrick Putnam retreated over the dam to what he had long called "my side of the Nepusi" and indicated that he intended to spend the rest of his days there.[1] It was a retreat into Africa, the real Africa, the world of the bush, and a rejection of the hotel and the European intrusion into Africa that it represented. Putnam no longer had himself carried around the village at Camp Putnam on the tepoy. When he wanted to see someone, he would summon that person to visit him in his hut. No one appeared before Putnam unannounced for any reason. It was considered unthinkable for anyone, even Anne, to drop in on him. Although his hut and the infirmary were only a few hundred yards from the hotel, psychologically they were a world away. The barrier between the hut and the hotel was an invisible but impregnable wall created by the power of one man's will.

For eight months Putnam remained across the river while Anne continued to manage the hotel. The occasional tourists who showed up were a welcome diversion for her, and two of them in particular, both young Americans, interested Putnam enough to be allowed extensive contact with him as well.

The first of these was Julian Apley, who hitchhiked to Camp Putnam in January 1952 and, liking what he found, stayed for a month. Apley took many photographs and was so charmed by Patrick Putnam that he was scarcely aware of his illness. He found Putnam living in the little hut near the medical clinic, wearing a dapper broadbrimmed fedora and surrounded by animals. The two of them had long conversations, smoked strong Astrid cigarettes, and drank whiskey until the road was blocked by fallen trees from a great storm, the supply of whiskey ran out, and they had to make do with banana wine. Apley found Putnam an "intellectual, cool, funny witty kind of guy" with a "great dry sense of humor."[2] Putnam's pet okapi, Lelo, died while Apley was there, and Putnam had him do an autopsy. Apley swam in the "gloriously beautiful" Epulu River and took day trips into the forest with pygmies, who marked the trail by dropping large leaves with the stalks sticking up. Anne took him with her to a pygmy camp where they saw part of a circumcision ceremony.[3] Like everyone else at Epulu he began to enjoy the surprise of seeing who would come down the single road that connected them to the outside world. One day it was a beautiful blonde woman on an enormous motorcycle, the editor of an architectural journal in Stockholm.

Apley described Camp Putnam as very primitive but "like a paradise," where everyone seemed happy and everybody told him not to worry about anything. Around the time he left, another young American arrived. Schuyler Jones stayed for three months in 1952 and returned for a similar stay in 1953. He was there long enough to see more of what was happening and to describe Patrick Putnam as "a Somerset Maugham story come to life."[4] But he too, as he left, called Camp Putnam "a real paradise, possibly the only one there is."[5]

Jones was at Camp Putnam on the night in February 1952 when Putnam operated on a native woman to remove a dead fetus. When the woman was brought in by her husband and her father, an arm of the fetus was already protruding from the birth canal. Putnam sent for Anne and had her do a preliminary examination and then bring him all the household tools she could find. She brought scissors, pliers, wire cutters, tweezers, and two silver soup ladels, which they sterilized in a solution of boiling water and bichloride of mercury. The operation took place in his hut, with cages of animals stacked on all sides: lemurs, forest rats, two duikers, horned vipers, and cobras. A drying baboon carcass hung above his head, filling the room with the stench of decay. Putnam sat immobile on his tepoy, and the woman was laid out on a low bed at his side. The only medicines he had were morphine and penicillin. The only light came from a car headlight and six paraffin lamps. Putnam worked for five hours, through the night, surrounded by the patient's family and several onlookers. He had never delivered a baby, but Schuyler Jones had helped deliver lambs in Kansas, so he was asked to assist. "Several times he [Putnam] was forced to stop, convulsed by fits of coughing. Then he would draw deeply on a cigarette and continue. Slowly, very slowly, we made progress."[6] They removed the dead fetus piece by piece. Within a few days the woman had fully recovered.

Some six weeks before this incident, in January 1952, Dr. Putnam had sent Pat a two-week course of medicine recommended for brucellosis by Dr. Vernon Knight of the Harvard Medical School. The prescribed treatment was Terramycin combined with an injection of one gram of dihydrostreptomycin at twelve-hour intervals.[7] Whether from the actual effects of the drugs, or a revived hope that Western medicine might still save him, or simply from the stimulating effect on him of the success of the operation he had performed and the admiration of his young visitors, Patrick's health improved suddenly in March 1952. He moved back to the hotel with Anne and once again took an interest in what was going on there. "At long last Pat is better than he has been for at least a year and is getting around in a tiepoy once again and for the first time in 8 months he has been around the hotel this past week. I can't tell you how good it seems to have him about, even though it means okapis and chimps sleeping in the living room," Anne wrote to

Marley, Putnam's sister.[8] At Easter she sent her parents a telegram: "Paradise Regained Happy Easter Anne Pat."[9]

But paradise regained was not to last. In June 1952 Putnam had his first mental breakdown. He turned on Anne one day and announced in his deep ringing voice, "Your reign is over."[10] From then on, for the last eighteen months of his life, he seemed to those around him to move in and out of madness. It is difficult to know exactly how sick he was, however, because his actions were extensions of the way he had always behaved, and his tirades were an expression of his helplessness and his frustration.

Visitors to Camp Putnam had already begun to marvel at the control that an invalid was able to exercise over the entire village at Epulu. From his chair Putnam diagnosed illnesses, dispensed medicine, supervised the hotel, repaired buildings and machinery, built animal cages, cared for animals, settled disputes, and arranged public festivities by giving a constant stream of precise and graphic instructions to his employees and his wives. He had always liked to order people about, as his mother had directed her large ménage of children, servants, and workmen. But now the power that he liked to exercise over people turned demonic.

He accused Anne of trying to wear the pants in the family. He accused her of taking over the running of the hotel. He accused her of trying to kill him, for their arguments left him exhausted and with no discernible pulse. He insisted that she be carried around the little village at Camp Putnam in a tepoy so that she would have to experience the helplessness and accompanying humiliation that were his daily lot. He told Anne that sex was his god and that nothing else mattered. Since they had had no sexual relations for the past year, owing to his shortness of breath, he seemed to be telling her that she was no longer of any interest to him. Anne, who was not a particularly strong or willful woman, nevertheless became for him the embodiment of the strong women he had struggled against all his life: his mother, first of all, and more recently his stepmother, who he felt had distanced his father from him. Moreover, in taking over the management of the hotel Anne had become in his mind a usurper of Mary's rightful place, for the Palais was Mary's creation and always to be associated with her. (Patrick had never allowed any of Anne's monthly allowance from her father, Eisner money, to be spent on expenses at the hotel; those had to be paid with Putnam money. It was the one bit of accounting he was scrupulously careful about.)

As Patrick turned against Anne, he also turned against the workers at Camp Putnam, even some who had been his favorites for twenty years. He ordered them around as if they were puppets. He began to swear, in marked contrast to the gentleman's disdain he had always shown for foul language, and to revel in the exercise of a kind of ruthless cruelty.[11] Anne, helpless and bewildered, alternated between retaliatory outbursts and cowed submission. Seeking peace, she acquiesced in his announcement that henceforth he would run the hotel. She was to confine herself to managing the pygmy shows for visitors, for the pygmies, he acknowledged, were and had always been her special interest.

In July 1952, in the midst of the upheaval, a reporter from New York arrived. Oden Meeker had been commissioned to do a book on Africa for Scribner and articles for the *New Yorker* and the *Reporter*. Belgian officials in Leopoldville, already aware via the colonial grapevine that something was amiss at Camp Putnam, had tried to discourage him from heading there. The American proprietors were eccentric, their pygmies were commercialized, and their lodgings nearly uninhabitable, he was told. Meeker turned in at Epulu anyway. He was welcomed by Anne Putnam, but she "explained that there might be a delay before lunch since her husband had fired all the old cooking staff and was now teaching the mason, the carpenter and a couple of other craftsmen to cook, measuring everything in grams, and getting his OK before serving it."[12] Lunch, when it appeared, was excellent.

The reporter spent a day or two at Camp Putnam, admiring an okapi that was tethered there and a chimpanzee, and visiting the nearby pygmy village. The night before he left, Putnam sent for him. He had had himself moved to the cookhouse, where in the dim light provided by wicks in tins and bottles of oil, Meeker could dimly make out a long-limbed figure with long, thin hands, a brown-gray beard, and large blue eyes. He was lying on a cot surrounded by bunches of bananas, test tubes, books, and a scale for weighing food. A stove smoked in one corner. Putnam explained that he was teaching the garage mechanic to cook: "It broadens their minds."[13] They talked about his years in the Congo, and Putnam told him he had thousands of termite-eaten notebooks, but that he had done little writing: "It's all in my head," he said.[14] Oden Meeker was sufficiently impressed to offer to act as his literary agent in New York for anything he did write. Putnam stayed up until two in the morning directing the baking of bread for breakfast which, Meeker reported, was "extremely good."[15]

Anne, in despair at what seemed to her an outpouring of hate, once again took refuge in the forest with one band of Camp Putnam pygmies. She left with them in early August and stayed for a month. The pygmy camp seemed a paradise. "Pygmies are not only a dream but real, real, real. They have all thats important in life. How long they'll be able to keep it one wonders. But its love, life, family, nature, the dancing, singing. It's not depending on outside things, though they like them too," she wrote.[16]

While she was in this camp, an old pygmy woman died. After a night of mourning and wailing the secret "animal" (a long trumpet, usually made of wood) was called out, and special songs, not heard at any other time, were sung. Anne, as a woman, was not allowed to see the "animal," but she was allowed to see the dancing through fire that Colin Turnbull would later describe. Salamini, the pygmy man whose mother had died, told Anne that after death pygmies stay in the ground where they are buried. They do not go toward heaven. "That there is only one God in Bongo [crazy], we don't believe there is a god. There are lots of Satanis," he told Anne.[27]

Anne Putnam returned from the forest to find the situation at Camp Putnam no better, and one difficulty after another arose that autumn. Little William J., the pygmy baby they had adopted, came down with infantile paralysis. Anne was bitten by a snake and spent a month in bed. While she was still laid up, she discovered that the government had made Camp Putnam an official dispensary for medicine for lepers. Consequently, lepers began to come to Epulu and kept coming until there were seventeen there and no place for them to stay other than in the workers' village. In desperation, Anne ordered the workmen at Camp Putnam to build a leper village a short distance away in the woods. Still unable to walk, she had herself carried into the woods in a tepoy to supervise the work. "I'm never much of a boss but I drove people to work in that period," she confessed to Allan Keller, the collaborator with whom she later wrote her book *Madami*, about her life in Africa.[18] Ten small houses were built for the leper population. Anne tried to keep them away from the tourists, but whenever the lepers had a grievance, they would come together to lament at the hotel.[19] Their grievances were frequent, for Patrick Putnam's way of keeping them in line was to deny them food until they did as they were told.

With relations between Pat and Anne so unpleasant, Anne decided to return alone to the United States for three months to visit her parents. Her long-held dream—to publish a book about her African experiences—seemed about to become a reality. An editor at Prentice-Hall, Monroe Stearns, had offered her a contract for a book based on her lively, vivid letters home and had arranged for a journalist to assist her. In New York she would be able to work with her coauthor. She also wanted to consult doctors about Patrick's breakdown and try to get a tape recorder to record some of what Patrick knew, since there was no longer any hope of his writing it himself.[20]

Patrick sent her off with his wry blessings. Then, with Anne gone, he did his best to convey to his family in America his side of the story and to ask for their help. He wrote first to his old confidante, Aunt Elsie, knowing that whatever he told her would reach his father and counting on her to be more sympathetic to his plight than his stepmother might be. Patrick told his aunt that though he had never before had suicidal feelings, "except for a few months after Mary died," he was thinking about taking his own life. His reason was that "this spoiling of the lungs is an unstoppable development, and to come to America and use tons of oxygen would only prolong slightly a life that is practically over."[21] Implicit in his letter was his hope that his father and aunt would think it worthwhile doing anything that might prolong his life and would pick up the suggestion he seemingly had rejected, that he be brought home for medical treatment.

In early January 1953, Putnam checked himself into the hospital at Irumu, about a hundred miles from Epulu. He was so ill at first that he did not recognize friends, but then he rallied. In mid-February he sent another poignant plea to America for help, this time directly to his father. He was sixty pounds underweight, he wrote, and had in addition to shortness of breath "a tiresome tingling in feet and legs and hands and occasionally around the head." He admitted to some mental symptoms: memory impairment, mental lassitude, neurasthenia, and "occasional craziness," but of his breakdown he wrote that he knew what he was doing, although perhaps it had been foolish to try "to abolish, over night, certain faults in a loved and loving wife and in twenty odd primitive Africans."[22] Putnam asked whether lack of oxygen could be causing his problems. He wanted his father to summon him home for tests by specialists. He also wanted his father to explain to Anne Eisner's family how physically ill he was, for he thought Anne did not realize this and exaggerated his mental illness. He wanted the Eisners to delay her return to Africa. It was a last desperate plea from a very ill forty-nine-year-old man to the eighty-three-year-old father who had always before come to his rescue.

18. *Patrick Putnam at Camp Putnam, c.1952. By permission of the Houghton Library, Harvard University.*

But this time Dr. Putnam could do nothing, neither cure his illness nor take an unwanted wife off his hands. Patrick had abandoned Emilie Baca Putnam to his father's care in 1941. Twelve years later, Dr. Putnam was not willing to take responsibility for Anne Eisner Putnam. Nor were he and Margo eager to bring Patrick home to New York, where his care would be a great expense and where they feared he would continue to resist, as he always had, the medical advice he sought.[23]

It was Margo who wrote to tell Patrick that his father could not help him. When the letter from his stepmother arrived in mid-March, Patrick was thrown back on his own resources. Physically, he was virtually helpless, and he had no money. What he had was his indomitable will to live and his will to control the way he lived. And he still had the African world he loved and in which he had made a place for himself, a world he no longer wanted to share with Anne.

In the hospital at Irumu in March 1953, Putnam analyzed his situation and tried to make plans for his future. He wrote a memoir on the state of his health which concludes, "The well known end of emphysema is some weeks in an oxygen tent or with an oxygen mask. Not being Christian, before arriving at this point I am going to commit suicide carefully and exactly as if I had a cancer. I hope that this day is not yet near!!"[24]

He wrote his father again, a long letter, asking him to have Anne postpone her return to Africa. They irritated each other, he wrote, and her presence would only result in more of the unpleasantness of the past year. He also cabled Anne's father, asking him too to persuade Anne to delay her return to Africa. He had already cabled Anne not to sign a book contract before consulting him.[25]

Anne ignored his commands, thinking they were new manifestations of his madness and feeling that no matter how strained the situation at Epulu, she could not abandon him. She returned to Africa in late March to find herself treated as an unwanted intruder. Putnam's occasional interludes of gentleness only served to heighten her uncertainty and despair.

Patrick had left the hospital in mid-March because his physician there, a Dr. Legrand, had gone to Europe temporarily. He moved into a rest house, arranged and paid for by a young white nurse, Nelle Henry, who had become his friend.[26] Ill as he was, he could still call forth all his old charm. Schuyler Jones had been visiting Pat for two weeks, "doing what I can to give a hand."[27] Three months of hospital care had strengthened Patrick, and he was determined to return to Epulu. He had received a general complaint from the head of the Provincial Medical Service about errors in the monthly reports from rural dispensaries. Although it was not addressed to Putnam personally, he took offense at it; he had started his career in Africa plagued by the demands of the Belgian bureaucracy and now felt he was ending it on the same note. Frustrated, he insisted on going back to Camp Putnam to tend the sick there, to organize his personal affairs, and "to prepare the sacred monthly report," as he put it.[28] Schuyler Jones met Anne at the airport, and they all returned to Epulu in an ambulance.[29]

Putnam moved into a hut on the small island in the Nepusi River near the infirmary, withdrawing once again into Africa. He took up his work at the infirmary and drew up long lists (which he called "Medical Notes") of things that needed to be done for the lepers and others. He also wrote many personal notes to himself. One dated May 4, 1953, reads, "Anne, birthday, wine and snails," apparently in reference to a delayed party for her April 13 birthday.[30] Others are lists of things for Mada, his African wife, to do: "Mada sew sleeve button and wash hands and legs and sift red flour and give clean upper garment."[31] Patrick had seemed happy to see Anne when she returned, but he soon made it evident that he did not want her around. He would allow only his African workers and Mada to take care of him.[32] Anne was increasingly banished from his presence except on the rare occasions when he would send word that he wanted to see her.

But sociable as always, he tried to find ways to see his other friends. He wrote to Captain Jean De Medina, who ran the government animal station up the road, inviting him to visit and urging him to spend the night, explaining, "I have become so fragile (and there is no one whom this disgusts more than myself) that I need . . . more than 19 hours of rest and sleep out of 24. I wake up early in the morning, around 6 o'clock, and feel fresh and well-disposed for 2 hours, during which inconvenient hours I like to see my friends. Then I try to do three hours of work from my bed or the tepoy, then I eat, then I sleep, and to see my friends from 5 to 8 in the evening I have to take injections of épédrine in order to have a little breath. Here then is the reason why I am sick (and unavailable) almost all day long. If you spend the night, you get up early, I believe, and I would be able to see you."[33]

Anne had opened the hotel again, and in May 1953, James and Ruth Chapin stopped to visit on their way to spend two years at IRSAC (the research institute) in Costermansville. Putnam was pleased to see them but exhausted by the effort their visit required. They in turn were visibly shocked by his appearance and grieved at his "distressing change in personality."[34]

With Patrick's worsening illness, the atmosphere at Camp Putnam changed until it seemed a threatening place and no longer a place of joy. As he became more helpless and felt more vulnerable, so did everyone around him. The violent storms that broke over the forest that spring seemed an echo of the turmoil enveloping all of them. Before a storm, as one Congo observer described it, the forest lies "motionless, silent, dark under the leaden sky." Then come distant thunderings, as "a shiver passes through the forest," then violent shafts of lightning, electric cracklings, and the cracking of wood. Next there is a new sound as of some great waterfall, a crash repeated by echoes; finally, "a cold nervous wind announces the rain, advancing majestically, with a powerful, diffused drumming on the leaves." It is a world of "thunderclaps, lightning flashes, trees swaying, vegetation in violent, wrenching movement, birds flying blindly, monkeys shrieking, buffaloes galloping, elephants in rapid, ponderous pursuit of shelter. Instantly the animal path on which one is walking becomes a stream."[35] Schuyler Jones and Anne Putnam hovered by the fire in the hotel during one such storm in May 1953, knowing that a falling tree could demolish the building. Afterward, Jones went to see how Putnam had fared. He found Pat sitting on his bed surrounded by pygmies, baboons, and two Maribou storks that were croaking and shaking their feathers.[36]

Camp Putnam became rundown, and to the outside world it was a seedy place. In July, Patrick sent for Legrand, the Belgian doctor in Irumu, who came with his wife and children. The wife was "scared to death of the place and all the time he [was] examining Pat she [was] calling to him in Flemish to hurry," Anne wrote to her parents.[37]

When the new young *agent sanitaire*, a man named Franssen, came out on his rounds, Putnam insisted that the agent do all his examining in Pat's dark, cramped, and stench-filled room, but Franssen refused. He examined the neighboring people in the carpenter's shop and left without looking at the Camp Putnam people. Putnam was nonplussed and furious. It was the first time in years that anyone at Epulu had challenged his authority.[38]

Patrick had overworked at the infirmary in May, June, and July and had had several breathing crises, which left him much weaker. He was very sick for a time in July but then "got physically stronger but still queer in the head," according to Anne.[39] Once again there were "humiliating scenes" in his hut.[40] Made of sticks and leaves with an earthen floor, the hut was a single room, six by fifteen feet, with a sloping roof five feet high at its tallest point and a doorway only three feet high. When visitors were summoned, they had to crawl in on their hands and knees and, once inside, could only crouch or squat. They found an interior lit by kerosene lamps and crammed with animal cages and benches and tables piled high with books, papers, boxes, and bottles. Against the back inside wall a small lean-to was attached where an African slept in case Putnam needed anything during the night. For this job he had hired an epileptic boy. Putnam told Schuyler Jones that he wanted to study the boy's frequent seizures,[41] but the reason for his choice was probably an African belief that epileptics had great magic powers.[42] Western medicine—including his father's—having failed him, he was turning to African tribal medicine.

Putnam also had a morose and complaining young girl, Helena, sleep in his room; she had "Flavian itch" and possibly leprosy. When he particularly wanted to torment Anne, he would have her favorite shirt or sweater brought for Helena to wear. Anne explained Helena's presence by saying that Pat "liked to have strays around."[43] They were like the abandoned children his parents had adopted when he was a child, siblings who would never compete with him for attention but on whom he could deflect attention when he chose to.

There were elaborate sickbed scenes with a clerk present to take down every word that was said and with Anne forbidden to answer back. "In the middle [Patrick] loudly calls for hot water bags and acts as though he were about to pass out. But as I say it is all done with all his stage props set, his voice loud, and he very dramatically closes his eyes and asks who [is] there. And he gets very angry if he notices that I seem to be paying no attention. . . . I think a lot of it is to make the days less monotonous for him," Anne wrote her family.[44] Patrick insisted once again that he wanted to run the hotel and give orders to the workers; Anne was to have nothing to do with it. He knew she was typing up the pygmy legends she had collected, so he took the typewriter away from her. He ordered that the weekly mail delivery be brought immediately to him and would not let her see it.

Anne thought that Patrick was just trying to make her life miserable, that in his sickness he had irrationally turned against her. She seems not to have understood the pattern that ran through many of those seemingly irrational acts in the last eighteen months of his life.

Anne had agreed to share Patrick with his African wife; she did not recognize that she also had to share him with a long-dead wife, with Mary. Patrick Putnam did not want Anne Eisner Putnam to continue to run the hotel, for he thought of the hotel as Mary's creation. And he did not want Anne to publish a book about their life in Africa. Taking away the typewriter and intercepting the mail were attempts to cut off communication between Anne and her coauthor in the United States.

In fact, Anne's writing had increasingly become an issue between them, although it was an issue that Anne never understood. She had gone to Africa as a painter, a vocation that Putnam was proud of and encouraged. Initially, he also enjoyed her vivid writing and speaking style. Around the time of their marriage he acknowledged to his stepmother that Anne could not spell but "has that wonderful command of our bastard language which I think intelligent people who don't know Latin often acquire to a greater extent than those who do."[45] When Anne returned to the United States for a three-month visit in 1950 he asked her to write him the same kinds of lively letters describing her day-to-day activities in America that she had been writing her parents from Africa. When Anne's mother first urged that her African letters be turned into a book, he had seemed encouraging.[46] Anne began work with a collaborator named Helen Gould during her 1950 visit to the United States, but nothing came of their joint effort, for they could not interest a publisher. But Anne's family and friends kept trying, and her brother-in-law, *Fortune* magazine writer John D. McDonald, had useful contacts. By the time of her second visit to America, from December 1952 to March 1953, Prentice-Hall had offered her a contract and found a coauthor, Allan Keller, to turn her letters into a publishable manuscript.

When what had seemed an idle dream suddenly became a reality, Patrick was aroused to persistent opposition. He was eloquent and meticulous in his use of language, both in conversation and in writing, and had not liked the result of his own attempt at collaboration with Carleton Coon. He had never been satisfied enough with his knowledge of Africa or any of her peoples to produce a major serious work, but he thought that a serious work was the only kind of book worth doing. He did not at all mind publicity about his life, but he liked to be able to denigrate and disown it. For his wife to seek public attention with a popular book about their life in Africa, and to do so with the help of a ghostwriter, became more and more distasteful to him. Once again, as with Emily Hahn, there was competition for the typewriter, Patrick not so much wanting it for himself as wanting to keep it from Anne.

Anne interpreted his hesitation simply as concern about accuracy. From Epulu she wrote her editor: "Pat has stressed the importance that this book also be of value to students of African life as too many books on Africa are so unreliable and we have spent our time trying to learn what really goes on."[47] She did not understand his other objections to her book, nor, for that matter, did she understand his opposition to her running the hotel. To her these were ways of bringing them some very much needed money. With typical generosity of spirit she planned to have the book profits benefit all of them at Epulu. In the summer of 1953 she wrote her collaborator that she and the workers at Camp Putnam were dreaming of what she would buy if the book made money. The workers wanted her to buy a Victrola. She explained, "It is a la mode. Last year it was bikes, for a few years before that sewing machines and before my day umbrellas."[48]

Anne not only wanted to make money for them, however; she also wanted to celebrate the glorious adventure that her life in Africa was and to share it with a wider audience than family and friends. And she wanted to assert herself as an authority on Africa. Anne Putnam never competed with Patrick Putnam in this or any other arena; she always wholeheartedly deferred to his much greater knowledge of Africa. But she did increasingly resent the tourists and journalists who came through Camp Putnam, spent a night or two, and then went away to write books about their adventures, based upon what Patrick and Anne had told them. "We have four aspiring journalists here," she wryly commented to her family in February 1952.[49] Publishing a book was a way for her to get some credit for herself as a person knowledgeable about Africa.

In the summer of 1953, because she felt that her very presence at Epulu was agitating Patrick, and because she did not want to seem to be interfering with his plans for running the hotel, Anne spent two weeks in the little nearby town of Mambasa. When she returned, around the first of August, she went off into the woods with the pygmies. The pygmies were holding their circumcision ceremony, a preparation for adulthood that lasted for three months (although in the old days it had taken three or four years). From the circumcision camp she went to Musafili's village nearby, where she spent several days observing and taking notes on a pygmy wedding.[50]

While Anne was away, another traveling journalist turned up at Camp Putnam. Olle Strandberg, a Dane, and his companion arrived late one evening. They were met by an African who said in a combination of broken French and English, "Putnam malade. Putnam very ill. Putnam dying." The man pointed into the darkness, "Putnam says scram!"[51] But the Danish visitors were too tired and curious to move on. They explained that they had their own food and beds and wanted to stay for the night. The hotel man disappeared, then reappeared after a time and silently beckoned the two Danes, who had already begun to prepare their food, to follow him. He led them into the living room of the Palais, where a fire had been kindled on the central fireplace and two plates of rice and duiker stew and four bottles of Stanley beer had been placed on a rough table. The hotel man pointed to a door through which they could see clean-sheeted beds and mosquito nets. Then he vanished as abruptly as he had appeared. Later that night the two visitors heard a flute, quavering and melancholy, and they saw a group of pygmies wailing around a mud hut from which an elderly native healer emerged. His body was painted with white clay, his neck was hung with chains of bones and teeth, and he was carrying herbs and a leather pouch.

The next morning the visitors were preparing for a hasty departure when they were summoned to appear before Putnam. And so it was, Olle Standberg wrote, that they came upon "the wreckage of a very original man and his life's work which had collapsed in misfortune and madness."[52] They made their way past the litter of empty beer bottles, whiskey crates, and rusty cages full of rats and shabby monkeys to Putnam's smoke-filled hut.

> Our eyes smarted and it was difficult to see in that room, in which was an indescribable jumble of animal skins, things in tins of formalin and dried plants. An old pygmy woman sat on the floor burning leaves in a fire bowl, and a half-empty bottle of Johnny Walker stood on a hippopotamus skull which did duty as a bedside table. Putnam himself was half-lying in a deck-chair. His face was pale and waxen, and he had a dirty, yellow-coloured, matted beard which reached well down over his chest; his long, slender hands lay powerless on his knees and his eyes were strangely young, light blue and anxious. He was fighting for breath the whole time, and in the end he signed to us to sit down on a seat. . . . "I want to finish reading the paper first," he gasped and picked up a mildewed copy of the *New York Herald Tribune* which lay beside him. After we had sat there in silence for a while, we saw that he was holding it upside down.

Strandberg understood that Patrick Putnam was trying one last time to shape his story for the world.

> It says much for his strength and charm that, even as a moribund wreck, he managed to give the impression of a remarkable and fascinating personality. In between bouts of agonizing and struggling for breath he told us something of his life, of how he had found the Noble Savage in the Pygmy of the virgin jungle and how he trusted to

the medicine of that jungle people to be able to cure him of the be-
witchment from which he was suffering. Because he wasn't ill—he
was bewitched. "We unwittingly commit so many crimes and injus-
tices which we do not understand, we white men in Africa," he
whispered, "and it is only natural that we should encounter hatred
and vengeance which we don't understand either. But if I am to die it
will be quick. Look here!"

Putnam gestured toward a large glass jar nearby that contained a poi-
sonous snake. "If I feel that I can't manage to fight any more," he told
them, "then I shall let it out, stroke it—and within five seconds I shall
be gone from the Ituri!"[53]

Strandberg and his companion spent most of the day at Putnam's
side, listening to his stories about the forest, the pygmies, and especially about an okapi he had tried to tame. "It didn't come off," Putnam said. "That damned Medina is the only one who has managed it."
By evening he had sunk into a stupor, helped along by the bottle of
Johnny Walker at his bedside. Putnam had urged his visitors to stay on
for a few days "so that you can tell the people I know in Nairobi that
I'll soon be all right again," but they decided it was time to move on.[54]
They spent the evening at De Medina's animal station a mile down the
road. There every night De Medina hooked up a film projector to a car
battery and showed old movies, given him by the King of Belgium, to
a spellbound audience of villagers and pygmies hiding in the bushes or
perched in trees.[55] Change was coming to Epulu.

By mid-October Anne thought Patrick seemed better. "Pat has
made an incredible recovery since I last wrote and has left his room in
a tepoy for the first time of his own volition for well over a year and a
half," she wrote Oden Meeker. "He got up a strange parade which involved the chimp, hospital people; his tepoy was covered with a palm
canopy. He looked a little like a Daumier Don Quixote, drums, horns,
the wheelbarrow full of old coffee pots, banana trees, the typewriter,
somebody carrying flowers, someone else carrying a lit lamp. It was all

very amazing. Though much much better he is still a little odd."[56] Others used stronger language. Dr. Boris Adé, a Swiss scientist, who had come to Epulu to measure pygmies and had befriended Anne, described life at Camp Putnam as "grand guignol-esque."[57]

Then, in late October, Patrick unleashed "a reign of terror" that lasted for four days.[58] When Anne came to see him, he grabbed her hands, struck her on the forehead, and threw a lit oil lamp at her. He threw dishes, knives, and wood at the African workers who were trying to take care of him, grabbing them by the throat and trying to kill them when they came near. In his fury Patrick destroyed virtually all the furnishings for the hotel: towels, mattresses, pillows, sheets, mosquito nets, silverware. He took away from Anne the lamps and oil that were her only source of light, as well as pots and pans, coffee, and flour. All she finally had left were the clothes she was wearing and a blanket.[59] The people at Camp Putnam watched this rampage of destruction with a kind of fascinated horror. Kenge, a pygmy teenager, had learned how to iron shirts and was working at the hotel as a valet. More than thirty years later Kenge could still vividly recall these violent scenes, including the way Patrick had destroyed the typewriter by hurling it against the wall.[60]

Anne rushed to Mambasa to get help, and Dr. Boris Adé and Mr. Klempener, the administrator, came back with her. Although none of them wanted to declare Patrick insane, they warned him that they would have to do so and send him away if he hit anybody again, and this finally quieted him. But he had "destroyed every sheet, pillow mattress dish spoon, knife," Anne wrote her collaborator. "There's nothing, nothing left. He's broken the spirit of every person here. To go through my workers village is a heart breaking experience. We all know he can't get better. Everything can only get worse. We all loved him otherwise we all would have left. There's nothing to stay for. But one can't leave a bed ridden invalid, and he's inhuman now. I can't leave because the boys would leave."[61]

Klempener had told Anne to stay away from Patrick, probably both for her own safety and because her presence so obviously agitated him. In despair, Anne went again into the forest with the pygmies. She almost had to force the pygmies to go camping, for it was the height of the rainy season, but once in the forest they were all glad to be there. The enforced exile from Epulu turned out to be Anne's most exciting pygmy camp ever, for the women had their girls' puberty ceremony, the *alima,* and the men, not to be outdone, called out their "animal." The camp was full of singing almost around the clock; it started at four in the morning and ended at three the next morning.[62]

Anne was to spend the next six weeks, the remainder of Patrick's life, in this and two other pygmy camps, with only occasional forays back (the camps were all within an hour's walk of Camp Putnam) to find out how Patrick was doing. She took a bodyguard with her, hidden, in case Patrick again became violent.[63] But the bodyguard was not necessary, for Patrick, about two weeks after his outburst, suddenly became clearheaded again. To Anne it seemed as if he had waked from a Rip Van Winkle sleep. He sent for her and apologized for his behavior, which he attributed to the morphine and laudanum (opium) he had been taking.[64]

One evening the two of them had dinner in the moonlight under an umbrella tree. Patrick had just received a letter from Paul Schebesta, who had read in a German newspaper an account of Putnam's camp in the Congo and wanted to visit the next year. Patrick was too ill to take much interest in the contents of the letter, but he was pleased to have received it.[65] He was finally being recognized as a colleague by the man whose pygmy studies were well known. Patrick was interested in Anne's accounts of what she had been experiencing in the pygmy camps, particularly the girls' *alima* ceremony. He told her that she was getting "wonderful stuff" that "no white man knows," and he urged her to be careful with her information because she could "get the pigmies in trouble."[66] Of his warning, Anne wrote in her notebook, "I had never thought of that angle."[67] She returned to the pygmy camp that night as uncertain about what was going on as she had been when Patrick had his first breakdown, for his sudden sweetness and gentleness toward her was as startling as his sudden cruelty had been.[68]

A day or two later Patrick learned that a new hotel was going to be built at Epulu, right across the road from Camp Putnam. Apparently wanting to make an immediate personal protest to the administrator, he ordered his bed carried out to the main road. He and two attendants stopped all traffic until finally they hitched a ride on a truck, with his bed and other possessions, to Mambasa.[69] In that small, dusty settlement with a permanent white population of under ten people, Patrick checked himself into the single hotel in town, Hotel des Pygmées, which consisted of a few bedrooms, a combination dining room, sitting room, and bar, and a small bookshop.[70] When Anne heard where he was, she came in to spend several days with him, and again his unexpected gentleness baffled her. Around December 5 she returned to the pygmy camp, wanting to think over what was happening to her. She was living in the pygmy camp but had come back to Camp Putnam for the market a week later when a pygmy messenger came for her. "Bwana is very sick and they have sent a truck to get you," he told her. Anne knew immediately that it was too late, for they would have sent a car if there had been hope. Then Ageronga, who had been with Patrick Putnam for twenty-three years, appeared. "Close your heart, Madame. He is dead," Ageronga said.[71] They walked on for a few minutes in silence. At the crossroads where the road to Camp Putnam met the main road, they saw the people of Camp Putnam, the entire village, standing silently, an honor guard, beside the truck that was to take her to Mambasa.

Patrick had left her a note:

> Anne
>
> Don't come in. It's really unnecessary. When I get strong enough
> to be able to do some good at the Epulu I'll be back and will get out of

this expensive hotel into a cheap place, because we're pretty broke. [Some instructions followed.]

I'm going to sleep 4 p.m. P.S. I sleep all night and almost all day. Appetite for normal food coming back only very slowly.

Jacques and Alili have it easy now, we turn in between 8 and 11, and one gets waked up about 2 A.M. because they will forget to tuck the blanket properly under the mattress.

I wake up anywhere between dawn and eight o'clock.

Shocking! Disgraceful! Positively UNMANLY!!!

PTLP[72]

Anne learned that in the last week of his life Patrick had been very sociable and had seen many people. The day before his death he had a slight case of malaria, and for four days he had an arm infection that *Agent Sanitaire* Franssen had been treating. Both Franssen and the Greek trader Rozos, a good friend, were with him until midnight on December 11.[73] He died a few hours later, at four o'clock in the morning December 12, 1953, in the Hotel des Pygmées in Mambasa. The official report of his death gave the causes as chronic bronchitis and emphysema, but Jacques and Alili's account led Anne to think that the immediate causes were malaria and the arm infection. As Jacques imitated each breath Patrick took and described how Patrick had had him take the watch and take his pulse and write it down on paper, Anne was convinced that it was not a story anyone could have made up. Patrick had died peacefully, not choking as he had always feared.[74]

Anne stumbled off the truck in Mambasa and went first to the hotel, not knowing what else to do. The hotel woman was kind but wanted to start disinfecting his room and was upset because Patrick had made some lamp contraption that had wrecked the mosquito net. Anne realized that she had forgotten to bring clothes for the burial and that she had no flowers. She was in "a daze of horror at the wrongness of it all," for Patrick Putnam had wanted to be buried at Epulu, which he loved and had made his life.[75] Instead, because of a Belgian Congo law stating that interment must be in the place of death and within twenty-four hours, he was to be hastily buried in Mambasa, a dusty town he did not like, in a flat and crowded cemetery full of weeds.

The burial took place at five o'clock that evening, in grave number three of the Cimitière de Territoire de Mambasa. Rozos, the Greek trader, was there with an old Egyptian trader, Sheriffe Mohammad, both of whom had known Putnam since his earliest days in the Congo. Dr. Woodhams, the missionary dentist and homeopathic physician who had first treated Putnam in 1928, was there with Mrs. Woodhams and the Franssens. There were many other Europeans whom Anne did not know and a great crowd of Africans, come not to honor the Patrick Putnam of the past year but the legendary Putnam.

The *Stanleyville Gazette* noted the passing of "a great friend of the Congo and one of its most original figures,"[76] and Governor General Léon A. M. Pétillon sent a telegram: "The colony of the Belgian Congo will hold for a long time the memory of this learned anthropologist who devoted his life to research and has conquered the heart and the esteem of the pygmies."[77] Putnam would have denied that he was a learned anthropologist or that he had devoted his life to research. He would not have denied what he was most proud of, that he had won the friendship of three bands of pygmies.

The most eloquent tribute came ironically from Dr. Boris Adé, who had known Putnam only in the last few months when life at Epulu had become, as he wrote, "grand guignol-esque." His tribute is also the truest, perhaps because he did not deny these months but saw through them to what had been there all along: Patrick Putnam's "genius, his extravagances, his contradictions and his miseries, . . . his mystical and at the same time skeptical character, his profoundly humane goodness and his destructive rages, his inhibitions and his pride." Adé wrote of the "kingdom" Putnam had created and called him "an astonishing man who had succeeded in creating a world to his measure, outside of time, outside of the rational, outside of the norms of civilization."[78]

Patrick Putnam's own explanation of his life touched on these same themes. In one of his last letters to his father explaining his recent tirades at Epulu, he reminded Dr. Putnam that he had written "Patrick Putnam, King of the World" in his grade school geography book and hinted that he had "escaped to Africa" where even he could be "King frog in a very little puddle."[79] He was the timid man who would be king. Only in an isolated spot in the tropical rain forest in colonial Africa, an Africa that is no more, could this twentieth-century scion of the Lowells and the Putnams and of Patrick Tracy, the Irish pirate turned merchant trader, find a kingdom to rule.

Aftermath

After Patrick's death Anne was determined to rebuild Camp Putnam. "There is no canvas that I could paint in a studio in New York greater than the living canvas he created here," she wrote Carleton Coon.[1] To restore the idyllic-seeming world-outside-of-time that Patrick Putnam had created (and destroyed) at Epulu was her greatest wish. It would give meaning to her life and to his, redeem her recent suffering, and ensure a future for her in Africa, at least temporarily.

The hotel workers and the pygmies assured her of their support, but the Belgian colonial government was less cooperative: within a few days of Patrick's death she was handed a thirty-day eviction notice. The lease for the concession at Epulu had expired four years before, on December 17, 1949. Since then Patrick had not renewed it or paid the rent—one more indication that he did not want Camp Putnam to survive him. Anne had discovered this lapse during the last year of Putnam's life and had tried to pay the back rent and sign a new contract, but government officials had insisted that only Putnam himself could do so. The Belgian colonial government had let him stay on without a lease and continued to give him medicines and money for the clinic, but with his death they became eager to develop the tourist potential at Epulu. The animal station specializing in okapis had already been built across the road, and the year before, when Patrick had asked to be suspended temporarily from medical work for reasons of health, most of the infirmary activity had been transferred there.[2] An elephant farm was being moved to the nearby village of Bandigby, and both the animal station and the elephant farm were intended to draw tourists who would need more elaborate accommodations than Camp Putnam offered. A Belgian entrepreneur, Jean David, had been given a lease to build an elaborate stone and brick hotel a short distance up the river in a clearing that Patrick and Anne considered part of Camp Putnam. It was the bulldozing for this hotel that Patrick had gone to Mambasa to protest two weeks before he died.

Faced with immediate eviction, Anne wrote frantic letters and at the last minute was given a new five-year lease. Her right to stay at Epulu was assured, but it was no longer the isolated forest paradise she had loved. "I only want to keep it going for a year or two," she wrote Aunt Elsie. "Africa is changing. It is an interesting change as civilization brings its materialism in and none of its culture and the Africans lose their traditions and get corrupted but that is not the Africa I am interested in studying. Also I feel as though in a few years the whole race problem will explode. I don't want to be in the explosion. I am a coward."[3] It was a prescient statement. Independence for the Congo was only six years away, to be followed by bloody civil war in the Stanleyville area in which thousands of people, both Europeans and Africans thought to be sympathetic to Europeans, would lose their lives. Conventional wisdom, however, was that independence for the Belgian Congo was at least thirty years off.

As 1954 opened, Anne gave the annual Camp Putnam New Year's party. The workers and the pygmies urged her to do it. As one pygmy said, "We are sick of crying."[4] Four hundred people, villagers and pygmies, came from the surrounding villages, and there was food, singing, and dancing.

Allan Keller sent Anne a draft of her book that spring, and she read it with mixed feelings. It seemed to her quite well written, but she was distressed that Keller had played up the dangers from wild animals and left out the pygmy wedding. Further, he had made Patrick Putnam a shadowy and dull figure—although it was difficult for him to do otherwise, since Patrick had distanced himself from the entire project. Anne sent her coauthor extensive pages of comments and corrections but did not see the final manuscript before it was published and grew increasingly worried about it. "I feel as though if he were alive he [Pat] would prohibit the publishing of this book," she wrote her editor in late summer.[5] Her uneasiness about *Madami: My Eight Years of Adventure with the Congo Pigmies,* as her book would be called, made her all the more eager to do a serious book about the pygmies, what she called an "authentic" book, that would make full use of her seven years and Pat's twenty-four years in the Congo. "I am now one of the two world experts on the pigmies," she wrote her editor, meaning that only she and Schebesta were left.[6] She tried unsuccessfully that winter to get a Guggenheim Fellowship in order to continue her studies.[7]

Colin Turnbull, who was preparing to return to Epulu when Patrick Putnam died, came on anyway and arrived at Camp Putnam in late May 1954. This time he was traveling with his cousin, Francis Chapman, a Canadian who worked for the National Film Board of Canada. They planned to spend the summer at Epulu, with Chapman making films and Turnbull making recordings of pygmy and villager music.

Anne was worn out, tense and exhausted, when they arrived, and their presence seemed at first a virtual godsend. Turnbull immediately launched a music festival, and people came from miles around to perform: Bilas, Ndakas, Budos, Nguanas, and even some Azandes who were working at the elephant training station. "I can't tell you how nice it is having Collin," Anne wrote her parents, and two weeks later she added, "It's incredible how much the natives love him and everyone wants him to have the best. The pigmies will come later which is good because he is about the only person who has come through who is interested in the real people [villagers]."[8] Anne fixed up the hotel, and visitors began to come again—day trippers out from Mambasa, and even some Americans. Mr. and Mrs. Lowell Thomas, Jr., came for ten days to film a television documentary. For one sequence Thomas took Faizi, the pygmy leader whom Anne called "Pat's and my favorite pygmy," for a ride in his private airplane.[9] Anne closed the hotel for the day so that everyone at Camp Putnam could go to the airstrip at Mambasa and watch Faizi being photographed on his first plane ride. The juxtaposition of music festival and filmmaking, involving an exuberant mix of work and play, made these weeks seem almost like the old days at Camp Putnam.

After Colin Turnbull had recorded the villagers' music at the festival, he wanted particularly to record the pygmies' music in the forest. When they invited him to join them at their circumcision camp, he went off with them for some six weeks, leaving Francis Chapman at the hotel with Anne.

Kenge, the young pygmy boy of about fourteen who had grown up around Camp Putnam, immediately appointed himself Turnbull's cook and companion. Kenge's father was the funny and vulgar Andonata, and his mother was the strongminded pygmy woman Bassalinde. Andonata had died when Kenge was young, and Bassalinde had gone back to her relatives' village, but Kenge stayed on at Camp Putnam. Patrick Putnam had encouraged him to make himself useful around the hotel, and Kenge eventually became a regular employee there, which was unusual for a pygmy. Kenge was clever and amusing and very much a pygmy in his behavior: independent, mercurial, uninhibited, and living always in the moment. At the same time he was inquisitive and curious about the visitors to Camp Putnam. He liked the tourists and visiting scientists. He knew the kinds of things they were likely to want to know and could get very interested in these matters himself, which was flattering to the visitors.[10] As Turnbull would soon discover, Kenge also had an uncanny way of making various facets of pygmy thinking concrete.[11] He soon became not only Turnbull's cook and companion but his virtually indispensable informant.

No village boys were the right age (nine to twelve years) for the circumcision ceremony, so only eight pygmy boys were in the camp. Only close male relatives of the initiates were usually allowed in the camp at night, but Turnbull was told he could stay because Putnam had said that Turnbull was to take his place. He ate and slept with the pygmy boys and men, and they taught him their language, a mixture of KiBila and KiLese. In the last week of the camp they called out their secret "animal," the *esumba*, and Turnbull began to learn about it. On the final day Faizi, the head pygmy, announced that they wanted to make Turnbull a real member of the camp. They made tiny tattoo marks above his eyes and in the center of his forehead and mixed a small amount of his blood with the blood of Capita, another pygmy man.[12]

While the circumcision camp was in progress, Anne one day tried to call Colin in to help her interpret for visitors, but he was reluctant to tear himself away from what he was experiencing and refused to come. Anne was angered by this and became increasingly discouraged about the future of the hotel. Many of the workers at Camp Putnam were getting old—some had been with Patrick Putnam for twenty-four years—and others were being wooed away by the nearby animal camp, where the pygmies too were in demand as workmen and hunters. Food prices were being driven up by increased demand from workers at the animal camp and the Hotel David. By midsummer Anne had had enough and decided to close Camp Putnam. On July 26, her sixth wedding anniversary, she and Colin Turnbull and Francis Chapman went to Mambasa to set out some special plants on Patrick's grave: a palm wine tree, some elephant's ear, and a King Solomon's scepter. Anne had designed a small stone to mark the grave, but when the administrator proudly showed them the large stone monument he had had placed there, she was too moved to object to it; she only asked him to have the large cross taken off.[13] Then Colin and Francis helped her pack up, and they all left via Kenya for Britain and America.

Camp Putnam was abandoned, but the aura that surrounded it continued to draw curiosity seekers. They came to poke around in the dust, to stare at the chesspieces set up on the bamboo table and at the crumbling books on the shelf. John L. Brom, a European big-game photographer, tried to imagine the now nearly legendary life of the "Sultan of the Bambuti," the wealthy American who "went native," who succumbed to the spell of Africa and tried to pit himself against her—a tall, thin man with a red beard, fading in and out of madness, doping himself with infusions of various plants, while his retainers waited, alert for the slightest call, outside his door.[14]

Another visitor was Max Lerner, writer and columnist for the *New York Post,* who made a pilgrimage to Camp Putnam with Jean De Medina, head of the animal station and Patrick Putnam's longtime friend, as his guide. Lerner described the Palais, "forlorn and abandoned," the big square fireplace of brick still standing, and next to it a kitchen shed, a tepoy, and parts of an old Chevy. "He died, as he had lived," Lerner wrote, "in the setting about which he had dreamed at Harvard. To the whites who knew him here he seemed a passive, indolent man who had given up the competitive struggle at home and found life with the pygmies less demanding. But they missed the inner fire that burned in him. By any Western standard he made little of his life. But he gave it in a spendthrift way to the despised and rejected whom he loved."[15]

Another visitor, early in 1955, was Paul Schebesta, who paid his respects at Putnam's grave in Mambasa, accompanied by the local administrator, and then went to Epulu. Anne Putnam had written Schebesta telling him which pygmies he would find most helpful, but Schebesta was put off by the Epulu pygmies. He found them bold and saucy, not shy and timid like those he was accustomed to; they eagerly sidled up to visitors, offering their services and wanting to buy cheap goods. "Nowhere else in the Ituri Forest have I found such pygmies," he later wrote in disgust.[16] Ever after, he would insist that the Camp Putnam pygmies had been so spoiled by American visitors that their original culture had decayed and that any conclusions based on them could not be trusted.

When Anne Putnam was asked about these remarks, she made an honest evaluation. "Certainly the Pigmies at Camp Putnam are spoiled superficially," she replied to Colin Turnbull, who was worried about Schebesta's denigration of the Epulu pygmies.

They are not timid and afraid of white people, as are most pigmies. Some but not all of them at Camp Putnam have learned to count and have found it is easy to get tourists to give them money. There is always a change whenever anybody comes, be it an outside pigmy, any bantu, or a white man. . . . Certainly the atmosphere changed at Camp Putnam depending on who was there. However the pigmies continue to be pigmies and following most of their traditions and a woman is still not allowed out of her room during the Essumba. A Mother still has to cut her own umbilical cord with an arrow. The parents can not eat meat until the child crawls. This is true even if there is a white person in the camp. . . . There are a number of pigmies at Camp Putnam who Pat and I did not know at all, there are other[s] we knew but who never showed up for tourist groups. The ones who may be most affected by their contact with the whites are the teenagers such as Kengay [Kenge], Kikiabo, and Faizi Kadoko.[17]

Anne Putnam returned to New York City to take up her life as a painter and writer. Her initial misgivings about *Madami* faded when the book was published in November 1954 and was well received. "The book has gotten marvelous write-ups," she wrote Turnbull. She accepted invitations for lectures and book signings and was amused to find herself "a genuine Prima Donna."[18] Dr. Putnam was not so pleased. He added to one letter that was mostly about settling Patrick's affairs a single comment: "I hope that you are still enjoying the novelty of being an authoress."[19]

In England, Colin Turnbull lectured on "pigmy music and ceremonial" before the Royal Anthropological Institute and the anthropology committee of the British Museum. The lecture was "a great success," he wrote Anne Putnam.[20] Between the lines of his letter, however, and of hers reporting her success with *Madami*, a subtle but growing rivalry is apparent over which of them was to be the heir to Patrick Putnam's title of "pygmy expert." Anne Putnam had seven years of firsthand experience living among pygmies and had probably spent more time in pygmy camps, living with pygmies who knew her well and trusted her, than any other European. Trained as a painter, she was a skilled observer, which she believed it was important for an anthropologist to be. For nine years, from the time she first met Patrick Putnam on Martha's Vineyard, she had listened to him talk about the pygmies. She had the will and the field experience to try to qualify as an anthropological expert. What she did not have was anthropological training or a temperament suited to dispassionate analysis. Turnbull felt that in discussions she often clung stubbornly to her own point of view and would not listen to other possibilities.

Although Turnbull's lecture to an audience of anthropologists was "a great success," and the text of the lecture was printed shortly thereafter in an anthropological journal, Turnbull knew he could not go much further without anthropological training. He wanted and needed to understand the social context of the music. Before his second trip to Epulu he had taken a single course in social anthropology, from Margaret Read at London University, and had read some of Schebesta's books.[21] In the fall of 1955 Turnbull enrolled in a two-year course at the Institute of Social Anthropology at Oxford University, where E. E. Evans-Pritchard and Rodney Needham were his teachers. From them he absorbed the emphasis on social structure and kinship lineages that was characteristic of British social anthropology.[22] He also began increasingly to think in terms of oppositions, contrasts, dichotomies. In part this dualism in his thinking came from his Oxford training in French sociology: Montesquieu, Emile Durkheim, and the structural anthropologist Claude Lévi-Strauss. In part it was the response of his own aesthetic temperament to the unruly reality of the mixture of human societies in the Ituri Forest. The same love of order, of rhythm, of contrast that lay behind his lifelong interest in music led him to try to make sense of the human interactions in the forest, to give them shape and structure. Patrick Putnam had conceived of Epulu as a loose mixture, almost in chemical terms, of villagers, pygmies, and Europeans living together in the forest, with each group retaining its separate identity. Turnbull increasingly saw Epulu as more like a chemical compound with each of the two major components, pygmies and villagers (Turnbull ignored the Europeans), interacting with the other, even playing off against the other, and in so doing developing and fulfilling a particular structural role. Turnbull began to conceive of the pygmies as moving back and forth between two opposite worlds with opposite values: the good world of the forest and the bad (superstitious, materialist, dirty) world of the village. In the village the pygmies were treated like second-class citizens, but the living was easy there, for they could expect to feast on all the vegetable foods they wanted, borrow cooking pots and tools, and bargain for tobacco, wine, and other luxuries. In the forest pygmy life was far more rigorous but purer and more cooperative. There they lived in harmony with the forest and with one another. When, inevitably, the harmony was disrupted by poor hunting, sickness, death, or social tensions, they had a religious ceremony, their sacred *molimo*, to restore the balance and set things right.

Colin Turnbull spent the summer of 1956 in New York City working over Patrick Putnam's notes. Anne Putnam was initially enthusiastic about this plan, and Turnbull had suggested before he started that they might collaborate on a joint work on the pygmies. But Turnbull grew increasingly restive with Anne's demands on his personal time and attention. She in turn accused him of taking advantage of her hospitality. They parted at the end of the summer on rather cool terms, though Anne continued to share her knowledge generously, and Colin tried to balance the obligations he felt: on the one hand to give public credit to the Putnams for their unique work, and on the other to satisfy academic standards and get on with his own career.

The difficulties of their collaboration can be seen in their one joint project. During her last year at Camp Putnam, Anne had collected two hundred pygmy legends, and she was eager to have them published. Colin was able to get them accepted by an anthropology journal but under his name as sole author. In the introduction he gave Anne Putnam full credit for collecting the legends, but he apologized for their incompleteness, noting that they had been collected by a person who was not an anthropologist and who had written down only the English translation without attempting to get the original texts. He also acknowledged that the legends lacked context and were indiscriminately labeled "pygmy" when in fact they might be villager legends simply being told by a pygmy.[23] It was a frustrating situation for both of them. The published legends were an embarrassment to Turnbull and did not give Anne Putnam the professional status she yearned for.

For his Bachelor of Letters degree from Oxford, Turnbull made a synthesis of all the available material on the pygmies of the Ituri Forest. He found most travelers' and explorers' accounts so vague and generalized as to be of little use. His two major sources therefore were "the Schebesta material" for the pygmy group Schebesta knew best— the archers who hunted with bows and arrows and lived in the eastern part of the Ituri Forest—and "the Putnam material" on the net hunters around Epulu in the central part of the Ituri Forest. In "Putnam material" Turnbull included Patrick Putnam's article from Coon's *Reader in General Anthropology* (which he called "the only original work in English dealing with the Mbuti"),[24] Putnam's personal papers and scattered notes, Anne Putnam's *Madami*, the two hundred legends she had collected, information from personal conversations with both Patrick and Anne, and his own experiences at Epulu in 1951 and 1954.

Turnbull made a synthesis of material from both his sources around two central themes: the differences between net hunters and archers (which Patrick Putnam had first pointed out to him), and the contrasting values between the pygmies and the villagers and between the pygmy world of the forest and the world of the village. Turnbull also made two changes undoubtedly influenced by his professional studies. Instead of "pigmy," the Victorian English spelling that Patrick Putnam had always insisted upon, he began to spell the word in the contemporary preferred form, "pygmy." But he went further than that: he began to call them the Mbuti (or BaMbuti), their name for themselves in KiBila, rather than "pygmies," the epithet that had come down in Western civilization from Homer and endured for 3,000 years. In the 1950s anthropologists generally began to prefer indigenous language terms over popular Western labels.[25]

In 1957 Colin Turnbull returned to Epulu for the third time, intending to follow one hunting band of Mbuti for a year. Newton Beal, who had been with him on his first trip, again accompanied him. Anne Putnam decided to return as well when she heard that Turnbull was going back. Turnbull and Beal drove in from Kenya. Anne took a freighter from the United States, shipped her Peugeot station wagon to Stanleyville, and drove on from there. They all arrived at about the same time in the summer of 1957. From the United States before she left, Anne had been able to renew the lease on the residential part of Camp Putnam, slightly more than two hectares—much less than the thirty-eight hectares of residential and agricultural land that had been in the old Putnam lease. She did not intend to open the hotel for guests; she planned simply to live there while she visited the three children she had helped to raise and gathered more information for her pygmy studies.[26]

Epulu was no longer the isolated spot in the Ituri Forest it once had been, with only Camp Putnam, the small village of about fifteen families of people who worked there, and two or three associated band of pygmies. Several hundred workers had been imported to build Jean David's hotel and to run the animal station, and they had built a separate village into which the Camp Putnam people were slowly merging. Six stores and a bakery now lined the road directly across from the entrance to Camp Putnam. Along with the Hotel David and the animal station, Epulu had a brothel—also called a "hotel"—located across the river; all three establishments were popular hangouts for tourists, colonials, and the local people. Upon her return Anne Putnam tried to ban marijuana (illegal under Belgian colonial law) from the hotel area, only to discover that there was a large crop of it growing virtually on her doorstep.[27]

With Colin Turnbull's and Anne Putnam's return to Epulu, many of the old villagers hoped that Camp Putnam was going to be revived, and Turnbull found himself in an increasingly uncomfortable position. Mada Gobaneka, the African wife who had been with Patrick Putnam off and on for more than twenty years and the only one he had allowed to be with him in his last months, reappeared at Epulu. She wanted Turnbull to build her a house and provide for her as part of his obligation as *Mepotea putnam* (Putnam's son), which was how the villagers classified him.[28] The villagers wanted him to settle disputes, treat illnesses, argue their cases with colonial administrators, attract tourists with money to spend, and do all the things that Patrick Putnam had done. When it became apparent that Turnbull would do none of these things, that he had come back to Epulu solely to live with one group of Mbuti for a year, his relationship with the older villagers at Camp Putnam deteriorated rapidly. His relations with Anne Putnam being already somewhat strained, Turnbull finally decided to stay away from the Palais as much as possible. He lived in the newly established village of recent immigrants to the area or went into the forest with the Mbuti. His empathetic portrait of the Mbuti in the book he would write, *The Forest People*, and his obvious dislike of the villagers were probably in part reactions to the villagers' growing dislike of him because he would not do what they expected of him. Turnbull played the buffoon in their eyes by going into the forest with the pygmies when what the villagers wanted was that he make himself responsible for them. Among the pygmies in the forest, too, he at first played the buffoon: the gangly outsized outsider who did not know the rules and needed to be taught like a small child, the perennial butt of jokes and point of diffusion of social tension.[29] Turnbull had found a role to play while acting as a participant observer in pygmy society, an admirable course of action from the point of view of a professional anthropologist. But the villagers correctly understood that they were getting much less from him than they had gotten from Patrick Putnam in his perhaps overtly less-admirable roles of powerful white man and village chief.

If the villagers at Epulu did not enjoy Turnbull's third visit, the pygmies, and especially Kenge, did. After Turnbull left in 1954, Kenge had taken a job as chief bugler at the animal station. When he found that Turnbull was back, he immediately gave it up and once again became, in Turnbull's words, his "general assistant, informant, guide, mentor, and censor."[30] Kenge was to be a central character in *The Forest People*, which is dedicated to him. In two striking incidents in the book Kenge becomes for Turnbull the personification both of the joyful relation between the Mbuti and their beautiful forest, and of the unexpected limitations the forest placed on them. On a brief expedition away from Epulu, Turnbull and Kenge drove to the eastern edge of the Ituri Forest and then to Ishango National Park in the Ruwenzori Mountains, where from a mountain peak they looked out over miles of rolling grasslands to Lake Edward far in the distance. Down on the plains a small herd of elephants, a few antelopes, and a large herd of some 150 buffalo were grazing. Turnbull thought that Kenge, who as a hunter was interested in animals, would notice them immediately, but he did not. Finally Kenge turned to him and asked, "What insects are those?"[31] Turnbull suddenly realized that in the forest the range of vision is so limited that its people do not learn to take great distances into account in judging the size of an object.

Not long after their return from the automobile trip, they went back into the forest. Very late one night when there was a full moon, Turnbull heard a curious noise as he was about to go to bed. Wandering over to a clearing to see what it was, he found Kenge "clad in bark cloth, adorned with leaves, with a flower stuck in his hair. He was all alone, dancing around and singing softly to himself as he gazed up at the treetops." When Turnbull asked him why he was dancing alone, Kenge turned around to look at him pityingly. "But I'm *not* dancing alone,' he said. 'I am dancing with the forest, dancing with the moon.' Then," Turnbull wrote, "with the utmost unconcern, he ignored me and continued his dance of love and life."[32]

Colin Turnbull and Anne Putnam both remained at Epulu for a year. Their departure in the summer of 1958 seemed a sad replay of events three years before. Once again Anne had called Colin in from the forest to help her; once again he refused; and once again she became very angry. She wrote him a note telling him he was no longer welcome at Camp Putnam and to clear out. A few hours later, still in a fury, she fell from her bicycle and broke her hip. Turnbull and Newton Beal helped her pack up and accompanied her home across East Africa and back to New York. The hotel keeper, Jean David, took over the remainder of her three-year contract.[33]

The Forest People was published in 1961. Although most of the events recounted in the book occurred during his third trip to Epulu in 1957–58, Turnbull has said that he got his best material, both information and emotional responses, on the first trip when everything was new and startling.[34] Six months after his first visit he had sent Patrick and Anne Putnam a 120-page book outline headed "Pigmies of the Congo," which contains the essence in feeling and tone of the published work. In his outline he wrote of the tremendous contrast between the villagers and the pygmies: the villagers rejoicing in the gifts of civilization, the pygmies tempted only by cigarettes and beads. "This probably explains why the Africans [villagers] are to be seen working all day long whereas the Pigmies just laze about, smoking old cigarette ends stuffed into leaves, idly whittling arrows and spear shafts," he noted. He described the pygmies' forest camp, where the smoke from a central fire filtered up through the leaves, caught up light from the hidden sun beyond, and sent it dancing down to the ground at their feet. "The whole clearing was alive with this magic light," he wrote. "The pigmies were in perfect harmony with their surroundings." At every dance "the frenzy of their excitement was magnificent . . . these little people and the immense forest their very own."[35]

The book Turnbull published nine years later captured in a similar way the overwhelming beauty and wonder of the African tropical forest, the flavor of pygmy life there, and the engaging humanity of the pygmies themselves—the quarrels, the jokes, the depressing times when it rains in the forest, the joyful times when an elephant has just been killed or a cache of honey discovered. Turnbull was able to do what Patrick Putnam, trying to be a rigorous empiricist, would not allow himself to do. He took a body of material and made of it a work of art as well as science. Like D. H. Lawrence, Colin Turnbull was able to put into vivid language his feeling about a place and a people. Jan Vansina, an African specialist, called *The Forest People* a masterpiece: "It makes us feel that now we know what it is to be a pygmy."[36]

Just as the emotional tone of Turnbull's book came from his first visit to the Ituri, so too did his key scientific ideas. In *The Forest People* he argued a particular hypothesis about the pygmies, that what keeps

them distinct from the villagers is not primarily their role in food exchange (meat for cultivated bananas) but their unique set of values. In
the forest, he said, they have a religion and a set of values distinct from
those they appear to live by in the village. The germ of this hypothesis
came from Patrick and Anne Putnam, from Anne's love for what she
called "the fairytale world" of the pygmies in the forest and from Patrick's matter-of-fact statement that the music the pygmies sang in the
forest was different from the songs they sang in the villages. Turnbull,
with his training in music and in Eastern religions, was able to make
the imaginative leap that Patrick Putnam could not make, from recognizing that the pygmies had two kinds of music to hypothesizing that
they lived in two different worlds, each with its own values. When
they were in the village, the pygmies took part in village rituals such as
the boys' circumcision and the girls' puberty ceremonies; they had
weddings and funerals in the village manner; when they were ill or in-
jured, they consulted the villagers' medicine men. But in the forest the
pygmies marked these life events and life crises in a different way, their
own way, and they had other ceremonies uniquely of the forest in
which they celebrated the forest and their life together.

Patrick and Anne Putnam's legacies to Colin Turnbull were three-
fold. They gave him the germ of his key idea as well as sharing generously with him in many other ways their knowledge, their feeling for
the forest, their curiosity, and their accumulated wisdom and experience. They provided him with a ready-made community, a research
base, in the Ituri Forest, a community of people who immediately accepted and trusted him because they so loved and trusted the Putnams. Finally, of course, in the person of Kenge, the talented young
pygmy who had grown up at Camp Putnam, they provided him with
his cook, "general assistant, informant, guide, mentor, and censor"
and, ultimately, his central character. Kenge was the local colleague
and co-worker every anthropologist might wish to have.

The Forest People is not the book that Patrick Putnam would have

written. Putnam was more matter-of-fact in his style and more historical in his approach than Turnbull.[37] He was more interested in material culture and economics and less interested in ritual and ceremony.
Putnam liked to deny that the pygmies had any religion other than
sympathetic magic, while the very core of Turnbull's work was a depiction of the pygmies' religion or, rather, their two religions: their
part-sincere and part-skeptical participation in the villagers' awe before the power of spirits and ancestors, and their own heartfelt worship of the benevolent forest. Putnam would have been far more sympathetic toward the villagers and less negative in his presentation of
them than Turnbull was. And yet it was in Colin Turnbull—the man
who stopped in at Epulu for a night, was persuaded to stay for two
months, and was drawn back again and again—that Patrick Putnam
found a voice.

When *The Forest People* was published, Anne Putnam wrote to
congratulate Turnbull for doing "a beautiful, important work." She
requested that if the book went into other editions, he use Pat's full
name or "at least his P.T.L.P.," instead of "Pat Putnam," as "he had
very strong feelings on the subject." Then, after being both generously
appreciative and slightly chiding in one brief note, Anne allowed a
third emotion to surface: she signed herself wryly, perhaps bitterly,
"Patrick's third European wife."[38] It was as if to say that Turnbull had
told some, but not all, of the Putnam story.

Paul Schebesta reviewed *The Forest People* in the journal of his
"Vienna school" of anthropology, *Anthropos,* commenting that it was
useful to have a single people studied by both a culture historian (himself) and a social anthropologist (Turnbull). He chided Turnbull for in-
vestigating only one group of pygmies, and the Epulu pygmies at that,
but he liked Turnbull's emphasis on the pygmies' values. To describe
what they valued as a way of describing what was original with them,
Schebesta thought, was an important contribution to the history of
culture. Above all, Schebesta admired the author's friendship with

Kenge. "Turnbull has much to thank Kenge for," he wrote. "In him he learned to know fully a pygmy personality."[39]

Paul Schebesta's own analysis of pygmy religion had evolved until it was not far from Turnbull's, although he used different terms. In 1947 Schebesta had described the pygmy god "Tore" as having the "double character" of both god of the forest and, at the same time, god of the dead or of the ancestors (in accord with the religion of the villagers). In this way, ingeniously, Schebesta could continue to call the pygmies monotheists while recognizing (as Turnbull did) two different belief systems in their religious thought, at least one of which was clearly not monotheistic.[40]

Anne Putnam published "My Life with Africa's Little People," about her 1957–58 return to Epulu, in the *National Geographic* in 1960. In that article she redressed the imbalances that she felt were in *Madami*. She wrote about her late husband, Patrick Tracy Lowell Putnam, a Harvard-trained anthropologist, *agent sanitaire*, and "expert woodsman," who had built a laboratory, animal-collecting station, and hotel at Epulu on land leased from the Belgian government. She described his "wild shock of hair," his "luxuriant beard of flaming red," his "gift for leadership" and "genuine concern for the Little People's welfare," all of which "combined to give him a godlike stature among the Pygmies."[41] She wrote about a pygmy wedding, a pygmy death, pygmy "medicine" for good hunting before an elephant hunt, and pygmy accusations of witchcraft. One of the photographs accompanying the article is a picture of a little pygmy boy "named Patrick for the author's late husband."[42] It was Anne Putnam's attempt to set the record straight: to make Patrick Putnam the public hero she felt him to be and at the same time to present to the public her own continuing work.

The *National Geographic* article was Anne Putnam's last writing on the pygmies, although she spent several months at the American Museum of Natural History documenting the Putnam collection of masks and other artifacts, which had been given to the museum. On January

28, 1967, at the age of fifty-five, she died of cancer in New York City. Colin Turnbull spoke at her funeral, recalling "her inexhaustible generosity of spirit," her warmth, and her kindness. For the benefit of Anne's friends who had known her only in New York, he described the mud hut she and Patrick had lived in in the Congo. They lived, he said, "in a simplicity that they transformed into magnificence, and in a poverty that brought them riches." Whatever they had, they put back into the community, and "it was returned to them many times over in the affection and loyalty of the people among whom they lived." Turnbull ended with the words of a song he said the pygmies sing at the death of a person who is believed to have lived and died well— which for them means surrounded by the affection of family and friends—a song expressing their belief that whatever happens is the will of the benevolent forest:

> There is darkness upon us;
> Darkness is all around,
> There is no light.
> But it is the darkness of the forest,
> So if it really must be,
> Even the darkness is good.[43]

Turnbull never claimed that *The Forest People* was anything other than a popular work addressed to the general reader. In 1965 he published a long ethnographic monograph, *Wayward Servants: The Two Worlds of the African Pygmies,* based on the same 1957–58 fieldwork and presenting ideas much the same as those in *The Forest People.* But the later book is organized topically with greatly expanded material and has the full scholarly apparatus of maps, kinship charts, tables of exchange, plans of village layouts, appendixes, glossary, and bibliography. The French anthropologist Maurice Godelier, noting the "exceptional quality and density" of *Wayward Servants,* was able to use it as the basis for a theoretical study of his own: a Marxist and structuralist analysis of the relationship between the symbolic practices of the

Mbuti and their "mode of production." He focused on the *molimo*, the month-long ceremony held by the Mbuti on the death of a respected adult in which they "rejoice" the forest and awaken it to their needs. During the *molimo* the Mbuti hunt more intensely than usual and then feast, sing, and dance throughout the night in communal sharing that binds the society together and dissipates social tensions. Godelier suggested that the Mbuti religion of the forest is not a fanciful appendage to their society but the very thing that makes it possible for the society to continue to function and to reproduce itself.[44]

Turnbull wanted to return to the Epulu in 1964 for more field-work, this time to concentrate on the villagers, but the Ituri Forest was by then no place for outsiders. Shortly after independence came to the Belgian Congo on June 30, 1960, a United Nations peacekeeping force moved into the country, to remain for four years. When they were withdrawn in June 1964, a rebellion against the government erupted in the northeastern part of the country. An army of rebels calling themselves Simbas (lions) under the spell of a witch doctor went on a rampage in Stanleyville, and for 110 days the city was caught up in a reign of terror. On November 24, 1964, Belgian paratroopers and white mercenaries were transported into Stanleyville by United States planes to rescue several hundred European and American hostages being held by the Simba rebels. They found the city a charnel house in which at least 60,000 people had been killed. Father Longo, the popular Roman Catholic missionary at Nduye, was killed with a spear.[45] De Medina, the head of the animal station at Epulu, was poisoned, and the few okapis and elephants left at the station were eaten by the rebels. An American missionary reported that more than 500 men and women were executed at the foot of Lumumba's statue in Bunia.[46] During the rebellion the villagers fled into the forest, and the pygmies fought for all sides: the rebels, the government, the peacekeeping troops. Not until the 1970s, when they were sure peace had been restored, did people slowly begin to come out of the forest and re-form their village communities.[47]

With the Congo closed to him, Turnbull went instead to a small group of nomadic hunters in the mountains of northern Uganda. The Ik had once traveled a regular route between Uganda, Kenya, and the Sudan, but since the 1940s they had been trapped by more efficient national boundaries in Uganda, where their traditional hunting grounds had been turned into a national game reserve. Turnbull found them trying to farm an arid mountain area and in a situation so desperate that virtually all social ties and human values had broken down. The Ik lived as isolated individuals, foraging alone for food and water adequate for survival. Children after the age of three were turned out by their parents to fend for themselves. Turnbull spent eighteen months with the Ik in 1964–66 and wrote a book about them called *The Mountain People* (1972).[48] Again he structured them as opposites. In *The Forest People* Turnbull had contrasted the happy-go-lucky pygmies, who lived communally and simply, with the more materialistic, greedy, and superstitious villagers. The Ik society contrasted even more sharply with the pygmies, who had seemed a close-to-ideal human society. In the Ik he found their opposite, the worst of human societies. Part of the reason for the popular appeal of *The Forest People* in the 1960s and for the stir caused by *The Mountain People* in the 1970s was that—in addition to being vivid portrayals of unique societies—they were intended, respectively, as an inspirating example of how life might be joyously lived, and a shocking warning about how inhuman human beings can become when a social order falls apart. Like his colleague Margaret Mead at the American Museum of Natural History, where he was curator of African ethnology between 1959 and 1968, Turnbull wrote out of his conviction that a knowledge of other societies should be used to help us improve our own.[49]

Today a third generation of researchers, a young anthropologist-biologist couple from the United States, live on the site of Patrick Put-

nam's hotel. John Hart read Colin Turnbull's *Forest People* as an undergraduate in Minnesota. When he was awarded a traveling fellowship
after graduation, he used it to go to Africa, where he lived for two
years, from 1973 to 1975, with a band of pygmies in the Ituri Forest. Later he returned with his botanist wife, Terese Butler Hart, and
young daughters to settle at Epulu on the site of Camp Putnam. Terese
and John Hart have studied meat hunting among the Mbuti, the botanical composition of the primary forest, the potential of the forest as
the sole sustainer of the Mbuti, and the forest duiker. For the past several years they have been making a long-term study of the okapi.[50]
The Harts' interests have turned out to be similar to Patrick Putnam's.
He was most fascinated by the material basis of pygmy life, okapis, and
historical changes in the incredibly beautiful Ituri Forest. So too are
they.

Kenge, now a man in his mid-fifties, is still at Epulu. He likes to
work with the visiting scientists, and he enjoys the measure of fame
that being depicted by Colin Turnbull brought him. He would like to
have Colin Turnbull return. And he remembers, as vividly as if it were
yesterday, Patrick Putnam's *méchant*, "wicked," actions in the last
days of his life at Epulu. Kenge remembers Putnam sending his workers out to kill a leopard that was harassing the village, an order that
terrified the workers because it was so dangerous and because it was
one more sign that the man who gave the order had become an irrational tyrant. And he describes Putnam picking up the typewriter, one
of the few and therefore much prized products of Western technology
available at Epulu, and hurling it against the wall. Kenge does not attempt to explain Putnam's action. To him it was but one more puzzling and inexplicable facet of Bwana Putunami's behavior.[51] Kenge
cannot have known the lifetime of frustration, the destroyed dreams,
and the final despair that lay behind that act.

Why did Patrick Tracy Lowell Putnam spend his life in central Africa? What was he fleeing? What was he seeking? At one level he may

simply have been fleeing his family. Several friends and relatives and at least one of his wives thought he went to Africa to escape from his adopted siblings, for they brought into the family a range of physical and behavioral problems. Patrick himself, however, never hinted at this, and he was genuinely fond of Sebastian and Marley. More likely he was fleeing the burden of what his parents expected of him. What his father wanted of his son was simple and straightforward: he wanted Patrick to take up some profession, preferably medicine, and to live up to the Lowell legacy, which meant to live and act as a gentleman and to make some contribution to the public welfare. What his mother wanted was more complex. She conveyed to Patrick the sense that he was special, so special that he would spend the rest of his life trying to live up to her view of him, trying to be the extraordinary person she thought he was. Patrick Putnam's almost legendary charm and his tendency toward exhibitionism may both have had their origins here, in the attempts of a small boy to delight and surprise his mother. She also wanted him to be a rebel—within limits—against social conformity, as she was. At the same time, all this was supposed to be simply his own idea, for her only expressed wishes were that he be happy and that he have everything he wanted. Patrick Putnam as a child had the rather daunting task of trying to figure out the complicated set of things his mother wanted of him, all the while pretending that he was merely satisfying himself. He had also to maneuver through the obvious conflict between the self-discipline and effort necessary for the professional career his father expected, and his mother's mandate simply to enjoy himself.

When Patrick changed his major in college from chemistry to anthropology, and then did only brief graduate study, he was taking a step in his mother's direction. He chose to be a dilettante, an amateur, literally: to do what he delighted in, what he loved, and only so long as he loved it. And yet the specter of his father's view that he ought to do something significant with his life hung over him. It is difficult to imagine a career choice in the United States that could have satisfied Patrick Putnam's demands that it require only casual effort, be constantly pleasurable, and yet lead to remarkable professional success. He had to go to colonial Africa to find a place where, for a white man, just such a career might be possible.

Putnam went to Africa at a time when Belgium was eager to make the Congo appear a model colony but without giving up any economic or political power there. He was allowed in because he could offer primary medical care in an isolated area under the auspices of the Belgian Red Cross. He was allowed to stay after leaving the Red Cross because his "dude ranch" fit the government's plans for development and tourism. Once established, he lived virtually like an African chief ruling over his village of workers at Epulu. But Putnam was no ordinary chief. He was a white man living on a government concession, and as such he had all the power and protection of the Belgian colonial government behind him.

Patrick Putnam fled from his doting parents' conflicting demands on him to a European colony half a world away. There he could live not only like a chief but like a gentleman, in an exquisitely beautiful place and surrounded by servants who, for $1.80 a month, would do his every bidding. No white colonial in the Congo ever did anything that a "boy" could be sent to do. No white person in the Congo ever carried anything anywhere. White persons were themselves carried, each in a tepoy with four bearers, whenever they tired of walking. It was a world in which all physical burdens were borne by others.

And it was a world that offered pleasures of many kinds. Patrick Putnam could take African wives as he pleased and send them away when he was displeased. He had the beautiful Ituri Forest all around him, a natural laboratory for any kind of scientific study he might like to do. He lived in a complex human mix of Europeans and Africans from several different tribal groups, whose varying languages and customs were continually fascinating to him. At Epulu he found the place where he could truly carry out his mother's dictum that he enjoy himself and all the beauty and interest that the world offered. Camp Putnam brought him interesting guests, among them journalists, authors, filmmakers, and wealthy big-game hunters. They in turn made him world famous by writing about him as an expert on the Ituri Forest and on the pygmies. The publicity helped him convince himself and his mother that he really was as remarkable and special as she thought. Meanwhile, when the local people came to him for legal or medical advice, Putnam was able to feel that he was useful, that he was making a contribution to the common good. He found a place where he could practice medicine, like his father, with no more training than a four-month course he had taken in Belgium.

Patrick Putnam did not just flee the demands of his family, then, but was drawn in a positive fashion to Africa. He was looking for adventure. He was looking for a kingdom to rule. Having found his kingdom, he was able to justify his position by the benefits he brought his people: modern medicine, help with legal problems, and access to the outside world via the motor traffic that stopped at his house.

It is ironic that Putnam, who disdained the use of a tepoy because he regarded it as a symbol of colonialism, did not recognize that motor traffic in Africa was equally colonial. The reason is surely that he himself, like many other young men in the twentieth century, was enamored of the automobile.

Henry Morton Stanley had had to hack his way through the Ituri Forest. When the Congo became a Belgian colony in 1908, road building was a first priority. The Belgians forced villagers to live along the roads, to build the roads, and to maintain them. The members of the Harvard Expedition of 1927 traveled by automobile or truck. They drove virtually everywhere, apart from a rare expedition on foot to a remote pygmy village. Meanwhile, the road building continued, pushing ever farther into the forest. In *Congo Solo*, Emily Hahn described European foremen and engineers driving their crews, under pressure to get the roads built as fast as possible, but with food supplies so inadequate that their workers were half starving. So many able-bodied men had been taken away from their plantations to do road work that there was a general food shortage throughout the area.

The roads were built by Africans. The roads were not built for Africans. Their purpose was to provide the Europeans with easy access into the interior in order to maintain order, increase trade, and get raw materials out. Africans were not supposed to travel except on official business. They had to have a permit to be on the road, an explanation of where they were going and why, written by a white man. The roads were for Europeans.

Patrick Putnam built his camp on the Epulu along the road he knew was coming, a road from east to west through the Ituri Forest. He chose the site with the road in mind and applied for an early concession. The success of his camp at Epulu depended on the road, which brought him paying and staying customers, and he also sold gasoline and repaired motor vehicles. A major drawing card for Camp Putnam was that it was a safe and "civilized" (European) place in the heart of Africa and easy of access: safe because of the iron discipline of colonial Belgium, easy of access because of the road.

But this road-world collapsed with the coming of independence and five years of civil war in the Congo. The Mobutu government had little stake in road building, partly because of its close association with colonialism, and maintenance of the roads stopped abruptly. Today automobiles and trucks travel through the Ituri at a maximum speed of fifteen miles an hour, instead of the fifty miles an hour of the 1950s, if they can get through at all. For the most part Zaireans have returned to their traditional travel routes, the Congo River and its tributaries.[52]

The dude ranch along the road was central to Patrick Putnam's identity. The first thing about himself that he told new acquaintances or reporters was that he was an innkeeper in the Belgian Congo. It was an intriguingly offbeat label and one that allowed him to keep his amateur status in all his other endeavors. But through most of his life he clung to a secret hope that he might someday write up what he knew, that he might astonish the world by producing a great work in anthropology. When he threw the typewriter against the wall in his last days at Epulu, he was acknowledging the collapse of this dream, this fantasy, and destroying the tool that for so long had haunted and even mocked him.

Why was Patrick Putnam unable to write the book he yearned to write? One obvious reason was his lack of self-discipline. He collected bits of information on many different topics and had large plans, but he seemed unable to outline a manageable project and carry it through to completion. He was unwilling to work steadily at a task he found boring or unexpectedly difficult. But these personality traits do not adequately account for his dilemma. More profoundly, Patrick Putnam's problem was deciding what stance he ought to take toward Africa and how he could represent what he had experienced there. These were issues he struggled with from his first publication in 1930 to the notes he sent from his deathbed in 1953. His was the dilemma of the self-aware white man in Africa in the twentieth century.

In his "Report from the Field" to the *New Yorker*, Putnam used a glib and sophisticated style, presenting himself as the shrewd and savvy observer of equally shrewd and savvy African pygmies and making fun of other white explorers and travelers in Africa. But that stance of European traveler in Africa more knowledgeable about the real Africa than other Europeans there was uncongenial to him, and he dropped it. Next he tried to be the anthropological data collector, in part to satisfy his Harvard professors. But he found that what he had collected among Abanzima's people was lamentably inadequate, for when analyzed it proved to be little more than what he had learned by living with a native woman.

Fifteen years later, working with Carleton Coon, Patrick Putnam again tried to define himself as a writer in relation to Africa. This time he was the field expert attempting to fit his knowledge into the categories defined for him by his academic colleague. But Putnam was unwilling to let the richness and contradictions of his experiences be rounded off into bland summations or worked into questionable theoretic schemes. He scarcely acknowledged the resulting publication.

Finally, Putnam tried simply to be a field resource person, to offer help to scientists, journalists, and whoever wanted to write about the Africa he knew. But he found increasingly that he himself was the subject, and he disliked what was written about him. He had been the Observer in Africa; now he was the Observed. His destruction of the typewriter was not only a sign of his own frustration and failed hopes. It was an attempt to keep his wife, Anne Eisner Putnam, from writing about their life in Africa. In the end he tried to reject writing altogether, along with the Western world of literary representation. He wanted simply to be allowed to have experienced Africa and then to disappear into the African silence.

Yet he knew it could not be so. He spent one of the last days of his life trying to shape the story that a passing journalist would write about him. He had been bewitched because of the white man's crimes in Africa, he told Olle Strandberg, but he was taking the medicine of the forest people and "I'll soon be all right again." In his last note to Anne he tried to shape her perception of him, to let her know that he was lucid and aware of how helpless, even pathetic, he appeared but that he was determined to carry on. He was sleeping almost around the clock, he told her. His last words were an ironic comment on his own condition: "Shocking! Disgraceful! Positively UNMANLY!!!" He wanted her to regard this as an uncharacteristic phase, to remember that he had been a Boston gentleman in the heart of Africa.

Patrick Putnam did not write a great book in anthropology. However, he made it possible for someone else to do so. That is contribution enough.

Notes

Introduction

1. Grace Flandrau, *Then I Saw the Congo.* pp.120–21.

2. Additional supporting, although obviously not conclusive, evidence is Putnam's belief that he was sterile. For the date and place of Lumumba's birth, see L. Kapita Mulopo. *P. Lumumba: Justice pour le héros,* p.25; and F. Scott Bobb, *Historical Dictionary of Zaire,* p.136. At birth Lumumba was given the name Isaïe Tassumbu. He took the name Patrice Lumumba in 1943 when he moved from Kindu to Stanleyville (now Kisangani). To make the move he needed a passbook, which he did not have, so he forged one, changing his name to mask his illegality. He took "Lumumba" from his mother's side of the family; "Patrice" may have been given him by a teacher or a missionary. His parents were converts to Roman Catholicism, but his first schooling was at a Protestant mission. (From Kapita Mulopo, *P. Lumumba.*)

Chapter 1. Journey into Africa

1. In 1917 Hooton founded the series Harvard African Studies with Oric Bates, a wealthy Harvard graduate who had taken part in excavations in Egypt, Tripoli, Nubia, and the Libyan desert. Bates died the following year, but Hooton carried on the series, which was intended to encourage research on Africa.

2. In 1926 Hooton sent the Rockefeller Foundation on a detailed list of projects for which he was seeking funding, titled "Research in Applied Anthropology at Harvard University" (Rockefeller Foundation Archives 1:1, ser. 200, box 340). The "vital essence" quotation is from a later request: Earnest A. Hooton, "Proposed Plan for Graduate Research in Anthropology at Harvard University," 22 Nov. 1930 (Rockefeller Foundation Archives 1:1, ser.200, box 339). In addition to supporting many of Hooton's projects, the Rockefeller Foundation and the Laura Spelman Rockefeller Memorial Fund provided major underpinning for British social anthropology with their support of the International Institute of African Languages and Cultures, founded in

London in 1926. The institute published the journal *Africa* and in the early 1930s provided seventeen fellowships for two-year field studies in Africa, mostly to Bronislaw Malinowski's students ("Appraisal of Program," July 1940, Rockefeller Foundation Archives 1:1, ser.475).

3. Earnest A. Hooton, "Progress in the Study of Race Mixtures with Special Reference to Work Carried on at Harvard University," *Proceedings of the American Philosophical Society* 65, no.4 (1926):316.

4. Earnest A. Hooton, "An Untamed Anthropologist among the Wilder Whites" (about C. S. Coon in Morocco), *Harvard Alumni Bulletin*, 2 Oct. 1930, p.34.

5. Frederick R. Wulsin journal, "African Journey, 1927–1928," vol.1, 19 Nov. 1927, Rare Book Room, Tozzer Library.

6. Frederick R. Wulsin, "Preliminary Report on an African Journey, 1927–29," pp.6–8, Rare Book Room, Tozzer Library.

7. Wulsin journal, vol.1, 30 Dec. 1927.

8. Author's interview with Milton Katz, 18 June 1988.

9. Wulsin, "Preliminary Report," p.10.

10. Wulsin journal, vol.2, n.p.

11. Wulsin journal, vol.2, p.88

12. My main source for Putnam's activities in this four-month period is his report to Wulsin: "P.T.L. Putnam's Report of his Work in the Belgian Congo, in 1928, and his Return from there in 1929," datelined New York, 13 March 1929, Patrick T. L. Putnam Papers, Houghton Library (hereafter Putnam Papers).

13. Putnam, outline for "The Mboli, a Forest People," Putnam Papers.

14. Putnam, "The Bamboli's Pygmies," Putnam Papers.

15. Putnam, report to Wulsin, p.10. Other accounts of this elephant goring are in Emily Hahn, "Stewart," p.141; and Harry B. Wright and George Vedder Jones, "Doctor Totorido and His Pygmies."

16. Putnam, report to Wulsin, p.10. Later, as governor, Bock helped Putnam get his infirmary.

17. Ibid., p.26.

18. Angelica Putnam to Putnam, 1 May 1926, Putnam Papers.

19. "Notes on Stanley's Darkest Africa, 1890 by C.R.L.P., at Arebi and Congo Belge, c. Nov., 1928," Putnam Papers.

20. Putnam, report to Wulsin, p.2.

21. Milton Katz interview, 18 June 1988. Wulsin's telegram was phrased gently: "important you return at once work up existing material your ethnological knowledge indispensable here for reorganization peabody museum now under way suggest nile route for sake of speed further congo material can wait several years very best regards frederick wulsin" (Wulsin to Putnam, 4 Dec. 1928, Putnam Papers). Angelica Putnam's telegram a day later (5 Dec. 1928) to her husband conveys the command she apparently got from Wulsin: "wulsin asked news terribly worried health mental effect period from experience advocate your unceasing supervision orders patiricho immediate return unless you treay [treating?] your advice Angelica" (Putnam Papers).

22. Putnam fits a recent description of the reckless sense of invulnerability sometimes displayed by a society's upper-class youth. See Nelson W. Aldrich, Jr., *Old Money.*

23. Putnam, report to Wulsin, p.40.

24. Ibid.

Chapter 2. The Family

1. See John Bartlett, *Familiar Quotations,* 16th ed., ed. Justin Kaplan (Boston: Little Brown, 1992), p.582.

2. Mary Caroline Crawford, *Famous Families of Massachusetts,* p.118. Other good sources on the Lowells are Delmar R. Lowell, ed. and comp., *The Historic Genealogy of the Lowells of America from 1639 to 1899* (Rutland, Vt.: Tuttle, 1899); Ferris Greenslet, *The Lowells and Their Seven Worlds;* and C. David Heymann, *American Aristocracy.* For the Tracy and Jackson families, see James Jackson Putnam, M.D., *A Memoir of Dr. James Jackson* (Boston: Houghton Mifflin, 1905).

3. Two good books on the early Renaissance humanism and the idea of the gentleman are Alan Bullock, *The Humanist Tradition in the West;* and Anthony Grafton and Lisa Jardine, *From Humanism to the Humanities.*

4. Anne Eisner to Putnam, 6 April 1948, Putnam Papers.

5. Ruth Rees to author, personal communication, 2 April 1988.

6. Emilie Baca Putnam, "Africa and return trip," 4 Dec. 1939, Putnam Papers.

7. Paul Boyer and Stephen Nissenbaum, *Salem Possessed.*

8. Author's interview with Gordon Browne, 25 Sept. 1989. On Israel Putnam, see John Niven, *Connecticut Hero: Israel Putnam,* Connecticut Bicentennial Series no.22, (Hartford, Conn.: American Revolution Bicentennial Commission of Connecticut, 1977).

9. Carleton S. Coon, *Adventures and Discoveries*, p.30.

10. *Vineyard Gazette*, obituary of Angelica Putnam, 1940, Albert Rathbone, *Samuel Rathbone and Lydia Sparhawk, His Wife;* and Albert Rathbone, *Gen. George Talcott and Angelica Bogart, His Wife.*

11. Author's interview with Augustus L. Putnam, 4 April 1988.

12. Gordon Browne interview, 25 Sept. 1989.

13. Obituary of Angelica Putnam, *New York Times*, 14 Jan. 1940; see also *New York Times*, 23 July 1913, 28 Dec. 1915; *Vineyard Gazette*, 20 April 1962.

14. Gordon Browne interview, 25 Sept. 1989.

15. *Vineyard Gazette*, 27 April 1973.

16. Author's interview with Emily Hahn, 23 Feb. 1987.

17. Gordon Browne interview, 25 Sept. 1989.

18. Putnam to C.R.L. Putnam, 19 Feb. 1953, Putnam Papers.

19. Putnam, "Essay for Amelia," n.d., Putnam Papers.

20. Ibid.

21. *New York Times*, 20 April 1962; clipping, *New York World*, 1922; C. C. Burlingham to Carleton Coon, 21 Dec. 1953, Coon Papers, National Anthropological Archives.

22. *Vineyard Gazette*, 27 April 1962; *New York Times*, 21 Aug. 1922, p.11, and 22 Aug. 1922, p.10.

23. Clipping, courtesy of *Vineyard Gazette*, 1922, citing a report in the *New York World*.

Chapter 3. Desiderata in the Choice of a Vocation

1. Coon, *Adventures and Discoveries*, p.30.

2. Heymann, *American Aristocracy*, p.43; Henry Aaron Yeomans, *Abbott Lawrence Lowell*, pp.176–77, 213.

3. E. A. Hooton, obituary of Dixon, n.d., Earnest A. Hooton Papers, Peabody Museum.

4. Gordon R. Willey, *Portraits in American Archaeology*, pp.272, 278–79; author's interview with Harry L. Shapiro, April 21, 1988.

5. Author's interview with Harry L. Shapiro, 21 April 1988.

6. Coon, *Adventures and Discoveries*, pp.23, 30.

7. Putnam, journal for summer 1924, Putnam Papers.

8. Putnam to C.R.L. Putnam, 15 Nov. 1924, Putnam Papers.

9. Author's interview with Dr. George Sturgis, 4 June 1987; Gordon Browne interview; also C. C. Burlingham to Carleton Coon, 21 Dec. 1953, Coon Papers.

10. Putnam to C.R.L. Putnam, 19 Feb. 1953, Putnam Papers.

11. *Boston Post*, 30 June 1927, clipping in Putnam Papers.

12. James Putnam to General Charles L. McCawley, 25 Oct. 1925, Putnam Papers.

13. *Boston Post*, 30 June 1927, clipping in Putnam Papers.

14. Putnam to Anne Putnam, 29 May 1950, Putnam Papers; Emily Hahn interview, 23 Feb. 1987.

15. Affidavit in Florence, Italy, 21 Dec. 1926, guaranteeing return passage home for Mohamed bin Tjatoer, Putnam Papers; Elizabeth Putnam, "Life of Patrick T. L. Putnam," 3 pp., Patrick Putnam Papers, Peabody Museum (hereafter Putnam Papers, Peabody).

16. Wright and Jones, "Doctor Totorido."

17. Putnam, "Desiderata in the choice of a vocation for myself," n.d. [1927], Putnam Papers.

18. Emily Hahn to Putnam, n.d. [summer 1945], Putnam Papers.

19. Alfred J. Kyle to Putnam, 21 July 1945, Putnam Papers.

20. Coon, *Adventures and Discoveries*, p.25; Hooton to M. Herskovits, 27 Feb. 1937; and Hooton to Elizabeth Dessez, 14 July 1927, Hooton Papers.

21. Hahn, "Stewart," p.142.

22. Jerome Beatty, "Great White Chief of the Congo," p.152. The book was probably Maurice Delafosse's *Civilizations négro-africaines*, a popularly written book published in 1925 in Paris. Delafosse was a French ethnologist, linguist, and colonial officer.

23. Putnam, "Mboli Science" (7 typed pages), "gleaned partly from divers members of the tribes during a three month's residence in one of their villages, and partly from an Mboli woman who was one of my personnel for nearly a year"; Putnam to D. Westermann, 5 March 1930, Putnam Papers. Although Putnam called it a three-month stay, it was less than two; he may have calculated that his travels with Abanzima were the equivalent of an extra month in the village.

24. English translations of the letters are given in James Henry Breasted, *Ancient Records of Egypt*, 5 vols. (Chicago: University of Chicago Press, 1906), 1:151.

25. Herodotus 2.32, cited in Georg Schweinfurth, *The Heart of Africa*, 2:125; see also A. de Quatrefages de Briau, *The Pygmies*.

26. Aïcha Ben Abed Ben Khader and David Soren, eds., *Carthage: A Mosaic of Ancient Tunisia* (New York: American Museum of Natural History and Norton, 1987), p.194.

27. Walton Brooks McDaniel, "A Fresco Picturing Pygmies," pp.260–71.

28. Homer *Iliad* (Fitzgerald trans.) 3.1–7 (Garden City, N.Y.: Anchor/Doubleday, 1974).

29. Pietro Janni, *Etnografia e mito*, has found Chinese and Mongolian, British Columbian, and Finnish versions of this myth. In 1930, Janni reports (p.131), Richard Danzel compared Kwakiutl and Tsimshian folktales with the Homeric legend and likewise concluded that it was these folktales, not an ethnographic reality, that inspired the Homeric reference.

30. Aristotle *Historium Animalium* 8.2, cited in Schweinfurth, *The Heart of Africa*, 2:124.

31. Schweinfurth, *The Heart of Africa*, 2:68.

32. Paul Broca, "Les Akka," p.282.

33. Sandra Puccini, "Gli Akka del Miani." On the discussion in Europe, see also Quatrefages, *The Pygmies;* and William H. Flower, "The Pygmy Races of Man."

34. Colin Turnbull, *The Forest People*, p.17.

35. *Encyclopaedia Britannica*, 11th ed., s.v. "pygmy"; H. von Luschan, "Sechs Pygmäen von Ituri," *Zeitschrift fur Ethnologie* 38 (1906): 716–31; James J. Harrison, *Life among the Pygmies of the Ituri Forest*. A group of pygmies were brought to St. Louis for the Exposition of 1904, and the story of one of them is told in Phillips Verner Bradford and Harvey Blume, *Ota Benga*.

36. Putnam, "Pigmies of the Ituri and Neighboring Forests," Putnam Papers.

37. The term "symbiosis" first appears in a two and a half page essay titled "Les indigenes," which Patrick Putnam copied apparently from a document in the Bureau des Affaires Indigenes in Stanleyville in 1928; in his report to Wulsin he mentions finding there "several typewritten reports from the territorial service of ethnological interest" (Putnam Papers). The Austrian pygmy

expert Paul Schebesta used the term without comment or attribution in his published work in 1938 and 1941; he may have picked it up from the same Belgian colonial service report.

38. Putnam, incomplete second version of pygmy essay marked "original sent to E.A.H.," Putnam Papers. As to the opposite question, "whether or not the pigmies could have gotten along without the products of the plantation is uncertain," he wrote. For discussion, see Robert Bailey et al., "Hunting and Gathering in Tropical Rain Forest"; David S. Wilkie and Gilda A. Morelli, "Pitfalls of the Pygmy Hunt," *Natural History,* Dec. 1988, p.33; and David S. Wilkie, "Hunters and Farmers of the African Forest," in J. S. Denslow and C. Padoch, eds., *People of the Tropical Rain Forest* (Berkeley: University of California Press, 1988).

39. Putnam, "Pigmies of the Ituri." Putnam was not the first to suggest that it was the pygmies' military skills that the villagers valued, feared, and wanted to control, but he was the first to make that and the pygmy-villager relationship in general the center of his analysis. For comments by early explorers on pygmies' military skills, see Gaetano Lasati, *Ten Years in Equatoria;* Guy Burrows, *The Land of the Pigmies,* pp.178–80; Wilhelm Junker, *Travels in Africa,* 3:85; *The Autobiography of Sir Henry Morton Stanley,* ed. Dorothy Stanley (Boston: Houghton Mifflin, 1909), p.365; Herbert Lang, "Nomad Dwarfs and Civilization," p.706.

40. Putnam's notes on J. A. Bethune Cook's *Sir Thomas Stamford Raffles,* Putnam Papers.

41. Putnam, outline of speech to Harvard Travelers Club, 26 March 1929, Putnam Papers.

42. Putnam, notes on interview with de Ligne, 30 July 1929, Putnam Papers.

43. Wright and Vedder, "Doctor Totorido," p.74.

44. Hahn, "Stewart," p.144; author's interview with Marley Putnam de Castro, 10 May 1987.

45. Angelica Putnam to Putnam, 8 May and 22 June 1930, Putnam Papers.

46. Angelica Putnam to Putnam, 8 June 1930, Putnam Papers.

47. Angelica Putnam to Putnam, 10 Aug. 1930, Putnam Papers. On the letter Putnam noted, "rec. Sept. 29, ans'd Sept. 29, 1930."

48. C.R.L. Putnam to Putnam, 24 Aug. 1930; cable, 13 Sept. 1930, Putnam Papers.

49. Putnam to William van Zuylen, n.d. [late 1930], Putnam Papers.

Chapter 4. *Agent Sanitaire*

1. Van Zuylen to Putnam, 19 March 1931, Putnam Papers.

2. Emily Hahn, *Congo Solo*, p.149.

3. Patrick Tracy Lowell Putnam, "Report from the Field," p.66.

4. One example is Lewis N. Cotlow, *Passport to Adventure*, p.103: "Pat Putnam was supposed to know more about pygmies than any man in Africa." Putnam was in the United States when Cotlow arrived at his camp.

5. Hahn, *Congo Solo*, p.34.

6. Ibid., p.55.

7. Ibid., p.149.

8. Ibid., pp.72, 108.

9. Emily Hahn interview, 23 Feb. 1987.

10. Hahn, *Congo Solo*, p.117.

11. Emily Hahn interview, 23 Feb. 1987.

12. James Chapin to Putnam, 15 Jan. 1932, Putnam Papers.

13. Hahn, *Congo Solo*, p.151; see also pp.69, 88.

14. Ibid., p.139.

15. Ibid., p.141.

16. Hahn, "Stewart," p.152.

17. Ibid., p.151.

18. Hahn, *Congo Solo*, p.103.

19. Ibid., pp.208–17. Part of this story is attributed to "an Englishman from South Africa" who was passing through Wamba, but the details fit Putnam's situation as Hahn later described it in "Stewart."

20. Hahn, *Congo Solo*, p.209.

21. Ibid., p.217.

22. Hahn, "Stewart," pp.157–59.

23. Hahn, *Congo Solo*, p.261.

24. Putnam, "Caves of the Bavaidu" and "A short description of my visit to the Caves in January, 1932, and the Preliminary Investigations which I made there," Putnam Papers.

25. Notes for 25 Jan. 1932, Putnam Papers. A list of letters, written the same day, includes "CRLP, Avion, news of firing."

26. Telegram, Putnam Papers.

27. Putnam, "Notes on the concession requested at the Ehulu [*sic*]" and "Supplement to 'Note sur la concession demandee a l'Ehulu," Putnam Papers.

28. Clipping from *New Bedford Times*, "Jungle Fever Proves Fatal" (obituary notice, Sebastian Putnam), n.d. [October 1931], courtesy *Vineyard Gazette*.

29. Hubert Smet to Putnam, 21 Aug. 1932, Putnam Papers.

30. C.R.L. Putnam to Putnam, 23 Dec. 1932, Putnam Papers.

31. C.R.L. Putnam to Putnam, n.d., Putnam Papers.

32. Putnam to Smet, Jan. 1933, Putnam Papers.

33. Putnam to Smet, 1 Feb. 1933; Smet to Putnam, 11 March 1933, Putnam Papers.

34. Emily Hahn interview, 23 Feb. 1987.

35. In 1934 Emily Hahn also published a novel, *With Naked Foot*, loosely based on her experiences at Penge. The story concerns an African woman (Mawa), a Portuguese trader (Fernandez), and a young American teacher (Adam Kemp).

36. C.R.L. Putnam to Putnam, 18 Nov. 1932, Putnam Papers.

37. C.R.L. Putnam to Putnam, Dec. 1932, Putnam Papers.

Chapter 5. Paradise on the Epulu

1. Hubert Smet to Putnam, 11 March and 4 May 1933, Putnam Papers.

2. Author's interview with Milton Katz, 12 May 1989.

3. Philip L. Rusden, "David Hunt Linder," p.134.

4. Gordon Browne interview, 25 Sept. 1989. Putnam was staying with Browne, a good friend and fellow anthropologist, who had been Jack Linder's freshman roommate.

5. Emily Hahn interview, 23 Feb. 1987.

6. Richard P. Strong, ed., *The African Republic of Liberia and the Belgian Congo*, 1:4–6, 154.

7. Augustus L. Putnam interview, 21 April 1988.

8. Milton Katz interview, 12 May 1989.

9. Coon, *Adventures and Discoveries*, p.125. Patrick and Mary Putnam, disguised as Mike and Mathilda, are mentioned also in Carleton Coon, *Measuring Ethiopia and Flight into Arabia*, pp.16, 17.

10. C.R.L. Putnam to Putnam and Mary Putnam, 24 Aug. 1933, Putnam Papers.

11. Author's interview with John and Terese Hart, 6 July 1987.

12. Gardiner Kline, "Recorder Cameraman Visits Ituri Forest of Pygmies," *Amsterdam* (N.Y.) *Evening Recorder,* 2 April 1928, p.7, clipping in Putnam Papers.

13. The best descriptions of Camp Putnam are in Beatty, "Great White Chief of the Congo"; Martin Birnbaum, "Mambau: An African experiment"; Martin Birnbaum, *Vanishing Eden: Wanderings in the Tropics* (New York: Rudge, 1942), pp.72–80; and Schuyler Jones, "The Forest," in *Under the African Sun.* See also Fred Hift, "Hotel in the Congo." Although Hift and other popular writers described Camp Putnam as located in a "jungle," technically it was in a tropical rain forest; jungle occurs only in Asia and South America.

14. Anne Eisner Putnam–Helen Gould MS, Anne Eisner Putnam Papers.

15. Beatty, "Great White Chief of the Congo," p.151.

16. Alex Shoumatoff, *In Southern Light,* pp.122, 134, 142, has vivid descriptions of pygmies; see also Turnbull, *The Forest People.*

17. Putnam-Gould MS, Anne Eisner Putnam Papers, describes the Epulu market. Emily Hahn in *Congo Solo* mentions Putnam's efforts to start a market while he was at Penge.

18. See Beatty, "Great White Chief of the Congo," p.152. "Unlike the missionaries, he didn't try to interfere with their beliefs" (Jones, *Under the African Sun*), p.77.

19. John Gunther, in *Meet Central Africa* (London: Hamish Hamilton, 1960), p.160, described Schweitzer's hospital as "positively obsessed" with stealing. Schweitzer arrived at Lambaréné in 1913, was still going strong in 1958, and died in 1965.

20. Quoted in James R. Daniels, "Manhattan Kaleidoscope," *The Outlook* (Woodstock, N.Y.), c. 1935, clipping in Putnam Papers. Patrick Tracy Lowell Putnam and Mary Farlow Linder Putnam, *Our Camp on the Epulu in the Belgian Congo,* 13 pp., privately printed, n.d. [1933?].

21. Putnam to Thomas Cook and Sons, New York City, 4 Feb. and 26 April 1935, Putnam Papers.

22. Patrick Putnam, "There Is Such an Animal." Putnam's unpublished MSS on the okapi include "La chasse a l'okapi" and "Situation Actual of My Attempts to Raise Okapi," both in Putnam Papers.

23. Notebook, "Registre-Hotel," Feb. 1934–Jan. 1935, Putnam Papers.

24. Hubert Smet to Putnam, 4 May 1933; and Mary Putnam to Putnam, n.d., Putnam Papers.

25. Putnam to James Chapin, 2 Oct. 1935, Explorers Club Archives.

26. C.R.L. Putnam to Putnam, 29 May 1935, Putnam Papers.

27. Marley Putnam de Castro interview, 10 May 1987.

28. Anabel Parker McCann, "Women Are in Great Demand in the Heart of the Belgian Congo," *New York Sun,* 23 Sept. 1936, p.36, clipping in Putnam Papers.

29. Putnam to Ryckmans, 15 March 1936, and early drafts; J. Henrard, Director of the Agriculture and Colonization Service, to Putnam, 13 July 1937, Putnam Papers (author's translations).

30. Putnam Papers.

31. *Class Reports,* Harvard College, 1931, p.147; 1935, p.169. In later years Putnam did not respond to the surveys.

32. E. A. Hooton to George Schwab, 15 Oct. 1937, Hooton Papers.

Chapter 6. Emilie

1. Clipping, 8 Oct. 1937, courtesy of *Vineyard Gazette.*

2. Marley de Castro Putnam interview.

3. Milton Katz interview, 18 June 1988, on the strain on viral pneumonia found only in the West.

4. Scrap in Putnam Papers.

5. Gordon Browne interview, 25 Sept. 1989.

6. Marley Putnam de Castro interview, 10 May 1987.

7. Putnam to Emily Hahn, 21 Jan. 1938, Putnam Papers.

8. C. C. Burlingham to Carleton Coon, 21 Dec. 1953, Carleton Coon Papers, National Anthropological Archives. Other information on Emilie Baca and the Baca family from author's interviews with Milton Katz, Gordon Browne, Josephine Baca (24 Sept. 1990), and Pen La Farge (24 Sept. 1990). Novelist Oliver La Farge married Emilie Baca Putnam's younger sister and wrote a memoir, *Behind the Mountains,* about his wife's childhood on the Baca ranch. La Farge described Doña Marguerite, his mother-in-law and Emilie's mother, as "small, very alive, intuitively chic"; she managed, he wrote, "to be at once perfectly French and perfectly Spanish, which is no small feat" (pp.3, 82, 88). Emilie apparently took after her. She is described by family members as an intellectual and a voracious reader and as having been her father's pet.

9. Emilie Baca Putnam to Marguerite Baca, 26 Oct. 1938, Emilie Baca Putnam Papers.

10. Putnam to Ronald Murray, Houghton Mifflin, 2 June 1940, Putnam Papers.

11. Putnam to unnamed correspondent, n.d., Putnam Papers. Putnam also challenged a negative mention of the Peabody Museum in the longer version. Beatty republished the article in *Americans All Over*, a collection of his *Reader's Digest* pieces.

12. Emilie Putnam to Marguerite Baca, 14 Dec. 1938, and 12 Jan. 1939, Emilie Baca Putnam Papers.

13. Emilie Putnam to Marguerite Baca, 28 Dec. 1938, Emilie Baca Putnam Papers.

14. Emilie Putnam to Marguerite Baca, 31 May and 2 Feb. 1939, Emilie Baca Putnam Papers.

15. Putnam to de Bergyck, 20 Dec. 1938, Putnam Papers (author's translation).

16. George Schwab and his editor George Harley, in *Tribes of the Liberian Hinterland*, pp.297–98, describe the leopard society and write, "It is impossible for us to realize the continual state of terror that exists where a society of these leopard people is known to exist." George Harley, *Native African Medicine*, p.139, recommends K. J. Beatty, *Human Leopards* (London, 1915), as the best book on the subject. An excellent later work in Paul-Ernest Joset, *Les sociétés secrètes des hommes-léopards*.

17. Beatty, "Great White Chief of the Congo." The district commissioner told the Putnams that 220 people had been killed in the area within the previous three to four years (Emilie Putnam to Marguerite Baca, 22 March 1939, Emilie Baca Putnam Papers).

18. Beatty, in "Great White Chief of the Congo," p.151, wrote that the penalty was likely to be a year of hard labor, which must be what Patrick Putnam anticipated. It was instead one week (Emilie Putnam to Marguerite Baca, 20 Dec. 1938, Emilie Baca Putnam Papers).

19. Angelica Putnam to Putnam and Emily Putnam, 29 July 1939, Putnam Papers.

20. Emilie Putnam to Marguerite Baca, n.d. [late December 1939], Emilie Baca Putnam Papers.

21. Emilie Putnam to Marguerite Baca, 31 May 1939, Emilie Baca Putnam Papers.

22. Marley Putnam de Castro interview, 10 May 1987.

23. Putnam, notes, n.d., Putnam Papers.

24. Marianna Torgovnick makes this point in *Gone Primitive: Savage Intellects, Modern Lives*, pp.42–72, "Taking Tarzan Seriously."

25. Erling B. Holtsmark, *Edgar Rice Burroughs* (Boston: Twayne, 1986), p.54. A good filmography is Manfred Bernhard, *Die Tarzan Filme* (Munich: Willhelm Heyne Verlag, 1983).

26. Interoffice memo, 27 April 1940, Putnam Papers. Putnam calculated that shooting 30 percent of the footage for these three films on location could justify the expenses of the trip.

27. Loose sheet, n.d., Putnam Papers.

28. Putnam to Bernie Hyman, 16 April 1940; to Merian C. Cooper, 2 pp., n.d., Putnam Papers.

29. C.R.L. Putnam to Putnam, 8 May 1941, Putnam Papers.

30. Emilie Putnam to Putnam, 8 July 1942, Putnam Papers.

31. Emilie Putnam to Putnam, 9 Jan. 1942, Putnam Papers.

32. Putnam, untitled essay, n.d.; Putnam to Mr. Jeksa [American Consul at Accra?], 16 June 1941, Putnam Papers.

33. Putnam to Farson, 17 Feb. 1941; Putnam's "treatment" for a film on Stanley, Putnam Papers.

34. Marley Putnam de Castro interview, 10 May 1987.

35. Putnam to Emilie Putnam, from Gold Coast, 6 April 1941, Putnam Papers.

36. Gordon Browne interview, 25 Sept. 1989.

Chapter 7. War and Rubber

1. *Bulletin Agricole du Congo Belge*, no.1–2, March–June 1942, clipping in Putnam Papers.

2. Putnam to C.R.L. Putnam, 5 Dec. 1942, Putnam Papers.

3. Several species of *Landolphia, Clitandra*, and *Carpodinus*. See *Encyclopaedia Britannica*, 11th ed., s.v. "rubber."

4. *Historical Dictionary of Zaire*, p.123.

5. *Encyclopaedia Americana*, 1987 ed., s.v. "rubber."

6. Putnam to Chief of Agricultural Service, Territory of Banalya, 12 June 1942, Putnam Papers.

7. Putnam, "Rubber Journal," n.d. [1942], Putnam Papers.

8. Putnam to Chief of Agricultural Service, 12 June 1942, Putnam Papers.

9. Putnam, "Guide practique poor l'identification et l'exploitation des essences caoutchoutifieres." Putnam also wrote a memoir based on his experiments: "Note on the happy medium between rapid coagulation and slow coagulation of latex landolphia as described in the manual CTC," Dec. 1943; Putnam to Delegué de la Commission de CTC, Stanleyville, 22 Feb. 1944, Putnam Papers.

10. Putnam, "Note pour Monsieur le Gouverneur General," 26 May 1944, Putnam Papers.

11. Putnam, "Dementi des dires tendencieus or mesongeres de Silberman et de De Vries," 26 May 1944, Putnam Papers (author's translation).

12. Putnam, news release, Leopoldville, 26 May 1944, Putnam Papers.

13. Putnam, notes on "treating Mada's wounds," May 1943, Putnam Papers.

14. Anne Putnam to Colin Turnbull, 15 April 1957, Anne Eisner Putnam Papers.

15. Anne Putnam to Allan Keller, 20 Nov. 1953, Anne Eisner Putnam Papers.

16. Ibid., and Anne Putnam to Allan Keller, 8 Dec. 1953, Anne Eisner Putnam Papers.

17. John L. Brom, *African Odyssey* (French ed. 1957; New York: Living Books, 1966), p.188. Brom was a European big-game photographer and filmmaker who visited Camp Putnam and wrote about it after Patrick's death. His summary of Putnam's life, though romanticized, is accurate enough to suggest that he got it from someone who had known Putnam well and over a long period of time—probably Jean De Medina, who ran the government animal farm across the road and was renowned as a good storyteller. Also Anne Putnam to Allan Keller, 8 and 20 Nov. 1953, Anne Eisner Putnam Papers.

18. Putnam to Provincial Commissioner, 13 March 1944, Putnam Papers. Putnam sent carbon copies to Temporary Agriculture Agents of Ligne and Wamba, whom he had praised for helping the pygmies make their camp.

19. C.R.L. Putnam to Putnam, July 1944, Putnam Papers. Baron von Zuylen mentioned Ryckmans's praise to Putnam (20 Aug. 1952, Putnam Papers). The rubber production figures for 1942 and 1943 are taken from a radio interview

that Putnam wrote (Putnam Papers) and apparently broadcast in the Congo, June 1944; the date is mentioned in Putnam to Monsieur de Chef de Service, 5 June 1944, Putnam Papers.

20. Putnam, draft of letter to Ryckmans, n.d. (original) emphasis, Putnam Papers (author's translation).

21. Putnam to Chief of Agricultural Service, 18 Dec. 1944, Putnam Papers.

22. Putnam, "Note sur Trouvailles personnelles sur l'exploitation de Ficus Vogelii (Nekbudu), "Stanleyville, 1 Jan. 1945; also Putnam, "Note pour Monsieur le Gouverneur de la province sur les possibilités de production caoutchoutifiere en 1945 and 1946," Dungu Territory, 7 Dec. 1944, both in Putnam Papers.

23. Putnam to Governor General, le Chef de Agriforests, Stanleyville, 1 Jan. 1945, Putnam Papers.

24. "Annexe au Contrat d'Engagement," Colonie of Congo Belge and P. Putnam as *agent agricole temporaire* from 22 May 1942 to 17 Dec. 1944, Putnam Papers; Anne Putnam to Allan Keller, 20 Nov. 1953, Anne Eisner Putnam Papers.

25. Father Longo to Putnam, 25 Jan. 1945, Putnam Papers. Father Longo started a well-known technical school at Nduye. Colin Turnbull, after visiting Father Longo there, called the big bearded priest in his white robes "the kindest, wisest, and most sincere person I had met in this part of Africa" (*The Forest People*, p.244). Longo was killed with a spear during the Simba rebellion in 1964, along with a group of nuns. A church in Mambasa is dedicated to him (John and Terese Hart interview, 6 July 1987; see also Shoumatoff, *In Southern Light*, pp.119, 121, 175).

Chapter 8. Writing about the Pygmies

1. Author's interview with Vivian Katz, 12 May 1989.

2. Milton Katz interview, 12 May 1989.

3. E. A. Hooton, Foreword to George Schwab, "Tribes of the Liberian Hinterland," p.vii.

4. Schwab did manage to write, as a courtesy to Firestone, a 70-page "Confidential Report of Conditions in Liberia" (Peabody Museum Archives).

5. Paul Cullery to E. A. Hooton, 30 July 1942; and Hooton to Cullery, 10 Aug. 1942, Hooton Papers. Cullery quoted the statement and asked Hooton where he had written it; Hooton replied that he agreed with the statement but could not remember where he said it.

6. Winifred J. Harley, *A Third of a Century with George Way Harley in Liberia,* p.61.

7. Anne Eisner to William J. and Florine Eisner, 13 Aug. 1945; Anne Putnam to Allan Keller, 20 Nov. 1953, Anne Eisner Putnam Papers. Anne was on Martha's Vineyard visiting her older sister, Dorothy, also a painter, who was married to the writer John McDonald.

8. The first draft of this manuscript (in Coon Papers) has the typed transcript of what Putnam said, pasted on sheets to which Coon added his own comments and information from Paul Schebesta's published accounts of 1933 and 1936. From this first draft it is possible to see almost exactly what Putnam told Coon.

9. Putnam to Coon, 21 Dec. 1945 Coon Papers.

10. Coon to Putnam, 24 Dec. 1945, Putnam Papers.

11. Coon to Putnam, 14 Feb. 1946, Putnam Papers.

12. Coon to Putnam, 14 Jan. 1947, Coon Papers.

13. Putnam to Coon, Kano [Nigeria], 7 Feb. 1949, Coon Papers.

14. Patrick Putnam, "The Pigmies of the Ituri Forest," in C. S. Coon, *A Reader in General Anthropology,* p.322. (Coon continued to like his own twice-as-long version and gave a manuscript copy of it to the Peabody Museum Library in 1957.)

15. Ibid., p.334.

16. Ibid., p.328.

17. Original "Pigmies of Africa" MS with Coon additions, Coon Papers.

18. Coon, *Reader,* p.323. Several paragraphs later, after Putnam's statement that the pygmies now were fulfilling only half their contract, Coon added another sentence: "Still both are satisfied." Again, this was contrary to Putnam's belief, but it fit Coon's interest in depicting a timeless state of mutual benefit.

19. Ibid., p.336.

20. See, e.g., Jean-Pierre Hallet and Alex Pelle, *Pygmy Kitabu,* p.62.

21. The literature on Schebesta includes Wilhelm Depré, "Paul Joachim Schebesta,"; Anton Vorblicher, "Professor Dr. Paul Schebesta SVD"; Rudolf Rahman, "Vier Pioniere der VolkerKunde"; Colin M. Turnbull, "Father Schebesta's Work among the Ba Mbuti Pygmies."

22. Martin Gusinde, "Wilhelm Schmidt, "S.V.D.," p.868.

23. Paul Schebesta, "Wilhelm Schmidt." Schmidt was influenced by the Swiss anthropologist J. Kollmann in choosing the pygmies as the original stock of the human race.

24. Robert Heine-Geldern, "One Hundred Years of Ethnological Theory," p.413.

25. Quoted in Jean Leyder, *Remarques sur l'Anthropologia et l'Etude scientifique des Pygmées du Congo belge* (Brussels: Government Printing Office, 1934), p.11.

26. Ibid. Vanoverbergh went to the Negritos of the Philippines; Martin Gusinde and Wilhelm Koppers to the pygmoids of the Terre de Feu; Peter Schumacher to the pygmies of Ruanda, Kivu, and Lake Albert; and Viktor Lebzelter to the Bushmen, while Wilhelm Schmidt and P. Trilles collaborated on a work on the pygmies of Gabon.

27. Paul Schebesta, *Among Congo Pigmies*, p.160. Some of this material appeared originally in Paul Schebesta, "Les conceptions religieuses des Pygmées de l'Ituri."

28. Schebesta, *Among Congo Pigmies*, p.161.

29. Paul Schebesta, "Colin M. Turnbull und die Erforschung der Bambuti Pygmäen, p.214; also Anne Eisner Putnam to Colin Turnbull, 11 April 1957, Colin Turnbull Papers (courtesy of Curtis Abraham).

30. Paul Schebesta, *Les Pygmées*, 1940, pp.87, 90. Schebesta's ideas about pygmy religion continued to evolve. The progression may be traced from "Les conceptions religieuses" in 1931, to Paul Schebesta, "Donées essentielles sur la religion des pygmées," *Congo* 1, no.3 (1936): 321–31 (rpt. in Schebesta, *Revisiting My Pygmy Hosts*, pp.186, 201), to Schebesta, *Les Pygmées*, 1940, pp.87–90, to Paul Schebesta, "Tore, le dieu forestier des Bambuti," pp.181–91.

31. Schebesta, *Among Congo Pigmies*, p.233; original "Pigmies of Africa" MS with Coon additions, Coon Papers.

32. Paul Schebesta, "La langue des Pygmies," *Zaire* 3, no.2 (1949): 119–28, cited in Serge Bahuchet, ed. *Pygmées de Centrafrique: Ethnologie, histoire et linguistique*, Bibliothèque de la Selaf, nos.73–74, (N.p.: Société d'Etudes Linguistique et Anthropologique de France, 1979), p.17. An excellent summary of the not very convincing evidence for Schebesta's classification of the pygmies and his arguments for a pygmy language is V. Van Bulck, "Ou en est le problème des pygmées de l'Ituri? *Zaïre* 2 (April 1948): 423–36. Van Bulck was also a priest. He spent ten days to two weeks working with Putnam at Camp Putnam in 1949 or 1950.

33. Anne Putnam to Colin Turnbull, 11 April 1957, Turnbull Papers (courtesy of Curtis Abraham).

34. Putnam to Coon, 16 June 1947, Coon Papers.

35. Original "Pigmies of Africa" MS with Coon additions, p.87, Coon Papers.

36. Putnam, "Pygmies of the Ituri Forest," in Coon, *Reader*, p.339.

37. Original "Pigmies of Africa" MS with Coon additions, p.105, Coon Papers.

38. Arnold van Gennep, *The Rites of Passage*, trans. Monika B. Vizedom and Gabrielle L. Caffee (Chicago: University of Chicago Press, 1960), pp.6–8, 13.

39. Original "Pigmies of Africa" MS with Coon additions, p.105.

40. Putnam, draft of letter to unidentified correspondent who had apparently inquired about Elisabethville, n.d. [c.1946], Putnam Papers.

Chapter 9. Anne

1. Anne Putnam to Allan Keller, 8 Nov. 1953, Anne Eisner Putnam Papers.

2. Putnam, "Sante Putnam," written in the hospital in Irumu between mid-Dec. 1952 and mid-March 1953, Putnam Papers. Putnam said the diagnosis was made in 1944. Gordon Browne remembers the doctor's report slightly differently: the diagnosis was bronchyectasis, and the prognosis was that Putnam had five years to live (interview, 25 Sept. 1989).

3. Illegible name [probably Dohogue, Putnam's immediate boss during his rubber work] to Putnam, 1 Sept. 1947, Putnam Papers.

4. Agreement of separation between Patrick Putnam and Emilie B. Putnam, 29 June 1945; C.R.L. Putnam to Putnam, 19 Dec. 1944, Putnam Papers.

5. Clipping on Dr. Putnam's second marriage, 9 July 1946, courtesy of *Vineyard Gazette*.

6. Putnam to Coon, 7 Feb. 1947, Coon Papers.

7. Putnam to Wessel Duval and Co., 67 Broad Street, N.Y., 21 July 1948, Putnam Papers; Putnam-Gould MS, Anne Eisner Putnam Papers.

8. Putnam to Coon, 16 June 1947, Putnam Papers.

9. Putnam, scraps of lecture notes, c.1945, Putnam Papers.

10. Ben Wolf, "The Dirty Palette," *Art Digest*, 15 April 1946, clipping in Putnam Papers.

11. Anne Eisner, journal, Anne Eisner Putnam Papers.

12. Putnam-Gould MS, Anne Eisner Putnam Papers.

13. Ibid.

14. Anne Eisner to William J. and Florine Eisner, 12 Sept. 1946, Anne Eisner Putnam Papers.

15. Anne Eisner to Margaret [De Silver], 13 Dec. 1946, in notebook, 1947, Anne Eisner Putnam Papers.

16. Anne Eisner, "Benin Page," and "Thanksgiving," Anne Eisner Putnam Papers.

17. Anne to Ben [Wolf?], 20 Nov. 1946, Anne Eisner Putnam Papers.

18. Anne Putnam to Colin Turnbull, 15 April 1957, Anne Eisner Putnam Papers.

19. Armand Denis to Putnam, 24 Aug. 1947; Anne Eisner to A. Denis, 22 Sept 1947; Putnam to Chief Secretary, Nigerian Government, 18 Nov. 1946, all in Putnam Papers. They bought carved masks, mostly from the Ibibio of Nigeria and from the BaCongo: BaChoko, BaPedi, and BaKuba (Anne Putnam to Peter Pollack, 6 Nov. 1955, Anne Eisner Putnam Papers).

20. Anne Eisner to William J. and Florine Eisner, 16 Jan. 1947, Anne Eisner Putnam Papers.

21. Anne Eisner to William J. and Florine Eisner, 17 Feb. 1947, Kano, Anne Eisner Putnam Papers.

22. Anne Putnam to Colin Turnbull, 15 April 1957; notebook, journey to Epulu; Anne Eisner to Denis, 22 Sept. 1947, all in Anne Eisner Putnam Papers.

23. Anne Putnam, notebook, 1953, Anne Eisner Putnam Papers.

24. Work charts and meal tallies, Putnam Papers; Author's interview with Colin Turnbull, April 8–9, 1987.

25. Anne Eisner to Charlotte [Klonis], 8 Nov. 1947, Anne Eisner Putnam Papers.

26. Anne Eisner to Via [Wood], n.d. [1947], Anne Eisner Putnam Papers.

27. Mada's year of birth, 1915, appears on a medical report sheet for her, diagnosing bronchitis, etc., dated "3-10-50," signed "P. Putnam, *Agent Sanitaire,*" Putnam Papers. Putnam's notes on a visit to the caves in 1931 show that Mada was then a member of his household.

28. Anne Eisner to William J. and Florine Eisner, 28 Jan. 1948, Anne Eisner Putnam Papers.

29. Anne Eisner to Putnam, 25 Feb. 1948, Putnam Papers; Anne to William J. and Florine Eisner, 16 Feb. 1948, Anne Eisner Putnam Papers.

30. Anne Eisner to Allan Keller, 23 Aug. and 28 Oct. 1953, Anne Eisner Putnam Papers.

31. Anne Eisner Putnam with Allan Keller, *Madami,* pp.50, 60, 173.

32. Putnam to William Mann, 14 Sept. 1948, Putnam Papers, Peabody.

33. Putnam to Anne Eisner, 24 April 1948, Leopoldville, Putnam Papers.

34. Putnam to Anne Eisner, 29 May 1948, Putnam Papers.

35. Anne Eisner to Putnam, 5 June 1948, Putnam Papers.

36. Anne Putnam to William J. and Florine Eisner, 28 July 1948, Anne Eisner Putnam Papers. The triple anniversary is noted in Anne Putnam to Dorothy Eisner [McDonald], 2 Aug. 1955, Anne Eisner Putnam Papers.

37. Colin Turnbull interview, 8–9 April 1987.

38. Anne Putnam to William J. and Florine Eisner, n.d. [1954], Anne Eisner Putnam Papers; Colin Turnbull, remarks at Anne's memorial service, 1967, MS in Anne Eisner Putnam Papers.

39. Anne Putnam to Colin Turnbull, 15 April 1957; Anne Putnam to Father Schebesta, 9 Nov. 1953; Anne Putnam to William J. and Florine Eisner, 4 Aug. 1948 and 24 March 1949, all in Anne Eisner Putnam Papers.

Chapter 10. At Home at Epulu

1. Putnam to Agnes and Alobe, n.d. [23 Dec. 1948, according to another letter from the same place] Gite Tembo, William Falls of the Kwango River, Territory of Kasongo Lunda, Kwango, Putnam Papers (author's translation).

2. Anne Putnam to Robert McGregor, American Consul at Leopoldville, 12 May 1954, Putnam Papers; Anne Putnam to William J. and Florine Eisner, Munene, 3 Nov. 1948, Anne Eisner Putnam Papers.

3. Ageronga to Putnam, 28 Sept. 1948, Putnam Papers.

4. Putnam, "Explanatory note," n.d., Putnam Papers, Peabody. The Ibibio live in the higher land of the Niger Delta; the Ijaw in the crocodile-infested mangrove swamps of the coastal belt of the Niger Delta; the Ngombe along certain stretches of the Congo and Ubangi Rivers.

5. Anne Putnam to Helen Gould, 11 Sept. 1950, Anne Eisner Putnam Papers.

6. Attempting to salvage something from what he had learned about African export crops, Putnam submitted an article on the growing of derris (a powerful insecticide and DDT substitute) to the *Courrier d'Afrique,* which during the war had printed his article on wild rubber but apparently did not publish this piece: P. Putnam, "Examen de quelques points de concertant en matiere d'ex-

portation du derris," 10 pp., Leopoldville, 25 May 1948; P. Putnam to Editor in Chief, *Courrier d'Afrique,* Leopoldville, 13 June 1948, Putnam Papers.

7. Putnam to A. Steven Bisser, 21 July 1948, Putnam Papers.

8. Putnam to Pan American Airlines, 27 Feb. 1949, and Putnam to William Mann, 14 Sept. 1948, both in Putnam Papers, Peabody; John Tee-Van, New York Zoological Society, to Putnam, 27 Sept. 1948, Putnam Papers.

9. Putnam to Washburn, 20 July 1948; Washburn to Putnam, 10 Aug. 1948, both in Putnam Papers, Peabody.

10. Putnam to Washburn, 8 May 1948, Putnam Papers, Peabody.

11. Putnam to J. O. Brew, 27 Dec. 1948, Peabody Museum Archives.

12. IRSAC was founded 1 July 1947 to promote the sciences of men and of nature in the Belgian Congo and in Ruanda-Urundi. Its administrative council included American astronomer Harlow Shapley, the Belgian ambassador to the United States, and directors of the Belgian-American Educational Foundation. Pamphlet by Alex Fain, *Vers nouveaux de l'Okapi,* (n.p.: IRSAC, 1950), Putnam Papers.

13. Putnam to Louis Van den Berghe, Sept. 1948, Putnam Papers.

14. Putnam to Monsieur l'Administrateur Territorial, 5 Dec. 1949; Putnam to Monsieur le Directeur [IRSAC], 30 April 1950, Putnam Papers. Among his papers there are several drafts of articles on the okapi, written in French, apparently c.1937. Putnam did publish his 1940 address to the Explorers Club on the okapi ("There *Is* Such an Animal"), but nothing after that date.

15. Putnam to Agnes and Alobe, 23 Dec. 1948, Putnam Papers.

16. Putnam to C.R.L. Putnam, 14 Jan. 1950; Woodhams to Putnam, 7 July 1950, Putnam Papers. See also Anne Eisner Putnam, *Madami,* pp.135, 254.

17. Putnam to C.R.L. Putnam, 14 Jan. 1950, Putnam Papers.

18. Putnam to C.R.L. Putnam, 27 March 1949, Putnam Papers.

19. Anne Putnam to William J. and Florine Eisner, 24 March [1949], Anne Eisner Putnam Papers.

20. Wright and Jones, "Doctor Totorido"; Putnam's stipend is mentioned in Anne Putnam to William J. and Florine Eisner, 19 Aug. 1950, Anne Eisner Putnam Papers. Jones, *Under the African Sun,* p.85.

21. Anne Putnam to William J. and Florine Eisner, 4 Dec. 1949, Anne Eisner Putnam Papers. Officially, however, Faizi's master was Ngoma, who lived in

Kopo's village about three kilometers away and was the real master of many of the Camp Putnam pygmies.

22. Colin Turnbull interview, 8–9 April 1987.

23. Putnam-Gould MS, Anne Eisner Putnam Papers.

24. Author's translation from French. Putnam's zoo labels in "Animals," folder in Putnam Papers, Peabody; also Anne Putnam to William J. and Florine Eisner, 7 Aug. 1949, Anne Eisner Putnam Papers.

25. Putnam to Tom Holly, 16 Aug. 1950, Putnam Papers; Anne Eisner Putnam, *Madami*, pp.7–20, 297. Tom Holly, an Australian photographer and correspondent, had written to ask if Putnam minded being quoted as saying, "Every man who lives out here has had relations with native women; and the ones who deny it are either liars or are impotent." Putnam suggested that Holly say "every bachelor" but added, "However, for you, psychologist, I may say that among what seem to me like my *most happily* married Belgian friends, the père de famille, to my certain knowledge, doesn't scorn a taste of black-meat now and then."

26. Anne Putnam to William J. and Florine Eisner, 9 Jan. 1951, Anne Eisner Putnam Papers; Anne Eisner Putnam, *Madami*, pp.152–56.

27. Anne Putnam to William J. and Florine Eisner, 4 March 1950, 29 Jan. and 11 April 1951, Anne Eisner Putnam Papers.

28. Anne Putnam to Helen Gould, 28 Jan. 1951, and Anne Eisner to William J. and Florine Eisner, 29 Jan. 1951, Anne Eisner Putnam Papers; Anne Eisner Putnam, *Madami*, pp.257–61.

29. Putnam to C.R.L. Putnam, 14 Jan. 1950, Putnam Papers.

30. Oden Meeker, *Report on Africa*, p.186; Anne Eisner Putnam, *Madami*, pp.283–85; Wright and Jones, "Doctor Totorido."

31. Kokoyoo's Baby Book, Putnam Papers; Anne Eisner Putnam, *Madami*, esp. pp.112–22.

32. Anne Putnam to Dr. Abraham Stone, 14 April 1955; Anne Putnam, comments on proof for *National Geographic* article, Feb. 1960, Anne Eisner Putnam Papers.

33. Putnam-Gould MS, Anne Eisner Putnam Papers.

34. Oden Meeker, "The Safari Industry," *Harper's*, Oct. 1955, pp.47–52; Tay Thomas and Lowell Thomas, Jr., "Flight to Adventure"; Wright and Jones, "Doctor Totorido."

35. Putnam to [name illegible], 1 March 1949, Putnam Papers.

36. Anne Putnam to Agence Maritime Internationale, 17 June 1953; Camp Putnam letter to Sabena agent, Nov. 1950, Putnam Papers. The rate for the pygmy show was 1,500 Belgian francs (about $6.00 American), net hunting was 200 francs (80 cents) per person, riding in a tepoy was 25 francs (10 cents) and in a pirogue 50 francs per person per hour.

37. James Chapin, ms obituary for P. Putnam, Explorers Club Archives; Anne Putnam to Oskar Eberle, 14 Jan. 1954, Anne Eisner Putnam Papers.

38. Anne Putnam to William J. and Florine Eisner, 24 Sept. 1953, Anne Eisner Putnam Papers.

39. Merlyn Severn, *Congo Pilgrim*, pp.178–84.

40. Ibid., p.181.

41. Ibid., p.184.

Chapter 11. Colin Turnbull

1. "Outsider" [conversation with Colin Turnbull].

2. Colin M. Turnbull interview, 8–9 April 1987. All further Turnbull quotations in this chapter are from this interview unless otherwise noted. Additional sources for biographical information are Turnbull, *The Human Cycle*, and the *New Yorker* interview titled "Outsider."

3. Anne Putnam to William J. and Florine Eisner, 6 May 1951, Anne Eisner Putnam Papers.

4. Colin Turnbull to Putnam and Anne Putnam, 5 May 1952, Putnam Papers.

Chapter 12. Withdrawal, Illness, and Death

1. Putnam to Anne Eisner, 31 May 1948, Putnam Papers.

2. Author's interviews with Julian Apley, 29 June and 26 July 1989.

3. Anne Putnam to Allan Keller, 28 Oct. 1953, Anne Eisner Putnam Papers.

4. Jones, *Under the African Sun*, p.101.

5. Ibid., p.70.

6. Ibid., p.90. Another description of this operation is Ron Talken, "An Incident at the Place of Putnam, March 4, 1952," ms in Putnam Papers.

7. C.R.L. Putnam to Putnam, 9 Jan. 1952, Putnam Papers.

8. Anne Putnam to Marley Putnam, 23 March 1952, Putnam Papers.

9. Anne Putnam to William J. and Florine Eisner, 10 April 1952, Anne Eisner Putnam Papers.

10. Anne Putnam to Allan Keller, n.d. [9 Nov. 1953], Anne Eisner Putnam Papers.

11. Anne Putnam to Putnam, 19 Oct. 1952; Anne Putnam to Allan Keller, 8 Nov. 1953 [first draft of 9 Nov. letter], Anne Eisner Putnam Papers.

12. Meeker, *Report on Africa,* p.181; Oden Meeker to Putnam and Anne Putnam, 28 May 1952, Putnam Papers.

13. Meeker, *Report on Africa,* p.186.

14. Ibid., p.187.

15. Ibid., p.186.

16. Anne Putnam, "Notes on Basa linda's death," 7 Aug. 1952, Anne Eisner Putnam Papers.

17. Anne Putnam, loose sheet of typed notes, n.d. [1952], Anne Eisner Putnam Papers.

18. Anne Putnam to Allan Keller, 28 Oct. 1953, Anne Eisner Putnam Papers.

19. Anne Putnam to Klempener, 24 March 1954, with bill for the leper camp, Anne Eisner Putnam Papers.

20. Anne shipped a used Webster wire recording machine, on loan from the Wenner Gren Foundation, from America, but it took months to get through customs. Putnam took it with him when he went to Mambasa two weeks before his death, but there is no evidence that he ever used it. (Anne Putnam to Monganza Swiss, 9 Dec. 1953, Anne Eisner Putnam Papers).

21. Putnam to Elizabeth Putnam, 12 Dec. 1952, Putnam Papers.

22. Putnam to C.R.L. Putnam, Irumu Hospital, 17 Feb. 1953, and a first draft [written Feb. 7?], Putnam Papers.

23. Margo Putnam to Putnam, [March?] 1953, Putnam Papers.

24. Putnam, "Sante Putnam," Putnam Papers (author's translation).

25. Putnam to C.R.L. Putnam, 18 March 1953; Putnam to William J. Eisner, n.d.; Putnam to Anne Putnam, 21 Jan. 1953, all in Putnam Papers.

26. Putnam to C.R.L. Putnam, 18 March 1953, Putnam Papers.

27. Schuyler Jones to Anne Putnam, 20 March 1953, Putnam Papers; Anne Putnam to William J. and Florine Eisner, 2 April 1953, Anne Eisner Putnam Papers.

28. Putnam to Nelle N. Henry, 17 April 1953, Putnam Papers.

29. Anne Putnam to Allan Keller, 8 Nov. 1953, Anne Eisner Putnam Papers.

30. Putnam, loose notes, 4 May 1953, Putnam Papers; Anne's birthday is cited from her passport, Anne Eisner Putnam Papers.

31. Putnam, loose sheet with others dated June 1953, Putnam Papers.

32. "[Mata/Mada] was there all the time and I saw her everyday": author's interview with Schuyler Jones, 10 Aug. 1989; also Colin Turnbull interview, 8–9 April 1987.

33. Putnam to De Medina, 6 April 1953, Putnam Papers (author's translation from French).

34. James Chapin to Anne Putnam, 28 Dec. 1953, Putnam Papers.

35. Attilio Gatti, *Great Mother Forest*, pp.184–86.

36. Jones, *Under the African Sun*, pp.84, 85.

37. Anne Putnam to William J. and Florine Eisner, 18 July 1953, Anne Eisner Putnam Papers.

38. Anne Putnam, journal, 30 July 1953, Anne Eisner Putnam Papers.

39. Anne Putnam to Allan Keller, 8 Nov. 1953; Anne Putnam to George, 1 Aug. 1953, Anne Eisner Putnam Papers.

40. Anne Putnam to Putnam, 19 Oct. 1952, Putnam Papers.

41. Jones, *Under the African Sun*, p.86.

42. Paul Schebesta, *My Pygmy and Negro Hosts*, p.263.

43. Anne Putnam to Allan Keller, 20 Nov. 1953, Anne Eisner Putnam Papers.

44. Anne Putnam to William J. and Florine Eisner, 18 July 1953; Anne Putnam to Allan Keller, 26 July and 8 Nov. 1953, Anne Eisner Putnam Papers.

45. Putnam to Margot Putnam, 22 May 1948, Putnam Papers.

46. Florine Eisner to Anne Putnam and Putnam, 31 Jan. 1950 (Putnam Papers), reports that an agent responded favorably to her query about the possibility of a book based on Anne's African experiences and conveys an offer for the sale of one of Anne's Vineyard paintings. On the letter Pat penciled: "9-2-50 Anne, I've read this nice letter and enjoyed it. good news—author and painter a real career [*sic*] woman, what!! PTLP" On wanting good letters from her, Putnam to Anne Putnam, 22 April 1950, Putnam Papers.

47. Anne Putnam to Monroe Stearns, n.d. [c.20 April 1953], Anne Eisner Putnam Papers.

48. Anne Putnam to Allan Keller, 1 July 1953, Anne Eisner Putnam Papers.

49. Anne Putnam to William J. and Florine Eisner, 4 Feb. 1952, Anne Eisner Putnam Papers.

50. Anne Putnam to Allan Keller, 28 Oct. 1953; Anne Putnam, notebook, 6 Sept. 1953, Anne Eisner Putnam Papers.

51. Olle Strandberg, *Jambo Means Hello*, p.68.

52. Ibid., p.70.

53. Ibid., pp.70–72.

54. Ibid., p.72.

55. Ibid., p.75.

56. Anne Putnam to Oden Meeker, 14 Oct. 1953, Anne Eisner Putnam Papers.

57. Boris Adé to Anne Putnam, 9 Jan. 1954, Anne Eisner Putnam Papers.

58. Anne Putnam, loose sheet, n.d.; Anne Putnam to Allan Keller, 28 Oct. 1953, Anne Eisner Putnam Papers.

59. Anne Putnam to Herbert Solow, 9 Nov. 1953; Anne Putnam, notebook, n.d. [c.20–29 Nov. 1953], Anne Eisner Putnam Papers.

60. John and Terese Hart interview, 6 July 1987. The Harts heard the story from Kenge at Epulu some thirty-five years after the event.

61. Anne Putnam to Allan Keller, 8 Nov. 1953; Anne Putnam to Herbert Solow, 9 Nov. 1953, Anne Eisner Putnam Papers.

62. Anne Putnam to William J. and Florine Eisner, Leilo Camp, 29 Oct. 1953, Anne Eisner Putnam Papers.

63. Anne Putnam to Allan Keller, 8 Nov. 1953, Anne Eisner Putnam Papers.

64. Anne Putnam to William J. and Florine Eisner, 28 Nov. 1953, Anne Eisner Putnam Papers; Anne Putnam to Goris, 30 Dec. 1953; and Putnam to Rozos, 12 Dec. 1953, both in Putnam Papers. Pat wrote Rozos that he had been taking little doses of opium regularly for six months.

65. Schebesta to Putnam, 25 Oct. 1953, Putnam Papers. The article he read called Putnam the "King of the Pygmies"; since Schebesta himself was often called the "Father of the Pygmies," and he suggested that the King and the Father ought to meet. He also mentioned Putnam's illness and Putnam's favorable comments on his own writings (Anne Putnam to William J. and Florine Eisner, 11 Nov. 1953, Anne Eisner Putnam Papers).

66. Anne Putnam to Allan Keller, 20 Nov. 1953, Anne Eisner Putnam Papers.

67. Anne Putnam, notebook, n.d. [c.20–29 Nov. 1953], Anne Eisner Putnam Papers.

68. Anne Putnam to Nelle Henry, 24 Dec. 1953, Anne Eisner Putnam Papers.

69. Anne Putnam to Carleton Coon, n.d. [Dec. 1953]; Anne Putnam to Goris, 30 Dec. 1953; Anne Putnam to Monganza Swiss, 9 Dec. 1953, Anne Eisner Putnam Papers.

70. Stuart Cloete, *The African Giant: The Story of a Journey* (Boston: Houghton-Mifflin, 1955), p.316.

71. Anne Putnam to William J. and Florine Eisner, 21 Dec. 1953, Anne Eisner Putnam Papers.

72. Putnam to Anne Putnam, 9 Dec. 1953; Anne Putnam, notebook, Anne Eisner Putnam Papers.

73. Anne Putnam to C.R.L. Putnam, 9 Jan. 1954, Putnam Papers.

74. Anne Putnam, notebook, Anne Eisner Putnam Papers; copy of Report of Death, American Consulate General, Leopoldville, Belgian Congo, 17 March 1954; Anne Putnam to Nelle Henry, 24 Dec. 1953, Putnam Papers.

75. Anne Putnam, notebook, Anne Eisner Putnam Papers; Anne Putnam to C.R.L. Putnam, 9 Jan. 1954, Putnam Papers.

76. *Stanleyville Gazette,* 28 Dec. 1953, clipping in Putnam Papers.

77. Pétillon telegram, Putnam Papers (author's translation).

78. Boris Adé to Anne Putnam, 9 Jan. 1954, Putnam Papers (author's translation).

79. Putnam to C.R.L. Putnam, 17 Feb. 1953, Putnam Papers.

Chapter 13. Aftermath

1. Anne Putnam to Coon, 21 Dec. 1953, Anne Eisner Putnam Papers.

2. Putnam to Dr. Legrand, 19 Nov. 1952, Putnam Papers.

3. Anne Putnam to Elizabeth Putnam, 3 Jan. 1954, Anne Eisner Putnam Papers.

4. Ibid.

5. Anne Putnam to Monroe Stearns, 25 Aug. 1954, Anne Eisner Putnam Papers. Anne's feelings about the book are in Anne Putnam to C.R.L. Putnam, 24 March 1954, Putnam Papers.

6. Anne Putnam to Monroe Stearns, 7 Jan. 1954; Anne Putnam to Allan Keller, 6 Jan. 1954; Anne Putnam to C.R.L. Putnam, 9 Jan. 1954; Anne Putnam to American Consul Robert G. McGregor, 1 Jan. 1954, Anne Eisner Putnam Papers.

7. Anne Putnam to Margo Putnam and C.R.L. Putnam, 10 Feb. 1954, Putnam Papers.

8. Anne Putnam to William J. and Florine Eisner, 30 May and 13 June 1954, Anne Eisner Putnam Papers. Two records from Turnbull's music collections were released on Folkway Records: FE 4483, *Music of the Ituri Forest* (1955); and FE 4457, *Music of the Ituri Pygmies* (1958).

9. Anne Putnam to Charl Ormond Williams, 11 July 1954; Anne Putnam to William J. and Florine Eisner, 30 May 1954; Anne Putnam to C.R.L. Putnam, 16 June 1954; Anne Putnam to Marley Putnam, 30 June 1954, all in Anne Eisner Putnam Papers. The Thomases' visit is described in Thomas and Thomas, "Flight to Adventure"; the photographs include one of Faizi in the single-engine airplane.

10. John and Terese Hart interview, 6 July 1987.

11. Turnbull, *The Forest People*, p.30.

12. Turnbull to Coon, 17 Sept. 1954, Coon Papers. Turnbull described this initiation camp in "Initiation among the BaMbuti Pygmies of the Central Ituri," emphasizing the change in the pygmies' attitudes toward the ceremony when the villagers were not around to make them take it seriously. Paul Schebesta, "Bambuti Initiation," challenged his account, suggesting that the initiation Turnbull participated in was so irregular that it must have been little more than a show performed on demand at Epulu for the benefit of visiting white people (i.e., Turnbull). Anne Putnam thought that the truth lay somewhere between Turnbull's and Schebesta's positions. "There is no doubt that you did witness a most unusual cir. ceremony where they did not seem to take it as seriously as usual. In fact I was shocked," she wrote Turnbull (15 April 1957, Anne Eisner Putnam Papers).

13. Anne Putnam to Elizabeth Putnam, 2 Aug. 1954; Anne Putnam to Schuyler Jones, 23 May 1954, Anne Eisner Putnam Papers.

14. John L. Brom, *African Odyssey* (New York: Living Books, 1966; trans. of French ed., 1957), pp.184–89.

15. Max Lerner, "The Putnam Story," *New York Post*, 24 June 1956, clipping in Anne Eisner Putnam Papers.

16. Schebesta, "Colin M. Turnbull und die Erforschung der Bambuti-Pygmäen, p.214. See also Paul Schebesta, "Pygmy Music and Ceremonial."

17. Anne Putnam to Colin Turnbull, 11 April 1957, Turnbull Papers (courtesy of Curtis Abraham).

18. Anne Putnam to Colin Turnbull, 15 Nov. 1954, Anne Eisner Putnam Papers.

19. C.R.L. Putnam to Anne Putnam, 27 Nov. 1954, Putnam Papers.

20. Colin Turnbull to Anne Putnam, 6 Jan. 1955, Anne Eisner Putnam Papers. Once published, the paper was immediately challenged by Schebesta. See Colin M. Turnbull, "Pygmy Music and Ceremonial"; Paul Schebesta, "Pygmy Music and Ceremonial," with Turnbull's reply following.

21. Turnbull to Coon, 17 Sept. 1954, Coon Papers.

22. Colin M. Turnbull interview, 8–9 April 1987.

23. Colin M. Turnbull, "Legends of the BaMbuti." Their relations that summer are reflected in Anne Putnam to Turnbull, 15 May 1956; Turnbull to Anne Putnam, 17 May, 22 Oct., 6 and 8 Nov. 1956, Anne Eisner Putnam Papers.

24. Colin M. Turnbull, *"The Mbuti Pygmies,"* p.145.

25. Schebesta called the archers in the eastern part of the Ituri the Efe, their name for themselves in KiLese, and some anthropologists have continued this usage. In general, the term Mbuti (or BaMbuti) is currently used by anthropologists to designate pygmies in the Ituri Forest; within this broad category distinctions are sometimes made between the Efe (in the east), the Sua or Mbuti (in the central Ituri) and the Aka (to the north).

26. Anne Putnam to Elizabeth Putnam, n.d. [Aug. 1957], Putnam Papers.

27. Anne Eisner Putnam, "My Life with Africa's Little People," p.287.

28. Colin M. Turnbull, *The Mbuti Pygmies: Change and Adaptation,* pp.74, 92; Colin Turnbull interview, 8–9 April 1987.

29. Colin M. Turnbull comments on his role as buffoon in *Wayward Servants: The Two Worlds of the African Pygmies,* p.12.

30. Ibid., p.11.

31. Turnbull, *The Forest People,* p.252. Emilie Baca Putnam made a similar observation in 1939: when they took one of the hotel workers with them on an outing to Stanleyville and went to the airport to see a plane land, the Ituri Forest villager was astonished that something so small in the air should be so large on the ground (Emilie Putnam to Marguerite Baca, 22 Feb. 1939, Emilie Baca Putnam Papers).

32. Turnbull, *The Forest People,* p.272.

33. Colin Turnbull to William J. and Florine Eisner, 17 June 1958, Anne Eisner Putnam Papers.

34. Colin Turnbull interview, 8–9 April 1987.

35. Colin M. Turnbull to Putnam and Anne Putnam, 1 Jan. 1952; "Pigmies of the Congo" MS, Putnam Papers.

36. Jan Vansina, review of Colin M. Turnbull, *The Forest People*, in *American Anthropologist* 64 (1962): 643. Vansina did have two criticisms. He chided Turnbull for not including a bibliography to show where his work fit in with earlier studies, and for being "too much a pygmy" and giving only an unsympathetic caricature of the surrounding villagers.

37. In the tradition of British functionalism, Turnbull assumed a static world in the Ituri Forest before the coming of Western colonizers, whose activities were only beginning to uproot ancient ways. In British social anthropology and social structure studies the task was to describe the functioning of a given social system, not to ask historical questions as to how it came to be.

38. Anne Putnam to Colin Turnbull, n.d., Anne Eisner Putnam Papers.

39. Schebesta, "Colin M. Turnbull und die Erforschung der Bambuti-Pygmäen," p.218 (author's translation).

40. Schebesta, "Tore, le dieu forestier des Bambuti," p.185.

41. Anne Eisner Putnam, "My Life with Africa's Little People," p.280. Anne Putnam wrote this article with the help of Monroe Stearns, her previous editor at Prentice-Hall. "Godlike stature" may be Stearns's phrase; it does not ring true as something Anne Putnam would have said.

42. Ibid., p.296. Colin Turnbull offered photographs for the article, but none of them satisfied the editors of the *National Geographic*.

43. Colin M. Turnbull, "For Anne, and her parents," MS, in Anne Eisner Putnam Papers.

44. Maurice Godelier, "Epistemological Comments on the Problems of Comparing Modes of Production and Societies," in Stanley Diamond, ed., *Toward a Marxist Anthropology* (The Hague: Mouton, 1979), p.79.

45. Bobb, *Historical Dictionary of Zaire*, pp.136–37, 221; Peter Forbath, *The River Congo*, p.ix; Shoumatoff, *In Southern Light*, p.175.

46. Lewis Cotlow, *In Search of the Primitive*, pp.91–92, 94. According to Cotlow, De Medina had earlier been lured to Stanleyville on some pretext, and when he returned to Epulu he found that many of the okapis and elephants had been killed for meat. Turnbull, *The Mbuti Pygmies: Change and Adaptation*, p.110, says De Medina was poisoned but gives the date as around 1970. The missionary making the report about Bunia was Bill Deans at Nyankunde, according to Cotlow.

47. John A. Hart and Terese B. Hart, "The Mbuti of Zaire." The Harts note that even though the village communities in the 1970s were reestablished, the traditional alliances were not. Newcomers—market-oriented farmers, local entrepreneurs, loggers, and others—had moved into the forest, and the pygmies frequently found it more beneficial to ally themselves with these newcomers than with their traditional "masters." For recent changes, see also Espen Waehle, "Ete (Mbuti) Relations to Lese Dese Villagers in the Ituri Forest, Zaire."

48. Colin M. Turnbull, *The Mountain People;* Colin M. Turnbull, "Rethinking the Ik."

49. In 1973 Turnbull described the two aims of anthropology as, first, to refine our understanding of social structure and discover significant generalizations (laws); and second, to relate to social problems, i.e., to suggest new ways to induce and control social change. He wrote that he wanted anthropology to be relevant "in a world desperately in need of all the guidance it can get." See Colin M. Turnbull, ed., *Africa and Change* (New York: Knopf, 1973), pp.5, vii. Turnbull did return to Epulu in 1970–72 and based the short book *The Mbuti Pygmies: Change and Adaptation* on the changes be observed. See also Colin M. Turnbull, *The Lonely African,* and *The Human Cycle,* both of which make use of his African experience.

50. See John A. Hart, "From Subsistence to Market;" Terese B. Hart and John Hart, "The Ecological Basis of Hunter-Gatherer Subsistence in the African Rain Forest"; Terese B. Hart, John A. Hart, and Peter G. Murphy, "Monodominant and Species-Rich Forests of the Humid Tropics: Causes for Their Co-occurrence," *American Naturalist* 133, no.5 (1989): 613–33; Terese B. and John A. Hart, "Tracking the Rainforest Giraffe," *Animal Kingdom* (publication of Wildlife Conservation International), Jan.–Feb. 1989, pp.27–32; John A. Hart and Terese B. Hart, "Ranging and Feeding Behavior of Okapi"; Terese B. Hart, "Monospecific Dominance in Tropical Rain Forests"; John and Terese Hart interview, 6 July 1987.

The "Ecological Basis of Hunter-Gatherer Subsistence" was designed in part to test Colin Turnbull's assertion that the pygmies could live independently of the villagers and solely on the products of the forest if they chose to (see, e.g., his *Wayward Servants,* p.28). The Harts concluded that it is unlikely that hunter-gatherers could or ever did live independently of village agriculturalists in the forest, because the forest lacks food of sufficient calories during at least five months of the year. The most food-rich areas of the forest are the savanna borders and the agriculturally derived areas of secondary forest. Robert C. Bailey et al., "Hunting and Gathering in Tropical Rain Forest," extended this argument to suggest that probably nowhere in any tropical rain forest have humans existed independently of agriculturalists or fisherman. A similar argument based on research among the Negritos in the Philippines and other data is Thomas Headland, "Hunter-Gatherers and Their Neighbors from Prehistory to the Present," *Current Anthropology* 30, no.1 (1989): 43–66.

Other current anthropological research in the Ituri Forest includes studies done by Robert Hailey and Nadine Peacock, at Ngodingodi, on nutrition, energy expenditure, time allocation, and fertility rates among the Lese villagers and the Efe (archer pygmies). Roy Richard Grinker, also at Ngodingodi, has been following a more Turnbull-like course, asking what the psychological and social (rather than economic and material) mechanisms are that keep the pygmies and villagers distinct. See Bailey et al., "Hunting and Gathering in Tropical Rain Forests"; Robert Bailey and Nadine Peacock, "Efe Pygmies of Northeast Zaire: Subsistence Strategies in the Ituri Forest," in I. de Garine and G. A. Harrison, eds. *Coping with Uncertainty in the Food Supply* (Oxford: Clarendon Press, 1988), pp.88–117; Roy Richard Grinker, "Images of Denigration," and his forthcoming *Houses in the Rain Forest*. Several Japanese anthropologists have done studies in the Ituri Forest, mostly on subsistence techniques of the Mbuti. Recent work by H. Terashima, T. Tanno, M. Ichikawa, and R. Harako has been published in *Kyoto University African Studies, Kyoto University African Studies Monographs*, and *Senri Ethnological Studies*.

51. John and Terese Hart interview, 6 July 1987.

52. Shoumatoff, *In Southern Light*, p.121; Kevin Duffy, *Children of the Forest*.

Selected Bibliography

Manuscript Collections

Houghton Library, Harvard University, Cambridge, Mass.
  Patrick T. L. Putnam Papers

Tozzer Library, Rare Book Room, Harvard University, Cambridge, Mass.
  C. S. Coon, and Patrick Putnam, "Pygmies of Africa," 1945, 130 pp.
  Frederick R. Wulsin, "African Journey, 1927–1928," 4 vols.; also 4 vols.
  of photographs

Peabody Museum Archives, Harvard University, Cambridge, Mass.
  Earnest A. Hooton Papers
  Patrick Putnam Papers

Explorers Club Archives, New York, N.Y.

Rockefeller Foundation Archives, Tarrytown, N.Y.
  Record Group 1:1, series 220 and 475

National Anthropological Archives, Smithsonian Institution, Washington, D.C.
  Carleton Coon Papers

Ministry of Foreign Affairs, Brussels, Belgium
  Archives Africaines

Private Collections

Ann Eisner Putnam Papers, courtesy of Christie McDonald

Emilie Baca Putnam Papers, courtesy of Josephine Baca

George Way Harley Papers, courtesy of Louis Wells

Published Works by Patrick T. L. Putnam

"Africa may solve Nazi food wants in this war," *Los Angeles News,* Monday, 1
  July 1940.

"Guide pratique pour l'identification et l'exploitation des essences caoutchoutifieres," *Le Courrier Agricole d'Afrique* no.22 (1942): 1–3.

"A Mangbetu Game." *Man* 30 (April 1930): 73–74.

• BIBLIOGRAPHY •

Our Camp on the Epulu in the Belgian Congo., Mary Farlow Linder Putnam, coauthor. 13 pp., illus. 1933?

"The Pigmies of the Ituri Forest." In Carleton Coon, ed., *A Reader in General Anthropology*, pp.322–41. New York: Henry Holt, 1948.

"Report from the Field: Wamba, Vele-Nepoko, Belgian Congo." *New Yorker*, 28 February 1931, p.66.

"There *Is* Such an Animal [okapi]." In Seward S. Cramer, ed., *Through Hell and High Water*, by Members of the Explorers Club, pp.345–53. New York: Robert M. McBride, 1941.

Books and Articles about Patrick Putnam and Camp Putnam

Beatty, Jerome. "Great White Chief of the Congo." *American Magazine* 128 (July 1939): 20–21, 151–53; condensed as "Dude Rancher in the Congo," *Reader's Digest* 35 (August 1939): 43–46; rpt. in Jerome Beatty, *Americans All Over* (New York, John Day, 1940).

Birnbaum, Martin. "Mambau: An African experiment." *Geographical Magazine* (London) 5 (1937): 339–50.

Chapin, James P. "Patrick Tracy Lowell Putnam." *Explorers Journal* 32 (1954): 30–32.

Chapman, F. Spencer. *Lightest Africa.* London: Chatto & Windus, 1955.

Cotlow, Lewis. *In Search of the Primitive.* Boston: Little, Brown, 1942, 1966.

Flandrau, Grace. *Then I Saw the Congo.* London: George G. Harrap, 1929.

Hahn, Emily. *Congo Solo: Misadventurers Two Degrees North.* Indianapolis, Ind.: Bobbs-Merrill, 1933.

———. "Stewart." In Emily Hahn, *Times and Places* (New York: Thomas Y. Crowell, 1970). First published in *New Yorker* (22 October 1966).

———. *With Naked Foot.* Indianapolis, Ind.: Bobbs-Merrill, 1934.

Hift, Fred J. "Hotel in the Congo." *Travel* 94, no.10 (1950): 30.

Jones, Schuyler. *Under the African Sun*, chap.2, "The Forest." London: Hurst & Blackett, 1956.

Longnecker, Bill. "I Lived with the White King of the Pygmies." *Bluebook* 96 (April 1953): 6–12.

Meeker, Oden. *Report on Africa*, chap.8, "Ituri Forest." New York: Scribner, 1954.

———. "The Safari Industry." *Harper's Magazine*, October 1955, pp.47–52.

Phillips, Albert Henry. *Cape Town to the Mountains of the Moon,* pp.198–207. New York: Madill McBride, 1949.

Putnam, Anne Eisner, with Allan Keller. *Madami: My Eight Years of Adventure with the Congo Pigmies.* New York: Prentice-Hall, 1954. Excerpted in *Reader's Digest* 65 (October 1954): 149–68.

———. "My life with Africa's Little People." *National Geographic* 117 (February 1960): 278–302.

Putnam, Emilie Baca. "The Romance of the Congo: Its Forests, Its Animals, Its People." *Anchora of Delta Gamma,* January [1941?], pp.123–28, and March [1941?], pp.243–46.

Severn, Merlyn. *Congo Pilgrim.* London: Museum Press, 1952.

Strandberg, Olle. *Jambo Means Hello.* Trans. Maurice Albert Michael. Boston: Houghton Mifflin, 1956. Originally published in Danish as *Jambo!* (1955).

Thomas, Tay, and Lowell Thomas Jr. "Flight to Adventure." *National Geographic* 112 (July 1957): 59–64, 73.

Wright, Harry B., and George Vedder Jones. "Doctor Totorido and His Pygmies." *True,* June 1953.

Other Books and Articles

Abruzzi, William S. "Flux among the Mbuti Pygmies of the Ituri Forest: An Ecological interpretation." In Eric B. Ross, ed., *Beyond the Myths of Culture Change,* 3–31. New York: Academy Press, 1980.

Aldrich, Nelson, Jr. *Old Money: The Making of America's Upper Class.* New York: Knopf, 1988.

Alonso, M. E., ed. *China's Inner Asian Frontier: Photographs of the Wulsin Expedition to Northwest China in 1923.* Historical text by Joseph Fletcher. Cambridge, Mass.: Peabody Museum, Harvard University, 1979.

Amory, Cleveland. *The Proper Bostonians.* New York: Dutton, 1947.

Ashley-Montagu, M. F. "Edward Tyson, M.D., F.R.S., 1650–1708, and the Rise of Human and Comparative Anatomy in England." *American Philosophical Society Memoirs* 20 (1943).

Bailey, Robert C., Genevieve Head, Mark Janike, Bruce Owen, Robert Rechtman, and Elzbieta Zechenter. "Hunting and Gathering in Tropical Rain Forest: Is it Possible?" *American Anthropologist* 91, no.1 (1989): 59–82.

Bobb, F. Scott. *Historical Dictionary of Zaire.* Metuchen, N.J.: Scarecrow Press, 1988.

• BIBLIOGRAPHY •

Boyer, Paul, and Stephen Nissenbaum. *Salem Possessed: The Social Origins of Witchcraft*. Cambridge, Mass.: Harvard University Press, 1974.

Bradford, Phillips Verner, and Harvey Blume. *Ota Benga: The Pygmy in the Zoo*. New York: St. Martin's Press, 1992.

Broca, Paul. "Les Akka, race pygmée de l'Afrique Centrale." *Revue d'Anthropologie* 3 (1874): 279–87.

Bullock, Alan. *The Humanist Tradition in the West*. New York: Norton, 1985.

Burrows, Guy. *The Land of the Pigmies*. New York: Thomas Y. Crowell, 1898.

Clifford, James. *The Predicament of Culture: Twentieth-Century Ethnography, Literature, and Arts*. Cambridge, Mass.: Harvard University Press, 1988.

Cook, J. A. Bethune. *Sir Thomas Stamford Raffles*. London: Arthur H. Stockwell, 1918.

Coon, Carleton S. *Adventures and Discoveries: The Autobiography of Carleton S. Coon*. Englewood Cliffs, N.J.: Prentice-Hall, 1981.

———. *Measuring Ethiopia and Flight into Arabia*. Boston: Atlantic Monthly Press, 1935.

Cotlow, Lewis N. *In Search of the Primitive*. Boston: Little, Brown, 1966.

———. *Passport to Adventure*. Indianapolis, Ind.: Bobbs-Merrill, 1942.

Crawford, Mary Caroline. *Famous Families of Massachusetts*. Vol.1. Boston: Little, Brown, 1930.

Depré, Wilhelm, "Paul Joachim Schebesta, 1887–1967." *American Anthropologist* 70 (1968): 537–45.

Duffy, Kevin. *Children of the Forest*. New York: Dodd, Mead, 1989.

Flower, William H., "The Pygmy Races of Men." *Journal of the Anthropological Institute of Great Britain and Ireland* 18 (1889): 73–91.

Forbath, Peter. *The River Congo*. New York: Harper & Row, 1977.

Gatti, Attilio. *Great Mother Forest*. New York: Scribner, 1937.

Geertz, Clifford. *Works and Lives: The Anthropologist as Author*. Stanford, Calif.: Stanford University Press, 1988.

Gide, André. *Travels in the Congo*. Trans. Dorothy Bussy. New York: Knopf, 1927. Rpt. Penguin Books, 1986.

Grafton, Anthony, and Lisa Jardine. *From Humanism to the Humanities*. Cambridge, Mass.: Harvard University Press, 1985.

Greenslet, Ferris. *The Lowells and Their Seven Worlds*. Boston: Houghton Mifflin, 1946.

• BIBLIOGRAPHY •

Grinker, Roy Richard. "Houses, Clans, and Cloth: Modeling an Inter-Ethnic Economy in Zaire." *Museum Anthropology* 16, no.3 (1992): 41–50.

———. "Images of Denigration: Structuring of Inequality between Foragers and Farmers." *American Ethnologist* 17, no.1 (1990): 111–30.

Gunther, John. *Meet Central Africa.* London: Hamish Hamilton, 1960.

Gusinde, Martin. "Bibliography of Pygmy Material," *Anthropological Quarterly* 3 (January 1955).

———. "Wilhelm Schmidt: 1868–1954." *American Anthropologist* 56 (1954): 868–70.

Hahn, Emily. *Africa to Me: Person to Person.* Garden City, N.Y.: Doubleday, 1964.

———. *China to Me.* Garden City, N.Y.: Doubleday, Doran, 1944.

Hallet, Jean-Pierre, and Alex Pelle. *Pygmy Kitabu.* New York: Random House, 1973.

Harako, Reizo. "The Cultural Ecology of Hunting Behavior among Mbuti Pygmies in the Ituri Forest, Zaire." In Robert Harding and Geza Teleki, eds., *Omnivorous Primates,* 499–555. New York: Columbia University Press, 1981.

———. "The Mbuti as Hunters: A Study of Ecological Anthropology of the Mbuti Pygmies." *Kyoto University African Studies* 10 (1976): 37–99.

Haraway, Donna. *Primate Visions.* New York: Routledge, 1989.

Harley, George Way. "Masks as Agents of Social Control in Northeast Liberia." *Papers of the Peabody Museum* (Harvard University) 32, no.2 (1950).

———. *Native African Medicine.* Cambridge, Mass.: Harvard University Press, 1941.

———. "Notes on the Poro." *Papers of the Peabody Museum* (Harvard University) 29, no.2 (1941).

Harley, Winifred Jewell. *A Third of a Century with George W. Harley in Liberia.* Newark, Del.: Liberian Studies Association of America, 1973.

Harrison, James J. *Life among the Pygmies of the Ituri Forest, Congo Free State.* London: Hutchinson, 1905.

Hart, John. "From Subsistence to Market: A Case Study of the Mbuti Net Hunters." *Human Ecology* 6 (1978): 325–53.

Hart, John, and Terese B. Hart, "The Mbuti of Zaire," *Cultural Survival Quarterly* 8 no.3 (1984): 18–20.

——. "Ranging and Feeding Behavior of Okapi (*Okapia Johnstoni*) in the Ituri Forest of Zaire: Food Limitation in a Rain-Forest Herbivore?" *Symposium, Zoological Soceity of London*, no.61 (1989): 31–50.

Hart, Teresa B. "Monospecific Dominance in Tropical Rain Forests." *TREE* [Trends in Ecology and Evolution] 5 (January 1990): 6–11.

Hart, Terese B., and John A. Hart. "The Ecological Basis of Hunter-Gatherer Subsistence in African Rain Forests: The Mbuti of Eastern Zaire." *Human Ecology* 14 (1986): 29–55.

——. "Between Sun and Shadow: The Vast Rain Forests of the Congo Basin Have Hidden the Elusive Okapi for Millennia." *Natural History* 101 (November 1992): 28–35.

Heine-Geldern, Robert. "One Hundred Years of Ethnological Theory in the German-Speaking Countries: Some Milestones." *Current Anthropology* 5 (1964): 407–17.

Heymann, C. David. *American Aristocracy: The Lives and Times of James Russell, Amy, and Robert Lowell*. New York: Dodd, Mead, 1980.

Janni, Pietro. *Etnografia e mito: La storia dei pigmei*. Rome: Instituto di Filologia Classica, Universita de Urbino, 1978.

Johnston, Harry H. "The Pygmies of the Great Congo Forest." In *Annual Report of the Smithsonian Institution for 1912*, 479–91. Washington, D.C., 1913.

Joset, Paul-Ernest. *Les sociétés secrètes des hommes-léopards en Afrique Noire*. Paris, Payot, 1955.

Junker, Wilhelm. *Travels in Africa during the Years 1882–1883*. Trans. A. H. Keane. 3 vols. London: Chapman & Hall, 1889–92.

Kalb, Madeleine G. *The Congo Cables: The Cold War in Africa from Eisenhower to Kennedy*. New York: Macmillan, 1982.

Kanza, Thomas. *The Rise and Fall of Patrice Lumumba: Conflict in the Congo*. London: Rex Collings, 1978.

Kapita Mulopo, L. P. *Lumumba: Justice pour le héros*. Paris: L'Harmattan, 1992.

Kaplan, Irving, ed. *Zaire: A Country Study*. Area Handbook Series. Washington, D.C.: American University, 1979.

Kuper, Adam. *Anthropologists and Anthropology: The Modern British School, 1922-1972*. Rev. ed. London: Routledge & Kegan Paul, 1983.

• BIBLIOGRAPHY •

La Farge, Oliver. *Behind the Mountains.* Boston: Houghton Mifflin, 1956; rpt. Santa Fe: William Gannon, 1974.

Lang, Herbert. "Nomad Dwarfs and Civilization." *Natural History* 19 (1919): 697–713.

Lasati, Gaetano. *Ten Years in Equatoria and the Return with Emin Pasha.* Trans. Mrs. J. Randolph Clay. 2 vols. London: Frederick, Warne, 1891.

Leeuwe, Jules. "On Former Gynecocracy among African Pygmies." *Acta Ethnographia* 9 (1962): 85–118.

Lumumba, Patrice. *Congo My Country.* Trans. Graham Heath. London: Pall Mall Press, 1962.

Marcus, G. E., and M. Fischer. *Anthropology as Cultural Critique: An Experimental Moment in the Human Sciences.* Chicago: University of Chicago Press, 1986.

Marquand, John P. *The Late George Apley: A Novel in the Form of a Memoir* (1937). New York, Modern Library, 1940.

McDaniel, Walton Brooks. "A Fresco Picturing Pygmies." *American Journal of Archaeology,* 2d ser., 36 (1932): 260–71.

Merriam, Alan P. "The Concept of Culture Clusters Applied to the Belgian Congo." *Southwestern Journal of Anthropology* 15 (1959): 373–95.

Morel, Edmund D. *Red Rubber: The Story of the Rubber Slave Trade Flourishing in the Congo.* London: Heineman, 1906.

Mulvaney, D. J. "The Anthropologist as Tribal Elder." *Mankind* 7 (1970): 205–17.

———. "The Australian Aborigines, 1609–1929: Opinion and Fieldwork." In J. J. Eastwood and F. B. Smith, eds., *Historical Studies, Australia and New Zealand: Selected Articles.* Melbourne, 1964.

Nadaillac, M. de. *Les Pygmées.* Paris: Jules Gervais, 1887.

Naipaul, V. S. *A Bend in the River.* New York: Knopf, 1979.

"Outsider" [conversation with Colin Turnbull]. *New Yorker* 42 (20 August 1966): 26–27.

Puccini, Sandra. "Gli Akka del Miani: Una storia ethnologica nell'Italia di fine secolo (1872–1883)." *L'Umo* 8, nos. 1–2 (1984): 29–58, 197–217.

Putnam, Emilie Baca. "Japan, Its Children's Welfare." *Survey* 88 (March 1952): 119–23; (May 1952): 196.

Quatrefages de Briau, A. de. *The Pygmies* (1887). Trans. Frederick Starr. New York: Appleton, 1895.

Rahman, Rudolf. "Vier Pioniere der VolkerKunde: der Patres Paul Arndt, Martin Gusinde, Wilhelm Koppers, and Paul Schebesta zum siebzigsten Geburtstag." *Anthropos* 52 (1957): 263–76.

Rathbone, Albert. *General George Talcott and Angelica Bogart, His Wife*. New York, 1937.

———. *Samuel Rathbone and Lydia Sparhawk His Wife: A Record of Their Descendants and Notes Regarding Their Ancestors*. New York, 1937; Supplement, 1941.

Rosenthal, Eric. *Stars and Stripes in Africa*. London: Routledge, 1938.

Rusden, Philip L. "David Hunt Linder, Sept. 24, 1899–Nov. 10, 1946." *Mycologia* 39, no.2 (1947): 133–44.

Schebesta, Paul. *Among Congo Pigmies*. Trans. Gerald Griffin. London: Hutchinson, 1933.

———. "Bambuti Initiation." *Kongo Overzee* 24 (1958): 136–61.

———. *Die Bambuti-Pygmäen von Ituri*. 4 vols. Brussels: 1938–50.

———. "Colin M. Turnbull und die Erforschung der Bambuti-Pygmäen," *Anthropos* 58 (1963): 209–23.

———. "Les conceptions religieuses des Pygmées de l'Ituri." *Congo* 1, pt.5 (1931): 645–66; 2, pt.1 (1931): 45–68.

———. *My Pygmy and Negro Hosts*. Trans. Gerald Griffin. London: Hutchinson, 1936.

———. *Les pygmées*. Paris: Gallimard, 1940.

———. "Pygmy Music and Ceremonial." *Man* 57 (1957): 62–63.

———. *Revisiting My Pygmy Hosts*. Trans. Gerald Griffin. London: Hutchinson, 1936.

———. "Tore, le dieu forestier des Bambuti." *Zaire* 1 (1947): 181–95.

———. "Wilhelm Schmidt, 1869–1954." *Man* 54 (1954): 89–90.

Schildkrout, Enid. "Art as Evidence: A Brief History of the AMNH African Collection." In *ART/artifact*, 153–60. New York: Center for African Art, 1988.

Schildkrout, Enid, Jill Hellman, and Curtis Keim. "Mangbetu Pottery: Tradition and Innovation in Northeast Zaire." *African Arts* 22 (February 1989): 38–46.

• BIBLIOGRAPHY •

Schildkrout, Enid, and Curtis A. Keim. *African Reflections: Art from North-eastern Zaire*. Seattle and New York: University of Washington Press and American Museum of Natural History, 1990.

Schwab, George. "Tribes of the Liberian Hinterland." Ed. with additional material by G. W. Harley. *Peabody Museum Papers* 31 (1947).

Schweinfurth, Georg. *The Heart of Africa: Three Years' Travel and Adventures in the Unexplored Regions of Central Africa, from 1868 to 1871*. Trans. Ellen E. Frewer. 2 vols. London: Sampson Low, Marston, Low, and Searle, 1973.

Shoumatoff, Alex. *In Southern Light: Trekking through Zaire and the Amazon*. New York: Simon & Schuster, 1986.

Stanley, Henry Morton. *In Darkest Africa*. New York: Scribner, 1891.

Stirpe, C. E. "Anthropologists vs. Missionaries: The Influence of Presuppositions." *Current Anthropology* 21 (1980): 165–79.

Stocking, George W., Jr., ed. *Colonial Situations: Essays on the Contextualization of Ethnographic Knowledge*. History of Anthropology, vol. 7. Madison: University of Wisconsin Press, 1991.

Strong, Richard P., ed. *The African Republic of Liberia and the Belgian Congo*. 2 vols. Cambridge, Mass.: Harvard University Press, 1930.

Thornton, Robert J. "Narrative Ethnography in Africa, 1850–1920." *Man* 18 (1983): 502–20.

Torgovnick, Marianna. *Gone Primitive: Savage Intellects, Modern Lives*. Chicago: University of Chicago Press, 1990.

Turnbull, Colin M. "The 'Elima': A Pre-Marital Festival among the BaMbuti Pygmies." *Zaire* 14 (1960): 175–92.

———. "Father Schebesta's Work among the Ba Mbuti Pygmies." In *Festschrift Paul Schebesta zum 75. Geburtstag*, pp. 1–5. Vienna-Mödling, 1963.

———. "Field Work among the Bambuti Pygmies, Belgian Congo: A Preliminary Report." *Man*, March 1960, pp. 36–40.

———. *The Forest People*. New York: Simon & Schuster, 1961.

———. *The Human Cycle*. New York: Simon & Schuster, 1983.

———. "Legends of the BaMbuti." *Journal of the Royal Anthropological Institute* 89.1 (1959): 45–60.

———. "Initiation among the BaMbuti Pygmies of the Central Ituri." *Journal of the Royal Anthropological Institute of Great Britain and Ireland* 87 (1957): 191–216.

• BIBLIOGRAPHY •

———. *The Lonely African*. New York: Simon & Schuster, 1962.

———. *Man in Africa*. New York: Anchor/Doubleday, 1976.

———. "The Mbuti Pygmies: An Ethnographic Survey." *American Museum of Natural History Anthropological Papers* 50, pt.3 (1965): 139–282.

———. *The Mbuti Pygmies: Change and Adaptation*. Case Studies in Cultural Anthropology. New York: Holt, Rinehart, & Winston, 1983.

———. "The 'Molimo': A Man's Religious Association among the BaMbuti Pygmies." *Zaire* 14 (1960): 307–40.

———. *The Mountain People*. New York: Simon & Schuster, 1972.

———. "Pygmy Music and Ceremonial." *Man* 55 (1955): 23–24, 31; 57 (1957): 62–63, 128.

———. "Rethinking the Ik: A Functional Non-social System." In Charles D. Laughlin Jr. and Ivan B. Brady, eds., *Extinction and Survival in Human Populations*, pp.49–75. New York: Columbia University Press, 1978.

———. *Wayward Servants: The Two Worlds of the African Pygmies*. 1965; Westport, Conn.: Greenwood Press, 1976.

Twain, Mark. *King Leopold's Soliloquy*. Boston: P. B. Warren, 1905.

Vallois, H. "La signification anthropologique des Pygmées." *Revue Lorraine d'Anthropologie* 7 (1934–35): 7–16.

Vorblichler, Anton. "Professor Dr. Paul Schebesta s v d." *Anthropos* 62 (1967): 665–95.

Waehle, Espen. "Efe (Mbuti) Relations to Lese Dese Villagers in the Ituri Forest, Zaire: Historical Changes during the Last 150 Years." *s u g i a* [Sprache und Geschichte in Afrika] 7, no.3 (1986): 375–411.

Willey, Gordon R. *Portraits in American Archaeology*. Albuquerque: University of New Mexico Press, 1988.

Winternitz, Helen. *East along the Equator: A Journey up the Congo and into Zaire*. New York: Atlantic Monthly Press, 1987.

Wulsin, Fredeick R. "An Archaeological Exploration of the Shari Basin." *Harvard African Studies* 10, pt.1 (1931).

Yeomans, Henry Aaron. *Abbott Lawrence Lowell, 1856–1943*. Cambridge, Mass.: Harvard University Press, 1948.

Index

Aba, 15
Abanzima, 11, 14, 19, 35, 40, 48, 51–53, 221; at Penge, 54–59, 61, 62, 65, 66, 79, 119
Abanzinga, 52, 143
Abercrombie & Fitch, 159
Accra, Gold Coast (Ghana), 97
Adé, Boris, 189, 193, 194
Adrian, Gilbert, 147
Africa (journal), 224 n.2
Africans. *See* Azande, BaNguana, Bantus, Bira, Bobua, Bushmen, Lese, Mbau, Mboli, Mbuti, Nasamonians, pygmies, Sudanese
Ageronga, 73, 143, 136, 156, 191
Agnes, 150
Akas (Akkas), 42, 129
Albany, New York, 24
Aldrich, Nelson W. Jr., 225 n.22
Alfani, 73
Alili, 192
Allies (World War II), 99, 100, 102, 110
Alobe, 150
American Geological Society, 35

American Magazine, 89, 92
American Museum of Natural History, 49, 53, 212, 215
Among Congo Pygmies (Schebesta), 127
Amory, Cleveland, 23
Andonata, 142, 198
André One, 143
André Two, 143
Angelique (pet baboon), 55
animism, 130, 131
anthropology, xiv, xv, 2; traditions in, 125, 215, 252 n.37
Anthropos, 126, 211
Apley, Julian, 170–71
Apropos, 21
Arab influence, 130
Arab slave traders, 46, 48, 96
Arebi, 15, 16
Aristotle, 42
Art Digest, 137
Art Students League, 118
Aruwini River, 14, 52. *See also* Ituri River
Ascham, Roger, 22
Astrid, Princess (Belgium), 65
Asumini, 59
auto race, 157
Avabi, Belgian Congo, 3

Avakubi, 54
Azande, 6, 131, 197

Baca, José, 87
Baca, Marguerite Pendaris, 87, 233 n.8
BaBila. *See* Bira
Bailey, Robert, 254 n.50
BaLese. *See* Lese
Bamako, 2
BaMbuti. *See* Mbuti; pygmies
Die Bambuti-Pygmaen von Ituri (Schebesta), 128
Bandigby, 196
bangi. *See* marijuana
BaNguana, 46, 48, 73, 74, 76, 103, 123, 147, 159. *See also* Nguana
Bantus, xi, 2, 10, 48, 74, 123, 129, 130, 143
Barnard College, 80
Bassalinde, 142, 198
Bas-Uele, 8
Bates, Oric M., 223 n.1
Batwa, 97
BaYaka, 146, 149
Beal, Newton, 163, 165, 166, 168, 170, 205, 208
Beatty, Jerome, 88
Bedford, New York, 50, 66
Behind the Mountains (La Farge), 233 n.8

• 265 •